Omar Zaid

Islam
in the Shadows
of the
New World Order

Islam in the Shadows of the New World Order
A Singular Perspective

By Omar Zaid, M.D.

© Omar Zaid – Omnia Veritas Ltd

All Rights Reserved

ozaidmd@gmail.com // ozaid@yahoo.com

Ph: +60178841809

Cover design by Dr. Omar
Photographer: Osama Al Zubaidi

Published by Omnia Veritas Ltd

contact@omniaveritas.org

"... a whole series of countries is now dominated by conditions which have destroyed the structural forms worked out by history and replaced them with social systems inimical to creative functioning, systems which can only survive by means of force. We are thus confronted with a great construction project demanding wide-ranging and well organized work. The earlier we undertake the job, the more time we will have to carry it out."

Political Ponerology:
A science on the nature of evil adjusted for political purposes
by Dr. Andrew M. Lobaczewski (1998)

And when the Word is fulfilled
against them (the unjust),
we shall produce from the earth a beast to
(face) them: He will speak to them,
for that mankind did not believe with
assurance in Our Signs.

Contents

Preface   The Impasse   viii

Overview   xvi

PART ONE

THE METAPHYSICS OF SPIRITUAL LAW

THE MEDINA PRINCIPLES   1
Spiritual Law & The Rights of God

Introduction to the Spiritual Law of Islam   2

The Three Principles of Spiritual Determinism or Pillars of Spiritual Law derived From Mohammad's Medina Speech

Obedience, Submission, Decay	14
Consequences or Inverse Determinants	19
Not Heeding the Fear of God	20
Disobedience	23
Forgetting God	27

The Greater Maxims

The Law of Grace	30
The Law of Unity	45
Unity & Power	48
The Muslim Polity as one Man: An Analogy	60
Power	63
Love, Goodness & the Caliphate	65
Islam As the 'Image' or Vicegerent of God	67

The Companion Maxims   72

Truth, Faithfulness and Mercy	72/77
Communion	78
Worship	83
Knowledge	88
Community	92
Humility	99

Guidance	103
Love	105

The Moral Imperative — 109

The Rights to Sin & War — 114

    Free-Will's Relation to Justice & Equity

Conclusion — 119

PART TWO

ESSAYS ON ISLAMIZATION AND ISLAMIC SCIENCE

Prologue: Mankind's Fallen Estate &   121
The Two Hands of the Satanic Worldview

Chapter One

Universal vs. Authentic — 129

    On the Matter of Tasawwuf — 134

Chapter Two

Islamic Science & Muslim Humiliation — 143

Definitions, Apologetics, Consequences, Admonitions,	143
Mysticism, Sufi-Claimers and the Crisis of Knowledge,	155
Mysticism vs. Sufism	164

Chapter Three

As I See It — 169

Why Muslims Neglect the Sword of *Hisbah*	169
The Surrender of Faith and Reason (IOK Failure)	181
Crimes Against Humanity:	195

    Mimicry & the Humiliation of Women

Realities Confronting Islamization Policies and Pundits	204
The Titanic Muslim Dilemma	216

    Authentic Pedagogues, Reactionaries & Enemies

The Masquerade of Authenticity — 227

Real Political Science and The Resting of My Pen	232
Jihad, Natural Muslims, Summary and Conclusion	

Appendices

Appendix I	244
On Transcendence;	
Neuropolitics: Thinking, Culture, Speed	
Appendix II	246
On The Universal Soul	
Appendix III	252
The Serpent Cult	
Appendix IV	
The World Parliament of Churches	254
Index	255
About The Author	270
Endnotes	272

OVERVIEW

Dear Reader,

I have attempted the impossible for which my life's experience seems to have prepared me. With great deference to any and all correction and admonition along the way, I embarked on a task that was compelled by daily encounters, readings, queries, discoveries and bewildering current events; not the least of which was the restraint that had descended on the pens and tongues of many colleagues.

My study of Islam is joined to a quest for truth that has been my companion from an early age. Even then it caused me to bite the many hands that fed me, hence, certain persons mentioned herein are subject to this beleaguering habit for which I apologize but without regret. I have done so because during the course of ceaseless studies I encountered contradictions in deed and doctrine for which no other remedy is possible, especially in light of the command given to Muslims to right that which is wrong and treat the enemies of Islam as such whenever possible. And though I have some reservations as I am yet a novice in the school of Islam's wisdom, I make this offering.

You may come across errors committed in ignorance and perhaps by neglect for which I beg forgiveness and humbly seek correction. Nevertheless, this effort is made in earnest and not without significant reflection and what I pray is true guidance.

May Allah be pleased and may readers become better informed on matters of knowledge that were, most likely, unknown to them.

Sincerely,

Omar Zaid
29 Jan 2012

Preface

The Impasse

Little effort is being made to get at the truth. The critical eye, as a rule, is not sharp. Errors and unfounded assumptions are closely allied and familiar elements in historical information. Blind trust in tradition is an inherited trait in human beings. *Occupation with the (scholarly) disciplines on the part of those who have no right is widespread.* But the pasture of stupidity is unwholesome for mankind — the common desire for sensationalism, the ease with which one may disregard reviewers and critics ... leads to failure to exercise self-criticism about one's errors and intentions, to demand from oneself moderation and fairness in reporting, to reapply oneself to study and research. Such let themselves go and make a feast of untrue statements. "They procure for themselves entertaining stories in order to lead (others) astray from the path of God." [Qur'an 31.6 (5)] This is a bad enough business.[i] - Imam Ibn Khaldun

An error does not become a mistake until you refuse to correct it. ... Without debate, without criticism, no Administration and no country can succeed and no republic can survive. That is why the Athenian lawmaker Solon decreed it a crime for any citizen to shrink from controversy.

John F. Kennedy, Waldorf-Astoria Hotel, New York City, April 27, 1961
From his famous 'Conspiracy Speech'

Ibn Khaldun's reference to "pastures of stupidity" is a scientific observation that comforts me because I use similar terms and, furthermore, the impasse of the same 'stupidity' was recently re-confirmed by an astute observer of human psychopathy in communist Poland. Dr. Andrew M. Lobaczewski went even further to confirm Khaldun's cycles of history and civilization without having read Al'Qur'an or Imam Khaldun's legacy. This, in itself, is empirical evidence that the Islamization of Science is a natural consequence of unbiased research carried out by numerous non-Muslims.

PREFACE

> We already know that every society contains a certain percentage of people carrying psychological deviations caused by various inherited or acquired factors which produce anomalies in perception, thought, and character. Many such people attempt to impart meaning to their deviant lives by means of social hyperactivity. *They create their own myths* and *ideologies* of over-compensation and have the tendency to egotistically insinuate to others that their own deviant perceptions and the resulting goals and ideas are superior.
>
> Dr. Andrew M. Lobaczewski, op. cit. (p. 86)

Across the pond from Britain's Greco-Roman *cum* Zionist elitists, Presidents Kennedy and Abraham Lincoln were assassinated by such politically correct myth-makers, much like Julius Caesar. All three fellows were in the process of dismantling rings of wealth confiscation facilities that served their respective senates of *poneros*.[ii] The creatures responsible for these and related murders have been working across fabricated East-West and North-South transgenerational divides for millennia. My research reveals that the felons who manage this lot of pathocrats and jinn are far more sinister than Neo-Cons, Zionists and pseudo-Muslim analogues. So it appears that this continuum of institutionalized wickedness implies that orthodox approaches to the analysis of mankind's history in terms of ideological striving and social dynamics are disingenuous hoodwinks and myopic delusions guided by psychopathic victors who rewrite texts, curricula, scripture and other narrations such as the New Testament. Indeed, such efforts are ongoing affairs conducted by trans-generational worldview programmers who have systematically qualified the initiation plenums of magi members of the Church of Luciferianism.[1]

> ... there is what Andrew Lobaczewski calls *Macrosocial Evil*: large scale evil that overtakes whole societies and nations, and has done so again

---

[1] A group of cults assigning either godhood or salvation status to Iblis as Lucifer, the bearer of enlightenment. For example: Freemasonry, OTO, Anthroposophy and various Gnostic persuasions.

and again since time immemorial. The history of mankind, when considered objectively, is a terrible thing.

Laura Knight-Jadczyk (ed)
Political Ponerology, op. cit.

... the despotism witnessed in Muslim history was a consequence of the dying away of [its] moral force. It also shows that the Muslim community failed to institutionalize it . . . we have thus managed to retain a fossilized society in the name of the Muslim community, whose basic religio-moral élan died down centuries ago.

S.M.A. Sayeed, The Myth of the Authenticity, New Delhi, 1999, 4.

Hence, in the absence of institutionalizing the Principles of God's Kingdom on Earth (as outlined in the next section), macrosocial evil is inevitable. When adding this fact of life to President Kennedy's admonition regarding his first hand acquaintance with the cult of evil as well as Imam Khaldun's assessment, Dr. Sayeed's remarks remain eminently relevant because, except for its imagination, there is scant evidence that the authentic religio-moral élan of nascent Islam has survived. This failure of what should have been a consequential political institutionalization of transcendent dominion in the affairs of men is what confronts the entire world today. Specifically stated, despite having a monopoly on the final revelation, Muslims failed to establish the Kingdom of God by running after booty. It may be said, therefore, that while they robustly observed/observe the rites of true religion like good fetishists, at the same time they neglect/neglected the *Rights of God* and his servants. This disregard is considerable as Muslims murder each other vigorously while repressing constituencies and women with the traditional universal frenzy of pious mania or pretense. Why is this?

Al'Qur'an qualifies the thesis by describing mankind's record as a struggle between 'Prophetic' and 'non-Prophetic' descendants of Prophet Adam who appears to represent 'homo sapiens sapiens'. This is to say that a contest exists between 'carefully cognizant' and 'pathologically heedless' groups of men and women that are multi-racial and cultural pluralities. Although creation should not be reduced in light of Islam's *tawhid*, we may consider this dualism a political struggle of 'non-transcendent' constituencies because both have failed to govern the earth righteously. In the end, and according to prophetic eschatology, these groups are forcibly divorced forever without any chance of reconciliation. Furthermore, and dreadfully so, the former group shrinks rather remarkably to only one per thousand (as per reliable Hadith), while the latter comprises an inverse complement bound for hell.

This being a rational perspective for spiritually sober servants of Allah swt, it is advisable for aspiring Muslim Scientists to review what Prof. William E. Connolly has called *The Neuropolitics* (micro-politics) *of the Body-Brain-Culture-Network*.[2] This is the now established scientific fact of social phenomenology to which Machiavelli referred when he offered the following counsel to his Prince:

> Conquered states that have been accustomed to liberty and the government of their own laws can be held by the conqueror in three different ways. The first is to ruin them; the second, for the conqueror to go and reside there in person; and the third is to allow them to continue to live under their own laws, subject to a regular tribute, and to create in them a government of a *few*, who will keep the country friendly to the conqueror. -
>
> *Neuropolitics: Thinking, Culture, Speed*, University of Minnesota & Press, 2000.

Presently these "few" include many who pose as patrons of Islamic Science but actually manage Rome's slaves via Body-Brain-Culture *PSYOPS*.[3] The latter are vain imaginations using mnemonics (semiotics) that persuade minions to peacefully pay tribute to the enemies of their well being or at least buy enough weapons to slaughter easily conjured enemies. This is a far cry from the Medina Constitution and offices of *Al'Hisbah* as described by Imam Hanbal's remarkable treatise on

---

[2] *Neuropolitics: Thinking, Culture, Speed*, University of Minnesota & Press, 2000.

[3] Psychological operations (PSYOP): Military Information Support Operations (MISO) are planned operations to convey selected information and indicators to audiences to influence their emotions, motives, objective reasoning, and ultimately the behavior of governments, organizations, groups, and individuals. JP 1-02 DOD Dictionary of Military and Associated Terms

Islam's *Khilafah*; especially in so far as it maximally defies the adjective 'Islamic', a word that does have degrees of qualification.

Al'Qur'an teaches us that 'illusions wrought by magicians [sorcerers] fail' and that these same 'wicked men [leaders] are placed in every city to burrow in their scheming'.[4] The good book further describes these fellows as a party of consummate hypocrites, which implies that many religious leaders attend their ranks. Why then do Muslim academics ignore frank statements of fact that imply the now scientifically established micro- and macro-political guidance of policy-making 'think tanks' for wicked scribblers? Could it mean that Muslim leaders haven't transcended the limitations offered by Dr. Connoly's science and subsequently abandoned the office of *al'hisbah* in deference to traditional political appeasements? It certainly appears that way. "That's Life" you say? I and others posit the contrary and go further to say that it is a clear path to the second death.

I submit, therefore, that both Muslim and non-Muslim academics have succumbed to a 'don't rock the boat' denial-syndrome that serves elitists in lieu of the *Rights of God*. They have turned their backs to men like Imam Ibn Hanbal and Malcolm X in deference to the cowardice that fulfills imminent gratification. I further submit that these same fellows and ladies entertain status-quo dialectics that have been conducted by murderous echelons since the 'Enlightenment' of a thoroughly Jacobin West.[5]

Without acknowledging such indictments in our search for an honest frame of reference, we cannot apply censure or other corrective actions and, hence, the advancement of truth and justice are summarily disallowed by an ongoing conspiracy of silence; one that promotes spineless rhetoric in micro- and macro-political theatres. The trickle-down effect is such that patriotic legions of post-Colonial Malays, for example, honor blackguards like Taib Mahmood and other

---

[4] In any society in this world, psychopathic individuals and some of the other deviant types create a ponerogenically active network of common collusions, partially estranged from the community of normal people. - *Political Ponerology*, op.cit. p. 138

[5] See: *The Hand of Iblis* by Omar Zaid; A. S. Noordeen, K.L. Malaysia (2010)

envoys of pathocracy who have licenses from London and Rome to systematically replace their native cultures with Western imprints while siphoning *Ali Baba* percentages offshore. In truth, they vicariously participate in transgressions against themselves and the 'Cause of God', much like those who have abandoned Islam to plague Syria or slaughter eccentrics like Colonel Khadafy for NATO *cum* Zionist overlords.

All of this is orchestrated by the 'Knights of Poneros[6] who murder or neutralize those who defy them, in addition to the merciless slaughter and rapine of all marginalized 'others'. They do this because typically colonized minds accept media bites and pay supportive taxes and sundry forms of *riba* laced tribute, as per E.W. Said's remarkable treatise, *Covering Islam*.[iii]

Notwithstanding this completely distasteful appraisal, the actual denial of their 'voluntary' participation in wickedness wounds the hearts of many a Muslim Academic and Imam. In turn, they seek balms of solace and 'world class' status in peer reviewed pretence; never minding, knowing or caring that such facilities are generally authored, mentored, managed and monitored by the enemies of their creed. Hence, when bearing in mind the inverted statistic cited earlier, the wisdom of such an ambition begs review.

Nevertheless, East-West North-South indifference is hardly ascribable to those who diligently attend the increasing divergence of affluence from rising levels of misery in the world. The plunders and devastations that accompany pan-cultural degradation reflect neo-imperialist efforts to create an attenuated (filtered) homogeny out of the controlled chaos of political and cultural pluralism. But the fact remains that this sociopathy is a form of insanity that escapes the micro-political cliques of politically-correct 'think-tanks' inhabiting mentally-colonized Islamia. The question, therefore, is 'Why'?

Neuro-Sociology actually defines the answer in simple and Islamically-correct terms:

---

[6] Greek for *evil*; current institution includes the Knights of Malta, for example.

> They have conformed to the left-brained sociopathy of sub-human ambition in pursuit of vain-glory, thereby becoming habituated to the perks that accompany its attainment at everyone else's expense. [7]

I'm paraphrasing of course, and no doubt this is a great insult to many who know me but it is of greater concern to those of us who are un-habituated to perks the righteous Caliphs would have scorned.

Surely solutions lie within the purview of Islam's eschatology and authentic traditions, along with its peerless universal doctrines. But nonetheless, and despite generations of Islamist hues, cries and obtuse mania, to find an authoritative political gauntlet represented by a *bona fide* Muslim voice is an exhausting if not fruitless pursuit. The donnish panaceas so far offered by pioneers of the Islamization-of-Knowledge (IOK) school seem not only unattainable and untenable but also arguable, divisive, uselessly academic, and, for the uninitiated, even patently absurd. Hence, this present study is an attempt at synthesis; one that steps beyond the particulars of reductionism and issue takers flaunting meaningless abstractions who have stood and presently stand impotent in the midst of a generic collegial resistance to courage and Divine Right. It is also offered as a remedy for the patented avoidance of acute sensitivities: a malady suffered by intellectual stars and Schools for Very-Very Important Scoundrels who are fed and watered by occult adepts behind curtains of pomp and circumstance.

At the transcendent level, and especially since attempts at objectivity are subjective reductions according to Prof. Connoly's research in agreement with Goethe, we must revisit the latter:

> ... to trace the phenomena to their sources, search out the point where they appear and exist, beyond which nothing further about them can be explained ... don't try to look beyond the phenomena. They themselves are the theory. Let the phenomena be very closely observed. Let the experiments be neatly performed. Let both them and their data be

---

[7] See: *Psychopathy vs. Antisocial Personality Disorder and Sociopathy: A Discussion* by Robert Hare; reviewed 2 Jan 2014,
http://www.cassiopaea.com/cassiopaea/psychopathy_aspd_sociopathy.htm

arranged in a definite order. Let one phenomenon be traced to another. Let a definite sphere of knowledge be outlined. Let views lay claim to certainty and completeness ... Let everyone draw his own conclusion— THEY PROVE NOTHING—certainly no 'isms and 'ologies. Opinions on all things pertain to the individual, and we know only too well that conviction depends not so much on insight as on inclination, no one grasping but what is within his ken and therefore acceptable to him. In knowledge, as in action, prejudice casts the deciding vote ... it is the spontaneous urge of our vital being toward truth as towards falsehood, toward all in which we feel in harmony.[iv] - J.W. Goethe

Accordingly, I have dispensed with the common academic pretense of dispassion in order to enhance this contribution with sufficient heart-pounding acumen to transcend academia's relations with knaves, deviants and time-honored projections of guilt and regret. The attempt is made with a view to focus on both compliance and non-compliance with Muslim responsibilities with but one caveat: 'to hell with sectarian and/or secular objections and objectors'.

For those who wish to consider thoughts on transcendence based on the perspectives offered by contemporary neuro-sciences and cognitive fields of inquiry, I recommend that you read Appendix One, which contains an excerpt that will surely demonstrate how far behind so-called Muslim "intellectuals" and "Alim" have fallen; including those with Master degrees in Islamic studies or some field or other that permits them to masquerade as scholars, scientists and even Physicians. I suggest you read it now so you do not become too un-nerved by the rest of this treatise. As for those who will indict me for hubris:

> The simple step of a courageous individual is not to take part in the lie. One word of truth outweighs the world.
>
> - Alexander Solzhenitsyn

Overview

> When a man has so far corrupted and prostituted the chastity of his mind, as to subscribe his professional belief to things he does not believe; he has prepared himself for the commission of every other crime. -
>
> Thomas Paine; "The Age of Reason", 1793

This ponerogenic maxim describes many Christian ministers as well as the Western allopaths who've trained the majority of Muslim doctors; which doesn't speak well for the next generation of Islamizers who will continue to poison their children with vaccines both physically and metaphysically with vain mnemonics. The sixty plus year palaver of 'Islamic Science' and its political front, the IOK movement (Islamization of Knowledge), is surely not insignificant and reflects Mr. Paine's concerns. The controversy is underscored by passages such as these:

> In Explorations in Islamic Science from 1989, Ziauddin Sardar describes the actors in the discourse by means of lines in, or titles of, songs from the world of pop and rock music. The headings of different sections are song titles. In this way the opinions of Seyyed Hossein Nasr are placed under the Beatles-inspired heading 'Nowhere Man'. Nasr is, according to Sardar, taking us on a 'Magical Mystery Tour'[8] and the part where Sardar

---

[8] S.H.Nasr's 'mystery tour' includes absurdities such as "God dwells in our heart" — a doctrine in keeping with religious romantics and those who wish Jesus or some higher power to reside there as well. Another of his doctrines is this: "The Sufi tradition contains a vast metaphysical and cosmological set of doctrines elaborated over a long period by Sufi teachers and masters of *gnosis*," ... as well as: "Sufism constitutes also a central link between the spiritual traditions of Islam and the West,' ... "Without the surrender of one's will, trust, and love for the *master, spiritual guidance is not possible*," which is a Jesuit cum Ismaili principle for blind following as required by Batinites and other sorcerers ... and of course the typical doctrine that all of us are essentially nothing: "Paradoxically, the greatest [Sufi] gift that has been given to us is the possibility of realizing our own nothingness;" part of the annihilation or *Fana* doctrine which he associates with Rudolph Steiner's *Akashic field*, a Hindu *cum* Freemasonic *cum* Theosophical doctrine ... all are serious statements of dangerous misguidance that have kept Muslims helplessly sanctimonious and piously romantic

summarizes Nasr's views is called 'Ground Control to Major Tom' after the first line in David Bowie's song 'Space Oddity' ... [v]

Muslim scientific productivity is very low. Indeed, if Muslims were to stop contributing to science, the rest of the world's scientific community would hardly notice. Moreover, Muslim cultures are marked by ambivalence about the modern scientific outlook. As a result, Islam harbors some very powerful pseudoscientific beliefs. Large numbers of Muslims from every nationality and sect are convinced that modern scientific and technological developments have been prefigured in the Qur'an. Evolution is almost absent from science education in many Muslim countries; Turkey has produced a very successful creationist movement. Some devout Muslim intellectuals have proposed that physics and biology be centered on divine design and that sociology and history be studied in a revelation-centered manner. Such pseudoscience is espoused by many university professors as well as popular religious leaders. Liberal Muslims would like to reinterpret their religion, but they are much more tentative than their Christian counterparts. So it is natural to ask whether Islam is incompatible with science."[vi]

Other perspectives are hard-hitting reactions to Columbia University's Dr. Saliba:

It was soon realized how emotionally charged individuals can become when it comes to a joint mentioning of religion, in our case, "Islam", with "science" – especially embodied in Dr. Saliba's usage of terms like "Islamic Science." The names and titles of the presentations by our worthy speakers were announced and individuals came up with responses like:

Some of the Muslims may derive motivation to seek knowledge by listening to the accounts of their ancestors' works. But then that's only a political gimmick, nothing more than bait.

And also:

---

rather than practical—even should they border on truth, which in this case, is readily mixed with lies and known liars. (see his, *The Garden of Truth,* pages, xv, xvi, 5, 134)

> The good thing about such a meeting is that you can get plenty of speakers who will be experts in this philosophical debate, but no real men or women of science.[vii]

Here is yet another writer with whom I sympathize:

> A variation on the same theme but purportedly salvaging the Muslim intellect from suffocating into the secularist void is the so-called Islamization of Knowledge. In its conceptual allegiance to Western science and technology it is no different from that of Muhammad Abdus Salam: It takes the value neutrality of knowledge as a monolith and spins an aura of Islamic terms and ideas around the corpus of substantive knowledge. Lest there be an accusation of harsh criticism, I should say their success in elucidating some aspects of Islamic economics deserves commendation. At the same time it serves to expose internal contradictions of the very idea by showing that any Islamization must address the crucial issue of values.[viii]

The "crucial" arena of 'values' is what I attempt to address with an uninhibited pen. Also, please note that the absence of "real [Muslim] men or women of science" in the debate—excepting a few such as Dr. Maurice Bucaille—is not a light consideration. As for my bias, I am compelled to favor the Saliba camp in opposition to what I perceive is an identity crisis on the part of those who generously accentuate Islam's contributions to Science, rich though they *were*:

> According to Dr. Saliba, modern science is a magnificent edifice made up of several building blocks. One of these many building blocks is Islamic Science.[ix]

As an informed critic of *Real Politics* and its manicured hypocrites, I have limited lenience for those who form NATO brigades of politically-correct 'No-Action-Talk-Only' conference-fiefdoms that are funded and managed by neo-Orientalists and institutions such as SCOPUS, the Freemasonic George Washington University, and Jesuits of Georgetown Ltd. Inc. et. alia. Though hard to come by, I much prefer the company of social-engineers and educators who practice authentic *adab* by putting things and people like history, liars, thieves, deviants, traitors and political sinners in proper place and perspective. Hence, I've consequently abandoned a polite 'tip-of-the-hat' to apologists who practice the fine art of casuistry. I do this in order to clear the no-man's land of dissimulation that permits ideologues to promote metaphysical cancer. But there are other reasons:

> My parents shipped me off to an Islamic school, or madrassa, in Lahore, to "get educated," as my mother said. I lived in a room with around 30 other girls—no chairs, no beds, no ventilation. In that room, we did nothing all day but study the Quran, pray, and listen to lectures on the prophet from a mullah, who stood behind a curtain. If a girl spoke out of turn, she would be publicly caned in the courtyard of the compound. Flies and vermin swarmed the washrooms. There were no sanitary napkins, just blood-stained towels. The toilet was a hole in the ground.
>
> Sabatina James
> *Why My Mother Wants Me Dead* (Mar 5, 2012)

How is it that the marvelous legacy left by Mohammad (pbh) has come to endure such a contemptible present? I venture to answer this with deference to any and all correction and admonition readers might offer along the way. I began the task when compelled by daily encounters, readings, queries, discoveries and bewildering current events; not the least of which were restraints that encumbered the minds, pens and tongues of many a colleague.

I address *Religio Perennis* as well as obstacles presented by various IOK sponsored definitions, after which I introduce extrinsic and intrinsic limitations as commanded by the very 'Real Politics' of very real Secret Societies. I touch firmly on the globalist conspiracy in relation to Frithjof Schuon *et alia.*, a movement that appears to be either sophisticated Tartufferie or blatant blasphemy from one of the darkest regents of Luciferianism. If you find the latter assertion fantastic I suggest you abandon metaphysics and envoys of the neo-Fascist Alliance—many of whom are advised and educated by Jesuits—until you don't.

The dissertation begins, however, beyond the pale of ritual religious discussion to present the challenges of 'Spiritual Law'. Rarely discussed as such in the traditional dialogue, these are followed by their inverse corollaries. I pray the reader will then come to realize divinely imbued principles that continually frustrate Islamists and utopian IOK fantasies.

I trust this is sufficient to wet appetites enough to not only read the analysis but also to sharpen red pencils and entertain foot and endnotes. By so doing, the reader might realize that the challenge of 'Islamizing Modernity' — an IOK plank — is a vain imagination. Why? — because neither Modernity nor Science can or need to be Islamized. To the contrary, it is the heart of men, women and most especially, children—beginning with so-called 'Muslims'—that require the disciplines attached to this process.

On the Present World Order

The Real Politics of the globalist conspiracy is well documented by far greater sleuths than I, including the unimpeachable Qur'an and authors of uncorrupt portions of Judeo-Christian scriptures and others. I also mention Drs. Steven Jones and Neils Harrit, who, together with numerous amply qualified scientists, have proven that seventy to one-hundred tons of the sophisticated military explosive known as nano-thermite brought down the three WTC towers rather than patsies assigned to Osama bin Laden's fictitious *Al'Qaeda*. Besides this, the BBC gave the entire scheme away when they announced the collapse of Building Seven ten minutes before it fell. It's high time, therefore, for Muslim academicians to acknowledge a most ancient conspiracy, as has Maulana Imran Hosein, a typically marginalized Qari scholar.

The Conspiracy's protagonist-retainers are represented today by the CIA, Mosad and MI-6 canailles, as well as by CFR Rogue Clintonians and Fulbright Scholars along with Papists, Bilderburger Palatines and Tavistockian Mind-Benders ala the Freudian mold of Freemasonic B'nai B'rith Zionists, *et alia* with campus extensions in Chicago, Columbia, Princeton, Yale and Harvard; not to mention the London School of Economics for masters of usury.

This alarming collective systematically inserts *ism* fabricators and facilitators with sophisticated instruments supported by Foundation Funds and IFIs within and without the fortress of Islam's beguiled defenders and supporters. They float aloft in the guise of round-table think-tanks, OIC representatives, and/or reformers in the mold of Gemal Attaturk (a Freemason and Crypto-Jew Sabataen), much like those who followed the Grand Master Al'Afghani into Masonic lizard holes of misguidance. Of such were the Freemasons Mohd. Abduh, the Egyptian Khedive, and Mohammad Rashid Rida. These devotees of Luciferianism comprised an elite (*khassa*) assigned by Iblis to the Rothschild consortium of affected Zionists, Romanist Knights of Malta, European nobility of the ancient Dragon Cult of Cain, and the sundry crypto-Jews who fund, navigate and arm the Globalist armada that assaults and impoverishes five-sixths of humanity daily.

Unfortunately, and as prophesied, many Muslims such as the Middle East 'Royal Mafia' have joined their cause. Others are slow to accept these facts or are caught by Arab gold in webs of deceit woven by professionally trained reform-artisans: a group of operatives who sedulously advance ideological 'fifth columns' within Muslim domains and unwittingly support their own demise.

Omar Zaid Abdullah, M.D.

21 Dec 2011
Chiang Khom, Thailand

PART ONE: THE METAPHYSICS OF SPIRITUAL LAW

THE MEDINA PRINCIPLES
& Spiritual Determinism

Spiritual Law & The Rights of God

Now, divine laws affecting men are all for their good and envisage the interests (of men).

This is attested by the religious law. Bad laws, on the other hand, all result from stupidity and from Satan, in opposition to the predestination and power of God. He makes both good and evil and predetermines them, for there is no maker except Him ... After one knows the principles of jurisprudence, one can enjoy, as its result, the knowledge of the divine laws that govern the actions of all responsible Muslims. This is jurisprudence ... whatever actions you perform and conversations you have should be in accordance with the Shari'ah (Divine law), because whatever the knowledge and actions of [God's] creations not in accordance with the Shari'ah (Divine law), are clearly misguided and keep them (i.e. creations/human beings primarily) away from the truth. [x]

Ibn Khaldun[9]

---

[9] Arnold Toynbee wrote, "He [Ibn Khaldun] conceived and created a philosophy of history that was undoubtedly the greatest work ever created by a man of intelligence...." . . . "So groundbreaking were his ideas, and so far ahead of his time, that a major exhibition now takes his writings as a lens through which to view not only his own time but the relations between Europe and the Arab world in our own time as well." - Caroline Stone, Cambridge, [Picture: Rembrandt; Ibn Khaldun with Tamerlane]

Introduction to the Spiritual Law of Islam

Premise:

The Three Principles of Spiritual Determinism or 'Pillars' of Spiritual Law

On the day of Mohammad's entry to Medina, the Prophet (pbh) gave a resounding speech containing several important principles that are directly associated with what Ibn Khaldun called 'predestination'. Three of these principles are crucial determinants for the successful establishment of any Islamic polity and College of Islamic Science. In addition, when understood and employed consciously and conscientiously, they preserve the union.

1. Fear of God

> ... "My words cannot be changed nor am I indeed unjust to the slaves." (Q 50:29) Therefore fear Him in this world and the world to come, in the seen and the unseen, since who fears Him, God grants him redemption for his sins and favors him with great reward. This person alone is highly successful. Fear of Allah saves man from His wrath, His punishment and anger. This will brighten the faces of people and elevate them on the Day of Judgment. Fear Allah, walk on the path of virtue and piety.

This principle, once established in the heart, is ground for all sober contemplations leading to truth and right action. It stands alone as the metaphysical rock upon which responsible decisions must be held forth in light of man's ultimate accountability. Therefore, the Muslim is compelled to "walk on the path of virtue and piety" in 'Fear of Allah' in order to succeed in this life as well as the next.

2. Obedience to God;

> Do not show any slackness in obedience to God. Allah has revealed the Book for your teaching and has made the right path clear for your guidance so that truth can be distinguished from falsehood. Just as Allah

has shown you His favor, likewise you should obey Him in right earnest. Look upon His enemy as yours and exert your best for winning His favor. Allah has chosen you for Himself and has given you the name of 'Muslims'. God has ordained that those who are to be destroyed will be swept away and those who are to survive, after the clear signs have come to them, would live with *insight* and on the *strength of evidence*.

This passage makes clear the right path for decision making, meaning the attentive and firm application of man's will towards choosing what is good by means of correct moral discernment. This faculty actively segregates what is beneficial from what is harmful and is only acquired as the result of obedience, which demands assiduous attention to the acquisition of knowledge via diligent activities and the avoidance of God's enemies.

3. Remembrance of God;

No power [political] is of any avail except the Power of Allah. Therefore, remember God as much as you can and live for the Hereafter. The man whose relation with God is based on sincerity, Allah will help Him against evil. None will be able to harm him [protection]. Allah's command is supreme over the people [authentic authority]. But people cannot command God.[10] Allah alone is Master of all men and men have no share in His lordship. Therefore, keep your relation with Allah on the right footing.

The establishment of this 'right footing' of remembrance in a person's life consequently leads the spiritually sober individual to choose treasures in heaven rather than 'the goods and chattels of deception'. But this does not imply that chanting like decadent monks is sufficient because such activities are egocentric and fall short of the real goal. Nevertheless, those who sincerely remember Allah live their lives for the Hereafter and in so doing they consequently discipline themselves to relentlessly choose what is ultimately and absolutely beneficial and

---

[10] Something many who practice form of sorcery think they are doing, including Christians who have been taught to speak forth a matter in the name of Jesus.

moral in the 'here and now'. Were Muslims so actively compliant rather than ritually pre-occupied, 'no harm' would come to them save for impediments that are soon balanced by the rewards granted to those who successfully meet life's trials.

The Contingency of Moral Imperatives

I will now establish that most of what Muslims experience at the hands of their enemies is judgment rather than trial. This negative estate represents inverse consequences leading to physical and metaphysical entropy.[11] The laws that govern this degradation are default determinants of spiritual laws inductively derived from the three principles just presented. But before discussing these estates of demerit, the required contingencies that attend divine grace is presented.

Wisdom is the specific knowledge of God that engenders the understanding of purpose. Man's discernment of right or wrong, good or evil, harm or benefit in a thing or creature 'scientifically' observed, devised, socially structured or physically manufactured is contingent on the acquisition of wisdom. Hence, moral idiocy encompasses secularism by Islamic standards as it compartmentalizes or ignores the remembrance of God, thus, making it a form of forgetfulness, and hence, irrational. This naturally follows the metaphysical inebriations that attend the neglect of spiritual laws since all positive consequences of mankind's deeds require moral actions. Inherent with the faculty of wisdom that 'begins with the Fear and Reverence of God' is the knowledge of our accountability and purpose in this world and in the world to come, this is to say: "the Meeting with Us", as oft written in Al-Qur'an.

---

[11] A measure of the unavailability of a system's energy to do work; in a closed system an increase in entropy is accompanied by a decrease in energy availability . . . In a wider sense, entropy can be interpreted as a measure of disorder; the higher the entropy the greater the disorder. - Oxford Dictionary of Science, 6th Ed, 2010

It is within this moral sphere of reflection and activity that the sciences, be they hard, soft, political or otherwise, lack wisdom. And though virtue is oft aired in theatres of pomp and circumstance, it is rarely applied consequently as justice in mankind's political, economic and social realms of exchange. This is because leadership autonomously defaults towards reprobation when the three principles described above are not consciously activated and maintained according to spiritual law. Furthermore, this activation and maintenance is not an individual task but a collective responsibility. Hence, when leaders, educators, advisors and *alim* et alia 'sell the purpose of religion' to unrighteous benefactors to whom they then owe their obedience, collective responsibility is abandoned and the default status of spiritual law immediately begins to fog the entire realm.

Such an estate invites *poneros* because it does not reflect fear or reverence for the three divine principles just cited. Furthermore, those realms that preach but do not practice these principles, reflect a collective form of hypocrisy.

> What makes it so plausible to assume that hypocrisy is the vice of vices is that integrity can indeed exist under the cover of all other vices except this one. Only crime and the criminal, it is true, confront us with the perplexity of radical evil; but only the hypocrite is really rotten to the core:
>
> Hannah Arendt - Political Philosopher

When integrity surrenders to such 'rottenness' it proceeds towards reprobation or, at the very minimum, sub-conscious repression as a natural course of human events and even mass denial. Although outwardly, things may appear otherwise, even normal, until calamity strikes and all is lost, including the reactionary reserve of conservative slogan mongers. This is very simple to comprehend because righteous dominion is abandoned along with moral imperatives while the Rights of God (the application of justice) are replaced by collective rituals that cover the communal pretense, which, in turn, only serves to nourish evil's progress towards dominion. Only those who withdraw in active protest are exempt from the natural consequences that follow the group's gradual repression and possible reprobation. A clear example of this is Prophet Noah. Meanwhile, those who protest but remain within the group are marginalized and repressed as per customary sub-human responses defined below as 'neo-patriarchy' and ponerogenesis according to social scientists who have intensively studied the matter. Although Muslims have been instructed to flee such oppression, the sad fact is that from the palace to the village hut, a majority of today's Muslims have become oppressors, even self-oppressors.

The extreme end of this determinant is reprobation, which is God's abandonment of man to his own devices. In the case of hypocrites, this retrogression happens in stages until the heart is blinded and completely given over to hypocrisy and open depravity as habits that progress towards instinctive behavioral patterns and a sense of shameless entitlement devoid of conscientious empathy. Many nations have, and are now following, this pattern of inevitable devolution; with the American government as a prime example of exceptionalism to normal human sensitivity.

To the contrary, the righteous dominion Muslims are meant to hold is contingent on the activation and maintenance of moral imperatives. What you are about to read is an examination of the process of their abandonment and the absurdity of denying the fact. This book therefore represents a morbidity and mortality report utilizing IOK and Islamic Science movements as tip-of-the-iceberg indicators of pathology whereby academics strain at gnats to justify elephants already swallowed. Here is an example of that effort from the Malaysian political milieu:[12]

> Yet they have also provided importance for the Administration's articulation of its vision of "right" Islam: as a "balanced, moderate and modernizing force that would not impede foreign investment, that was accepting of certain secular Western forms and that has taken account of current political realities in the Muslim and outside world." In the PM's

---

[12] *Islam in Malaysian Foreign Policy*, by Shanti Nair, p 116, 117.

view, "true" *dakwah*, unlike "the wrong interpretation of Islam" is distinguished by its reason, logic and sound argument. A real resurgence of Islam needed a solid foundation of contemporary ideas and analysis derived from the Quran and Sunnah, which could only emerge if there was "true" 'ijtihad.

You might imagine my chuckle as I read this because it is the position Muslims leaders have taken for quite some time, especially the part about the 'wrong interpretation of Islam'. To hear the leader of a profoundly corrupt political party whose Minister of Religion is not a *qari"* espouse such sublime thoughts is, well ... as I've already explained.

Never mind that the "right" approach to Islam demands that authentic *mujtahids* and *qari* sit on dais of power and practice the authentic *'ijtihad* that would impeach two-thirds of most Muslim political parties. Hence, politically-correct parties admit religiously-minded substitutes who are suitably attired in sensitive cultural garb on pulpits paid for by the State. Sounds fairly Anglican (essentially Catholic) to me and is exactly what the enemies of Islam desire. Perhaps you do not agree:

> ... that even while it was promoting greater values in society, this was "contradicted" by its pursuit of an intensive pace of economic growth and development that continues fundamentally to be based on secular Western models and to be over-concerned with material acquisition.[13]

Take a mortgage from one of these "Islamic Banks" and compare your final costs to a loan from a non-Islamic Bank and see how much you haven't saved. My old friend, Haji Taufek in Kuching (God rest his soul) did exactly this with a Dakwah Project that required a mortgage and became absolutely furious (in my presence) when he counted the cost as 50% higher than a mortgage from a pagan Chinese lender. I personally know an 'Economic Hit Man' sent to the country by a well known Boston firm responsible for a new IT development and capital

---

[13] Ibid.

city project. He reported to me personally, in 2010, that after his firm received their fees for extremely sophisticated planning, during the years that followed, greater than fifty percent of the tax funded project meant to benefit the people never materialized. I imagine the money disappeared into coffers of a more "correct" interpretation of Islam'. Naturally his superiors in Boston were disappointed because they had anticipated future takings.

As distinct from sophists[xi] and politically-correct impresarios of abstraction and Orwellian spin — sociopaths Dr. Lobaczewski calls 'spellbinders' — it is clear that only the pragmatic application of monotheist wisdom via the strong arm of *al'hisbah*[14] qualifies a people as fully Islamic. In addition, as knowledge is morally neutral until man willfully acts on it in order to reap its reward, it is also clear that the term 'Islamic' does not qualify as a scientific adjective unless any actions applied to such knowledge are moral. Furthermore, and to the contrary, failure to enact moral imperatives qualifies the inaction as immoral. Hence, moral ends cannot possibly be achieved by 'talking heads' at Islamization conferences with Jesuit-friendly Universalists where pundits are underwritten by those who hold the offices of *al'hisbah* at bay and, at the same time, control pulpits that endorse acceptable versions of "true" *ijtihad* that justify their political party's tenure. I witnessed several such forums at the Jesuit stronghold called IAIS in KL, Malaysia. This group substituted '*Islam Hadhari*' for the '*One Malaysia*' slogan, literally overnight, for these very reasons.

To comprehend the indictment, one must remember that 'Islam' is not a term that applies to God but to man. It is also a conditional term that infers obligations towards God, creation and each other. These duties are what I refer to as the 'Rights of God' because it is He, the Almighty, who defined them and taught them to us as moral imperatives. Hence, if you think of these contingencies as an assignment owed to your teacher you will reap the everlasting point of the matter. Hence again, without meeting these indispensable

---

[14] The enjoining of good and forbidding of evil in concert with the fear of Allah (SWT) balanced by the hope of His grace.

conditions by willfully applying moral action, man neglects the 'Rights of God' even if he keeps religious ritual.

Pol Pot and Peking's Gang of Four killed their respective majorities of traditional educators after which they systematically replaced them with suitably attired substitute teachers as part of the Comintern's Twentieth Century experiment. David Rockefeller is actually on record for having acknowledged the success of *their* 'social experiment' in China. The 'silencing' and relegation of sound traditions and human voices that define higher culture to museums and text books is what 'Black Hats' do with exceptional expertise; another reason *Islam Hadhari* programs suffered the stroke of a pen from 'One Malaysia' slogan mongers. *PSYOPS* strategists who prosecute the Western Cultural War refer to this process as 'neutralization': an operation that has several degrees and may require a wide range of agents from the Penthouse to the jackal's den.

An analogy that describes the dilemma IOK presently confronts is that of a man who promises a woman at age twenty that he intends to marry her but sixty-five years later has not done so. In this case, consider IOK proponents the groom and the office of *Al'Hisbah* the bride or at least a lady in waiting. Does this qualify as moral action, immoral inaction, just plain idiocy, or despicable hypocrisy—being the non-deed of those who claim Islam as their 'complete' religion? How much more impotent then are those who claim to defend Islamic Science without annihilating the evil in their midst? Perhaps they even fail to perceive or acknowledge it? After all, 'Black Hats' and their Magi really are that good in the propaganda departments of deception.

Hence, I posit that conferences on Islamic 'anything,' whether Science, Islamization, ritual or food are indeed moot or at best academic in light of the principles described by Mohammad (pbh) and the endemic Muslim failure to impeach the evil in their midst and treat the enemies of God as their own. To the contrary, they have actually ignored or denied these evils while embracing God's enemies, especially the latter's money.

Mere indictment is, therefore, grossly insufficient when the evil is institutionalized well enough to inhibit the fruits of moral activity.

Under this condition, the adjective 'Islamic' applies only in its passive and most debilitated sense. To pretend otherwise is pathetic stupidity, yet this very denial is something many have succumbed to. It actually represents a lack of collective resolve and the inability to effectively confront Islam's true enemies, which includes the person in the mirror. This inadequacy is one that Talmudic magi refer to as psychological gelding. Hence, it is no small wonder they particularly hold Muslims in contempt while tipping over dominoes in the Arc of Crisis. If this were not the case, their advances into Iraq, Afghanistan, Libya, Egypt, Syria, Muslim Banking and shopping malls would not have been prophesied or recorded.

During the Golden Age of Islamic civilization, the fear of God permeated the physical and metaphysical sciences along with the community. We might even justifiably call this period the 'Age of Islamic Science', but not because science needed Islamizing; although the term was never utilized until Sayyed Nasr's 1948 thesis. Contemporary Muslims of the time were imbued with a moral force that freely and actively chose what was good and beneficial while seeking the highest chairs of ethics and scientific achievement.[xii] Sadly, this is presently not the case at all. The fear of God's wrath has given way to ritual browbeating on Fridays followed by traditional sin till the next kutbah. The present state of affairs confirms this with horrific crimes of 'Muslim on Muslim' slaughter, honor killings, rape, and the sexual outrages of incest and pederasty, not to mention disguised *riba*. All of this is accompanied by patrons of garish pomp and the common embarrassment of congregations that lack well informed imams as well as Allah's protection and guidance.

The faculty of spiritual discernment most society's lack is absolutely dependent upon the maintenance of institutions that are disciplined to obey Divine Revelation. This, in turn, and as I shall clearly demonstrate below, allows men to grasp and maintain the guidance of divine inspiration collectively. Without such disciplined institutions, communal attendance to authentic intuition (i.e., divinely inspired common sense) is blocked as it simply cannot penetrate beyond veils of ignorance, apathy, lethargy and crimes against self and heaven.

Under such circumstances the communal zeitgeist is bound by conformity to evils that are not even recognized as such and to activities that are mistaken as beneficial. Such errors are antithetical to Allah's formative word of creation and, hence, activate predetermined inverse determinants that lead to illness and malignant dissolution, individually and collectively.[15]

Think of this activation as a kind of metaphysical 'reverse' switch that is highly specific and pertains to either individual or community. In cases of abject reprobation such as Cain (*Khabil*) or that of Sodom, the disintegration of creative formative powers becomes fixed on predetermined paths that are essentially hardwired into the fabric of the universe. Such cases as these are far beyond the more pliant trails that remain amenable to remediation after repentance, which is the changing of one's ways as described in the parable of the Prodigal Son. Politically, abject reprobation crystallizes to crusty fascism or becomes monstrously deformed and morbidly tumescent like Imperial Rome, or catatonically vegetative as were Arab and Ottoman chauvinists during their pre-Colonial nap, or hyperactively Dionysian like Africa and India or Western night-life in Washington D. C.

Within each nation's degenerative cycle, one finds all of these processes with one holding dominion over the others depending upon predisposed temperaments conformed to respective misguidance. In Italy you can visit Fascism in its Temples and Dionysius in Vatican abodes, alleys and penthouses. This crystallization *cum* dissolution process happens socially, physically, cognitively, psychologically, politically, religiously, metaphysically and intellectually until chaos is king of all systems of devolution though they appear otherwise — such is the case presently in the United States.

Under the governance of any such spiritual reversal, man is forced to accept and rationalize the acceleration of national morbidity because it is the inevitable result of misdeeds and misrule. Yet he is quick to say: "that's life" when in fact it is death, after which the

---

[15] For a dissertation on this process with regard to human sexualization and abnormalities, see: *The Taqua of Marriage*, A. S. Noordeen (2011)

second death follows. Examples of such irrational apathy are the conundrum of nuclear waste control with Fukushima's fallout or the extensive co-lateral damage of modern warfare or even free-trade agreements that destroy the order that follows local autonomy. But readers should realize that although the current devastation of an exploited environment and populace is caused by the monetized mindset of Wall Street profiteering that has raised 'occupation' levels of streets and minds, this so called awakening or rebellion reflects little more than a kind of misplaced hyperactivity such as what occurred during the so-called Arab Spring. The same process accompanies carbuncles, allergies, anxiety ridden histrionics, and even irritable alimentary systems. It is symptomatic rather than curative or palliative. It is not medicine. To find the cure one must make an intimate companion of logic.

Wisdom is what our modern scientists and governors lack in metaphysical diets and the basis for the deficiency are ideologies that imply human autonomy, such as Humanism. Humanism is the very same "illumination" sponsored by Jacobin pluralism and the promotion of abstract concepts such as liberty, equality, unity and justice, all of which were promoted without scientific definitions. Hence, logic was replaced with emotionally based rationalism, a phenomenon any psychologist will tell you is pathological; most especially in the absence of divine revelation and wisdom — my apologies Mr. Paine. What happens in such a vacuum is that it quickly fills with the wicked cunning that, if unopposed, generates all pathocracy.

Furthermore, as it is clear that constructs from the Enlightenment gave license for Western elites to artfully create Nation States [16] for plunder, the person with common sense who perceives the error naturally asks: "*Quidnam rector universitas est*? Who then is Master of the Cosmos and how do I honor Him instead of the cronies and exalted felons of this Empire of Cunning?" I will now attempt to explain the 'hows' and 'whys' in support of the already known 'Who', according to

---

[16] B. Anderson described nations and nationalisms as "imagined communities." See *Imagined Communities: Reflections on the Origin and Spread of Nationalism*. London : Verso, 1983.

laws that comprise the spiritual determinism that is sometimes referred to as predestination.

I. The Law of Obedience:

God does not grant the legacy of prophetic authority to the disobedient.

And we bestowed on Moses evident authority. [An-Nisa, vs. 153]

There are two apposite but opposing types of authority in the earth; both are legitimate but only one is blessed with divine approbation and grace. When a person obeys God's Commandments as related by His Prophets or through inherent common sense (*fitrah*), God, as his King, grants him or her the grace of divinely approved validation and vicegerency with the dignity of *as-Sakkinah* (peace and security). The existential validation of this maturation is something we strive for and is what the various initiation rites of indigenous peoples have tried to represent from time immemorial. This fundamental need for validation actually drives men with tyrannical ambitions to excel and seek peace and security by means of an illicit hegemony that never grants it. Men of sloth, on the other hand, simply go through the motions of phallic wielding fully expecting validation to be handed to them. Both types easily regress to anger and rage—for different reasons—when those under their hand do not endorse their presumed authority on cue. Others, when faced by frustration or repeated failure, often turn to dissipation to ease the pain of inner-shame, while pitiful persons turn to the ultimate indignation of suicide. In any event, men desire to govern; it is their nature—whether hovel or mansion matters not. However, only one type of human governs successfully and that is the obedient believer, Muslim or not.

The question is: 'What is the measure of their success'?

The answer is *as-Sakkinah*. Such people are content in the now and certain of joyful tranquility in the hereafter. Their bearing is the unassuming and unassailable *dignitas* that brooks all offence. Persons validated by Allah are those who strive to live to the fullest of their potential without fear of other men—not being the least bit concerned for the latter's approbation unless it is a matter of righteous admonition. These are people of God's blessed and authentic Authority—otherwise called the 'Salt of the Earth'. Their counter-parts in the other legitimate kingdom have, on the other hand, submitted to the league of Satan's illusion of validation. These folk require medals, certificates, degrees, trophies, secret initiations and the pomp and circumstance of public accolades. It really is that simple, nor is it a facile assessment.

Men in positions of authority without God's validation (guidance), whether in shanty or presidential chair, are persistently troubled by the lack of voluntary submission by persons under their hand, whether wife and children, employees, political adherents or religious congregations. They become renegades from truth who regress to tyranny, Wagnerian propaganda, oppression, and ultimately, megalomania, to greater or lesser degrees depending on capacity.

To the contrary, obedient folks of Godly authority carry the big stick of peaceful integrity. Such people are not troubled by the petty complaints of spouse or child. Their subordinates and companions quickly fall into line as well—as I did whenever my sixth grade teacher silently walked into class. Disobedient men do not carry such a rod of authority because they haven't put forth the effort of to get one. It's a supra-natural grace gift that is simply not made available to them.

II: The Law of Submission:

Those who do not submit to God's prophetic guidance, submit to misguidance by default. There is no divine help for them.

> Even if thou (O Muhammad) desirest their right guidance, still Allah assuredly will not guide him who misleadeth. Such have no helpers. [An-Nahl, vs. 37]

The Qur'an also teaches that Allah gives such people jinn for *walliyah*. They receive no help from God, neither in this world nor on the Day of Judgment. Temporal respite is the only grace available to them, presenting a hopeless situation filled with endless trouble.

Exceptions are compliant servants of righteous men and women and communities submitted to such people. These folk perform ritual but take little thought beyond their remuneration schedules. Most are shallow souls: decent people following commonly acceptable patterns of living who fail to seek out the things or knowledge of God and universe. They rarely pray with comprehension or perhaps attend communal prayers with a sort of self-effacing embarrassment; often not knowing what they recite or why they bother except for the illusion of safety that conformity provides. The world is filled with them and I pray the mercy of God will embrace the limited measure of will they do give to His cause in the earth.

Nonetheless, complacent communities that do not rise to the command of preventing evil or even migrating from its dominion will certainly not be spared the judgment of God's Hammer should it fall on their earthly domain as it did in Baghdad twice within the last millennium or recently in the voodoo haven of Haiti where 250,000 were killed in a few moments, or in shaman saturated soils where a tsunami took an even greater toll without warning, or in the domains of neo-patriarchy where bombs and bullets fly indiscriminately.

III: The Law of Decay

If man does not consciously attend to diligence, whatever he possesses and governs will decay prematurely.

> But Satan whispered evil to him: he said, "O Adam! shall I lead thee to the Tree of Eternity and to a kingdom that never decays?"
>
> Surah 20. Ta-ha, vs: 120

We may also call this the 'Law of Neglect'. This law is implicit in the thermodynamic principle of entropy: the tendency towards disorder or better said, towards the energy of chaos (unformed created potential). Here we have our call to work in order to maintain what we have acquired by God's leave, whether it is material or spiritual in nature.

Without diligent maintenance a marriage will sink just as easily as a poorly tended aircraft falls from the sky. This law is also the inverse of the 'Law of Husbandry'.

Husbandry is an Adamic responsibility especially incumbent upon leaders (Imams). Neglect at any level of human activity fails to conserve economy or effectively utilize resources and causes waste, something Allah hates.[17] When leaders are not vigilant their divine liability increases because waste increases as do the crimes of their citizenry who otherwise would have little opportunity or impetus to cross bounds that should have been set and enforced.

Criminal activity in itself is waste and illicit activities such as immorality or betrayal of the public trust are direct results of lax husbandry (al'hisbah) which exposes the unredeemed nature of a nation's government and people. Righteous husbandry is police work and governance of the highest order. In Islam it is the enjoining of good and the forbidding of evil. It's cloak is that of the shepherd and calls for watchful eyes and the dispassionate administration of swift justice:

> [*Hisbah*] is a broad principle of public law that entitles everyone to take a vigilant attitude towards corruption and abuse ... The head of state and government officials are under an obligation ... to discharge their trusts faithfully and justly:
>
>> No servant of God to whom God has made custodian over others dies without this predicament: God will forbid the countenance of paradise to him if he has died while betraying those who were in his custody.[xiii]

This also applies to men who lie to wives and children as their Imam. A majority of Muslim men are loathe to be good shepherds or actually choose to remain untrained for the position and hence ignorant of their duties. As a direct result, and as I will demonstrate, they have also become intolerant chauvinists who fail to recognize and support

---

[17] "... But waste not by excess: for Allah loveth not the wasters."
Surah 6. Cattle, Livestock vs: 141 (a recurrent statement)

righteous leadership so that betrayal of the public trust is now the Muslim norm.

Allah SWT intended for Islam to alter this predisposition for recurring social disorder by perfectly designing the Islam of Prophet Mohammad (pbh) to do so. If not for the neglect of her Imams, we would not have witnessed the decay of Muslim civilization as an inevitable consequence. They have done and are doing injustice to themselves and to their constituencies and arrogantly refuse to repent of the negligence.

In light of this fact, there is small need for conferences on Good Governance unless it is to bring leaders to their knees by means of the truth. This is an authentic Alim's duty. Where are they?

Consequences

Any correct focus of ultimate concern for Muslims is not hard science, which is inherently Islamic, but rather the implementation of the Medina Principles in support of all scientific pursuit. This existential need may be described as a pre-existant requirement for the development of beneficially moral, intellectual, social and institutional dynamics that consequently and naturally support a worldview in which science flourishes for the cause of man's authentic success. To the contrary, and as adequately demonstrated by the present melee of "Common Word" ismology conferees and mayhem in the several 'Arcs of Crisis', without a re-orientation towards such a sobering synthesis, the ongoing decline of Muslim culture describes a devolution towards primitive comfort zones that marshal pragmatic social conformity towards destructive applications of scientific knowledge.[xiv] Such moral, social, spiritual and physical decay is divinely preordained and has many historical precedents. This is because it is constitutionally incorporated in the fabric of mankind's nature and cannot be avoided. No matter what we attempt in our many flights from truth, every such exodus arrives at the same terminus of futility.

The absence of these applied principles in the life of any Muslim reveals a profound lack of understanding even in the presence of ritual effort. If the negation of these principles applies to those who conduct and determine the course of governance along with scientific pursuit, then education and the exploitation of the knowledge gained can only fall short of beneficial utilization for the absolute good of the polity. This is the legacy of all reductionism as the antithesis of a *tawhidic* faith-based epistemology whose foundation or "footing" is Revelation and the conscientious application of the three pillars of Spiritual Law. Hence, and for example, those endorsing pre-occupations such as *Religio Perennis,* as I will demonstrate in Part Two of this thesis, actually subsume Revelation rather than elevate it.

Therefore the divine sunnah's inverse set of predetermined dynamics only bring harm as presently reaped globally. This is because the course of man's cognizant faculties and subsequent behavior and choices are innately pre-determined by inverse consequences that autonomously attend any neglect of imperatives described by Mohammad (pbh) in Medina. This is the consequent default state of human reason when heedless of revelation and common sense. The manifestation of this unavoidable estate is articulated by well defined principles I have called the 'Inverse Principles of Divine Law'. Such carelessness successfully pilots societies towards substituting imperious sanctimony with its abasement of human dignity for genuine piety, inevitably leading to the following outcomes.

Inverse Determinant of Principle One:

Not Heeding the Fear and Remembrance of God:

The psychogenesis of successful *gestalt* reflection and contemplation begins with the Fear-of and Reverence-for God. The inverse or default status of this law implies a non-gestalt quality or insufficiency of thought and contemplation. This diminished capacity automatically leans towards reduced cognizance which, in turn, obviates revelation and inspiration and, hence, removes the excogitator from divine guidance. Even in the face of great intellect, divine guidance does not penetrate the heart as it is automatically veiled by ignorance as well as Allah's neglect because such individuals have neglected God by rejecting instinct and their pre-incarnate covenant with God as described in Al'Qur'an. The result is that they are given over to delusions with reprobate jinn as helpers who suggestions they then serve as identity and dignity markers until repentance or the grave. This is *shirk* (idolatry).

This inverse principle is what determines the course of numerous schools of reified materialism which (i) is the misapplication of Newtonian Physics and (ii) promotes morality's divorce from scientific endeavor, much the same as Humanism's alienation of church from the state. It manifests currently as the false religion of secular pluralism complete with icons like the Olympic Torch of Mithras, Eye of

Horus, Pyramids, Harry Potter and Lord of the Rings Hobbit romances, etc.

Attending this negative estate is a serious malady that affects the production of so-called 'scholars' whereby political considerations and 'special interests' discard the riper fruits of moral criticism and honest enquiry. Hence, standards are lowered or modified according to the reigning philosophically tenured bias of sycophancy. In turn, this allows incompetents, intelligent toadies and Freemasonic satraps like Pres. Eisenhower or Mohammad Abduh to be promoted over more worthy and righteous contenders.

What then follows is a tradition whereby personal inadequacies of intellectual, moral and ethical character are segregated and actively suppressed from public notice.[18] For example, plagiarism is rampant in many Muslim institutions which permits incompetents to sit in chairs of pretense as the result of cronyism, nepotism, racial quotas, apathy and ignorance. It also allows Institutional Governors to attend non-Islamic ideations such as Humanism or Illuminist sponsored [xv] ecumenical universalism—exactly as warned against in surah Al-Baqarah vs. 120, 145:

> Never will the Jews or the Christians be satisfied with you unless you follow their form of religion. Say: "The Guidance of Allah—that is the (only) Guidance." Were you to follow their desires after the knowledge which has reached you, then would you find neither protector nor helper

---

[18] Under such conditions, no area of social life can develop normally, whether in economics, culture, science, technology, administration, etc. Pathocracy progressively paralyzes everything. Normal people must develop a level of patience beyond the ken of anyone living in a normal man's system just in order to explain what to do and how to do it to some obtuse mediocrity of a psychological deviant who has been placed in charge of some project that he cannot even understand, much less manage. This special kind of pedagogy — instructing deviants while avoiding their wrath — requires a great deal of time and effort, but it would otherwise not be possible to maintain tolerable living conditions and necessary achievements in the economic area or intellectual life of a society. Even with such efforts, pathocracy progressively intrudes everywhere and dulls everything. - Political Ponerology, op. cit. p. 195.

Author's Note: There are 'degrees' Pathocracy that approach but do not reach the Totalitarian norm of a Stalin or Chairman Mao.

against Allah ... Even if you were to bring to the people of the Book all the Signs (together), they would not follow your Qiblah; nor are you going to follow their Qiblah; nor indeed will they follow each other's Qiblah. If you after the knowledge has reached you, were to follow their (vain) desires—then were you indeed (clearly) in the wrong.

And in Al-Anam vs 144:

> But who does more wrong than one who invents a lie against Allah, to lead astray men without knowledge? For Allah guides not people who do wrong.

The consequences of this grievous knowledge vacuum are spiritual defaults that are antithetical to mankind's benefit that indelibly lead to (i) the loss of Allah's Guidance; (ii) the loss of Allah's protection as per Qur'an's admonishment; and (iii) great harm.

When men forget to fear God's judgment by promoting incompetence, self-aggrandizement, ignorance, tribalism and identitarian favoritism, the reality of *akhira* becomes veiled even if intellectually acknowledged. The only possible result is failure rather than success. This antithetical estate is readily revealed by the following dictum: 'The greater the pageantry presented by the institutions so influenced, the greater their heedlessness of true scholarship and just governance'. For this reason, Hadrat Umar removed Khalid from his post because opulence and its trail of elitism, privilege and waste are hallmarks that announce the malady of grand pretense. The truth of this matter is endorsed by the following hadith:

> A silken Faruj was presented to Allah's Apostle and he put it on and offered the prayer in it. When he finished the prayer he took it off violently as if he disliked it and said: "This garment does not befit those who fear Allah.[xvi]

Hence, affectation and its sibling, pride, are signs of men and women who are heedless of fearing God even when they think this is not so because their actions betray intentions that are imprisoned by the sub-conscious pathology. As a result, they reject the counsel of guided individuals and knowledgeable people who present them with critical truth and sound scientifically derived directives. The latter advice includes the ecology of conservation, minimal standards of pollution, sound urban development and Islam's magnificent directives for munificence regarding fiscal restraint and equitable distributions of Allah's largess; including the prevention of riba, monopolies and mercantilism.[xvii] To the contrary, such leaders protect feudal estates as rulers (*khassa*) of exploitation and power broking and will not elevate disagreeable servants of truth to equitable status. Hence, they institutionalize wicked examples that are then accepted by respective polities submitted to the traditional sponsors of ponerogenesis.

Inverse Determinant of Principle Two:

Disobedience to Allah

Divine Guidance (i.e. *fitrah*, revelation and inspiration) is required if man is to discern good and evil. Disobedience to divine laws activates the inverse determinant or default status of Principle Two by removing man from Divine Guidance. This slowly leads to degrees of nihilism, idolatry and chauvinist hero worship and narcissism. Hero worship is the essence of Humanism, a construct that deifies man. The Apotheosis of George Washington as god-man of the U.S. Capitol is one example, the 'Perfect Man' of the Ismai'ili and Nazi cultus is another and both equate with essential forms of Satanism.

The consequences of persistent disobedience to *Shari'iah* are many but the main result is a specific type of spiritual blindness that promotes correlative neglect of the commonwealth's better interests. Naturally this paves the way for the ponerogenesis of the third law's default in favor of sociopaths who masquerade as shepherds of the flock; i.e., the governing elite and those who finance and the sycophants who serve them. This elite clique prefers to marginalize and persecute 'others' who do obey God. Essentially, this is Fascism as manifest in Zionist, Neo-Con, Wahhabi and related cults of extremism. It is also an expression of tribalism or *assabiyah* and represents the manufactured social consensus of repressive conformism that justifies the marginalization of 'others' for exclusion, oppression and profitable manipulation to the detriment of environment, fauna and flora.

The effects of disobedience are manifest in all systems of tribalism that establish a VVIP class who perfect the arts of propaganda, pretense and favoritism, after which they avoid criticism and eventually become incapable of recognizing errors. By then they are too proud and addicted to perquisites to repent, as was King Nimrud.

> Another type of individual, on the other hand, may achieve an important post because they belong to privileged social groups or organizations in power while their talents and skills are not sufficient for their duties, especially the more difficult problems. Such persons then avoid the problematic and dedicate themselves to minor matters quite ostentatiously. A component of histrionics appears in their conduct and tests indicate that their correctness of reasoning progressively deteriorates after only a few years' worth of such activities. In the face of increasing pressures to perform at a level unattainable for them, and in fear of being discovered as incompetent, they begin to direct attacks against anyone with greater talent or skill, removing them from appropriate posts and playing an active role in degrading their social and professional adjustment. Upwardly-adjusted people thus favor whip-cracking, totalitarian governments which would protect their positions.
>
> *Political Ponerology*, op. cit, p. 75

They begin to believe their own lies are and devote themselves to bald-faced impunity. Disobedience therefore elevates the wicked regency of Lord Poneros. It is the Legacy of Cain. Rationalism minus revelation thus prevails at the cost of truth and falsehood become tradition throughout the realm as an acceptable a form of histrionic insanity. Eventually, this ruling class (*khassa*) and the majority that supports it (*amma*) blind themselves to inconvenient truths via comforting cultural mores' that embrace the narcosis of human denial as a conspiracy of silence regarding 'sensitive' issues. At this point they collectively oppress or ignore people of discernment and ability by promoting similarly blinded compatriots (cronies) who conform to vanities that comprise the legal brief for their damnation:

> Lo. The hypocrites seek to beguile Allah but it is He who beguiles them. When they stand up to worship they perform it languidly to be seen of men, and are mindful of Allah but little; swaying between this and that, belonging neither to these or those. He whom Allah causes to go astray, thou (O Mohammad) wilt not find a way for him. [Al-Nisa, vs: 141-142]

Hypocrites, may seek and support each other's company in secret but will betray confederates the moment it is advantageous. Presently, this self-engrossed narcissistic consciousness (i.e. "belonging neither to these or those"), is the estate of many Muslim institutions in the name of reform and even charity.

In such vacuums of authenticity, *Al'hisbah* is systematically thwarted and deviation thrives. In its entirety, the estate of disobedience precludes the requisite 'insight' referred by Mohammad (wslm) in his Medina speech. Leadership develops a specific inability to accept criticism (admonition) which manifests as an all pervasive impunity attached to scorn. In turn, and in time, this completely prevents the incarnation of divinely guided inspiration. All is then systematically encapsulated by the mnemonics of semiotic icons and slogans chosen as memes to represent the realm's national denial of truth as they elevate the illusion of self-rule or liberty. This then crystallizes as patriotic loyalty to myth and its royalty mongers.

The result is that wisdom is replaced by cunning as the community forgoes profitable institutions of everlasting merit in deference to service (slavery) to temporal icons. Indeed, it is a form of idolatry:

> "And none receive admonition except men of understanding."[xviii]

To the contrary, people of understanding obey all three precepts: Fear of God, Obedience to Divine Law, and the Remembrance of God in all things. They do not need icons as they scientifically seek after knowledge rather than the idolatry of pomp and circumstance. With few exceptions, the ummah of Mohammad has failed to advance the cause of science and knowledge, and, hence, also Islam in any substantial form for the last five-hundred years. Now you know why.

Hundreds upon hundreds of precious manuscripts lay untranslated while sultans of sin refuse to fund what Occidentals eagerly achieve. These imams of booty take the ummah's wealth and profit from slavery while womanizing in Western nightclubs and penthouses. They build palaces and 'Old Ben' mimes in Mecca as they mimic the mafia model they have chosen to emulate. This criminal misguidance permits intimacy with Romanists, Cabbalists and Freemasons as they import usury and satanic sub-cultures. They then call these crimes against heaven, self and constituents, 'progress'.

To summarize and historically recap the existential consequence of this inverse determinant's effect: a genuinely mystified *ullama* with imams of opulence took over the 'Dark Age' insolence of Catholic pretenders of authenticity. During the subsequent Reformation, a marvelous Protestant surge of prestige and materialist industry usurped the once sacred domain and dominion of a formerly obedient Muslim polity. The entire lot is now subject to the scourge of the Counter-Reformation's monist materialism under Jesuit auspice. This spiritual blindness attends the PSYOPS of cunning fascist propaganda and the oppression of fiscal imperialism along with ghastly barbaric incursions—all of which were predicted by the Prophets, most especially Nabi Isa and Mohammad (wslm).

Presently, and in the name of secular humanism's tolerance, Muslims do not treat Allah's enemies as their own according to Principle Two. To the contrary, they make alliances with them and disingenuously trust in dialogues espoused by Satan's obdurate dons of deceit:

> The hour will not be established until my followers copy the deeds of the previous nations and follow them very closely, span by span and cubit by cubit . . . You will follow the ways of those nations who were before you, span by span and cubit by cubit, so much so that if they entered the hole of a mastiquire (lizard) you would follow them ...[xix]

Inverse Determinant of Principle Three:

Forgetting the Remembrance of God:

The remembrance of God is far more that ritual because it requires far more than religious knowledge. It is the ability to correctly apply free choice towards what is good and this is a faculty that depends on applying disciplines that establish metaphysical and physical templates (habits) for that purpose. Such habits repeatedly reinforce the mindfulness of God and His law and they must be meaningful and articulate—e.g., 'prayer with understanding' as taught by the prophet in contradistinction to rote recitations of a foreign tongue which is now the acceptable norm in non-Arabic speaking nations. Another is keeping the environment, mind and body unpolluted which requires far more knowledge and effort than what attends ritual ablution. This assessment unfortunately implies that Islam has become the lazy man's religion for the majority of its adherents.

The inverse determinant or default status of this spiritual law is initiated by the lack of meaningful (i.e. knowledgeable) discipline which, in fact, is a form of ignorance. This occurs because ignorance inhibits discernment due to the absence of cognitive acquisitions which, by definition, must include purpose and purpose is contingent on knowledge. Therefore, and as an example, the practice of ritual prayer and recitation in an un-comprehended foreign language again parallels the Catholic 'Dark Age'. Ignorance, therefore, empirically and naturally invites harm and inhibits divine protection which otherwise is a normative provision when one is obedient to prophetic directives and purpose by pursuing knowledge. If this were not so the following positive results would have occurred:

1. the discernment of good and evil, benefit and harm would
2. allow knowledge of proper *adab* to surface to man's consciousness as 'understanding' which would
3. permit the capacity to assimilate and implement pertinent knowledge well enough to

4. establish and maintain institutions and relationships that appropriately forbid evil and positively facilitate what is beneficial.

The corollary here is that: ignorance aids and abets evil. To reiterate and substantiate this position from other sources, I quote the following passage:

> ... the disciplined life and piety are not complete when there is ignorance. Imam Buran al-Din, author of *The Hidayah*, recited a poem by an unnamed author:
>
>> An immoral man of learning is a great evil, yet a greater evil is an ignoramus leading a godly life. Both are a trial everywhere to whomsoever clings to his religion."[xx]
>
> "Knowledge" as its center also hardened Muslim civilization and made it impervious to anything that did not fall within its view of what constituted acceptable knowledge.[19]

Unfortunately, the rule of thumb for Muslim societies at present is this: 'immoral men of learning' at the top with religious 'ignoramuses' (zealots) at both ends. Evidence for this is everywhere despite claims of a 'renaissance', though I've no doubt the latter occurs to limited degrees.

Nonetheless, efforts to correct Muslim ignorance of its own religion as well as the hard sciences and the exquisite benefits of the Humanities are indeed ongoing despite the impedance of a cadre of spoilers who refuse to invest Allah's money for sufficient R&D—i.e. to spend of what they do not need according to the prophet's directive in order to promote authentic progress. For example, in 2002 Germany spent 4.7 % of its GDP for R&D while Malaysia spent 0.2%.[xxi] I believe this is much too little and far too late when added to habitual Ali-Baba piracy.

---

[19] as-Samânî, *Adab al-imlâ*, M. Weisweiler (ed), *Die Methodik des Diktatkollegs*, 2 (Leiden 1952).

In Summary

If these fundamental principles and their inherently pre-determined qualities are diminished by neglect during the rational processes of governance, national development, scientific investigation, education, contemplation (religious and otherwise,) and political decision making, then scientists, politicians and executives proportionately default towards inverse determinants described. In this situation, subjective errors and misguidance naturally follow as they utilize whatever knowledge for development. This reductionism surely leads to material progress but it also prevents the actualization of what is truly beneficial for success.

Rather than benefits, therefore, the ummah is constantly offered choices between evils that are dialectically controlled by occult initiates of an elite *khassa* that is self-governing and thus blinded to truth. Progress under such auspices is not the 'progress' it is lauded to be as we observe social, physical, criminal and emotional ills running rampant among "Muslim" nations.

THE GREATER MAXIMS

The Law of Grace

> "In the name of Allah, Most Gracious, Most Merciful ... that the People of the Book may know that they have no power whatever over the grace of Allah, that Grace is entirely in His hand, to bestow it on whomsoever He wills. For Allah is the Lord of Grace abounding." [LVII: 29]

The Law of Grace may be stated as follows:

HONOR ALMIGHTY GOD CONSCIOUSLY AND HE WILL BESTOW HIS GRACE ON YOU ACCORDING TO YOUR EFFORT.

God's Grace is a reality arrogantly assumed by some, abused by many, and vainly pursued by others in the guise of 'good luck', but It is not a topic commonly discussed by Muslim exegetics. As a matter of fact, in the nine years I've been a Muslim academic I have never heard it discussed.

Grace is God's favor, the dispensation of His Divine Will as made manifest to us in the *cosmos* ['orderly arrangement of creation']. Its personal manifestation transcends ordinary human comprehension as a serenity of spirit and the unshakeable resolve that rests within the hearts and minds of God's servants in the face of any circumstance. All that exists has come into being by virtue of God's infinite grace, yet no one but the innocent receives the 'Peace of God' without submission to His will and the disciplines of mind, body and spirit that accompany the *conscious* acknowledgement of this fact of life.

The skeptic may ask if evil is a manifestation of God's Grace and the answer is 'yes' because without evil there is no challenge to man's exercise of 'free will'. But this does not in the least imply that God is partly evil as teach Freemasons and Gnostics who have adopted ancient Persian dualism. The essence of ponerogenesis (ontogeny of evil) is the conscious disobedience to Divine Law that results in harm or loss. As a matter-of-fact, disobedience to God is the only sin, all others are sub-categories. Since it is inconceivable, therefore, for God to disobey His own Law, He can neither be, nor desire nor aspire to evil. He does however create and condone it, or better said, 'permit' Satan to challenge men whereby evil deeds legitimize consequent judgment. This owes to the fact that evil is *an* unavoidable corollary of all disobedience. The following passage delineates the reality:

> "I swear by man's personality and that whereby he has been formed, God has engraved into it its evil and its good [whereby it can guard itself against moral peril]. He who makes personality pure, shall be successful, while he who corrupts it shall be in the loss." [91: 7: 10]

Therefore, for man to guard himself and overcome the 'potential' for the evil created *within him* he necessarily requires God's assistance. If humanity has inherited aught from Adam besides intelligence, likeness and the terminal tryst with God on Judgment Day, it is the challenge of this trial of our faith and test of common sense.

> "Every man shall taste of death, and the evil and good which befall you are a trial for you. ... 'Oh Jews, if, as you pretend, you are the friends of God and His elect of all mankind, wish for death that you may prove your sincerity.' But they never wish for death, for rejoining their Lord; and that is because they know that their arms have wrought evil and injustice."
>
> [2: 177, 183]

God does indeed create and determine the horrid consequences of wickedness both here and hereafter. Whether temporal or eternal, these consequences are Divine Judgments that represent God's disfavor. Hence, we may consider them the inverse of Divine Grace, that being 'Divine Curse'—a coin with two sides. Similarly, these distasteful consequences manifest in degrees of allocation (e.g. seven layers of hell) according to the severity of disobedience. Therefore, every Spiritual Law holds potential for gradations of good and evil effects. Hence, when spiritual Law is dismissed as an immaterial consideration in the affairs of men, the inverse of the dismissed law with its antithetical forces immediately and autonomously come into play by God's design and inevitably lead towards progressive degrees of harm and perhaps damnation. This is the essence of predestination.

It is therefore important to realize that the ubiquitous disregard for Spiritual Law is the cause of all war and lack of justice or peace in the affairs of men. it is also the reason Muslim's have suffered both the demise of their autonomy and the loss of God's protection.

There is no trial of faith without evil's challenge because the Grace of God extends to an immortal after-life in a newly structured cosmos of pristine excellence with an absolute *absence* of evil. For man to enter this wondrous estate his perfected submission to God's Will or at least his/her acknowledgement of God's absolute autonomy are thoroughgoing requirements for the franchise. Confessions of God's divine right and autonomy, by thought and/or deed, cannot be attained by unselfconscious automatons because predestined coercion would have contravened to negate the principle of free will. Hence, the Law of Grace demands man's free and favorable assent or self-conscious self-subjugation to God's infinite benevolence; and this is in order to avoid inverse consequences both here and in the hereafter.

This is the essence of Faith and the purpose of its trial during our earthly life. Without such faith we cannot please God nor can we enter the peace filled Grace of His Kingdom either here or in the hereafter. Our only free choice, therefore, lies between good or evil; blessing or cursing—there is no third option or neutral position.

To reiterate, the essence of evil is not its potential but rather the conscious denial of our pre-primordial covenant to acknowledge God's sovereignty by obeying His Law. Hence, evil is disobedience to what we instinctively know is good for us. Therefore, when men awaken to temptation and succumb to Satan's invitation rather than God's, it is they who welcome and perpetrate the wickedness. Hence, it is myopic for men to blame God or Satan or neo-cons, etc. for evil.

Of their own free will such people reject the additional grace of *peaceful* prosperity in the earth (*as'Sakkinah*).[20] This principle explains why it is that the *un-peaceful* prosperity commonly called 'progress' is filled with anxiety as the majority of men and women choose to worry about earthly possessions as they pile up booty. This includes deluded spouses who think their husband or wife 'belongs' to them, but even this sad condition is grace-filled until the first death brings an end to the fantasy. So then:

(1) if there is naught without grace, and
(2) if both good and evil proceed from this grace by virtue of our having even the ability to choose, it behooves the believer to
(3) understand the *Laws* written by the Eternal Cause of all causes, as well as the
(4) *trial* of our earthly life
(5) *before* the latter is terminated and we write an abidingly self-incriminating verdict in the Book of Deeds.

There inevitably come frequent trials to journeymen on the road of faith. Each trial, though it may hold evil is actually an act of grace because the option held forth is an opportunity to obtain additional favor that exceeds the potential of the evil.[21] For this reason, Prophet Isa instructed his disciples to rejoice in persecution and trouble. To the contrary, if there is no trial of faith in a man's life the implication is that God has withdrawn the promise of this enhanced potential and left the recalcitrant fool to his doom. These people are called *Kufr* or *Kafir* in Al-Qur'an and are to be avoided by believers whenever possible. Again, one should ask why.

The Qur'an often speaks of people whose 'case' or 'trial' *is no longer considered* by God. These are folk who no longer consider God while lusting after the finite benefits of His material world. These

---

[20] "God made you a true promise whereas I made you a false promise. I had no power over you but only invited you to error and you accepted my invitation. Do not blame me but only yourselves." - Satan Speaking (14: 22)

[21] Hence: the challenge to Prophet Job and suffering of Muslims prior to *Hijra*.

people repeatedly and assiduously choose evil's potential until they became addicted (habituated) to it.

> "... whoever seeks the advantage of the other world will receive the same and more of it. Whoever seeks the advantage of this world will receive the same, but he will have no share in the other." [42: 20]

'Materialists' do not strive for the Kingdom of God's eternal bonus nor seek the metaphysical light of additional guiding grace while they live on earth.[22] This includes spiritualists who opt for the numerous forms of idolatry. As a result, God actually shuns them once they've repeatedly refused His Call to Grace. This is, unfortunately, an inverse consequence of ignoring the Law of Grace for too long. As heedless reprobates, even if religious, they live exclusively by the ordinary benevolence of temporal respite—which has its own natural 'law of the jungle' so to speak—rather than the appreciating support of advancing Divine favor. Hence, they fail the test by dismissing the Law of Grace and are but vaguely aware, if at all, that they've also rejected faith.[23] As a result, they reject God's additional goodwill. For them one can do nothing.

Therefore, when evil is upon you, after you recover from the knowledge of its presence you should seek the attendant grace in the matter as it is hidden and awaits discovery. If you are in sin, seek the grace of forgiveness. If you are in perplexity, seek the grace of guidance. If you are in persecution, seek the grace of deliverance (even if it means death), etc. Each of these circumstances requires the initial grace of *fitrah* with which we are all born before we turn once more to

---

[22] "O ye that believe! fear Allah and believe in His Messenger, and He will bestow on you a double portion of His Mercy: He will provide for you a light by which ye shall walk straight in your path, and He will forgive you your past ... " [LVIII: 28]

[23] There are others who believe but do not act on their belief. This, unfortunately, is equivalent to unbelief. In the Qur'an, Faith is inextricably married to good deeds. See V2:112 for example, "Yes, but whoever submits his face to Allah and he is a Muhsin [a good doer who performs good deeds totally for Allah's sake without any show-off or to gain praise or fame] then his reward is with his Lord, on such shall be no fear, nor shall they grieve." Even Paul said: "Faith without works is dead."

God in supplication for His additional favor. Only the proud and arrogant refuse this option. There is no other way to obtain God's additional favor except in the following condition. This proviso is faithful service to a man or woman of faith whereby portions of the grace given to them by virtue of their perfection will naturally fall upon the servant—a bit like a dog and his master. In such cases, even an ignoramus gains favor with God.

To obtain grace, all one has to do is ask and then wait in submissive conformity-with and patient service-to Divine Law until the grace is given. It is a very simple matter. An example in my own life is this book and the few others I've written. Outwardly during the years of their research and writing my life appeared destitute of God's additional grace. I was unable to practice my profession as a Physician and finances remained extremely hard pressed. Even my clothing became tattered and often we had little to eat. At the present moment of this revision (Jan 2014), I have been without regular monthly salary for eight months. I initially cursed the officials who refused me the professional privileges I thought I deserved. But one day it occurred to me that had I been working as a Doctor I would never have sought God with such earnestness; nor would I have studied, nor learned, nor written what He bestowed upon me during that very trying time by His Grace. This then brings up a contingent to the Law of Grace, which is a very interesting corollary.

The Law of Reception

The reception of grace is a *conscious* function that is completely contingent upon one's religious conviction. Al'Qur'an segregates this matter by calling it 'certitude', an attitude that does not equate with mere submission:

> "Some Arabs of the desert have claimed that they have achieved religious conviction. Say: 'You have not achieved such conviction. You have been converted to Islam and have acquiesced in it, but religious certitude and conviction have not yet found their way to your heart and consciousness.'" [49: 14]

This passage describes those whom consider the *belief* in God but remain uncertain. This *uncertainty* is a barrier that is only overcome by trial and the resultant effort made to rise above the trial's challenge. There is no other path to the realm of religious conviction and increased favor with Allah. Therefore, to simply acquiesce and make no further effort to attain certitude is a slippery path flanked by murky pools of suspect motivation. Unfortunately, this describes many believers and shepherds. Were this not so, the grace of God's favor would have been maintained and increased in Islam such that the unity and power of its polity would never have waned. Such is the Law of Grace. This last statement is endorsed, I believe, by the following passage:

> "Rather, God grants you the favor of guiding you to religious conviction if only you are sincere (genuine)." [49: 17]

Sincerity of heart is a legal prerequisite for the activation of Grace as metaphysical guidance or 'light' in anyone's life. When the trials of sincerity are won, the real journey of grace along the path to wisdom begins:

> "And if my servants ask you of Me, tell them I am near and that I respond to the caller who calls upon me. Tell them to pray to Me, to believe in Me. That is the way to wisdom ... Seek further assistance by patience and prayer. The latter overtaxes none but the irreverent and the proud. It is a force of genuine assistance ..." [2: 186, 45-46]

Hence, grace is assistance from God, an actual 'force' that is attained via the marriage of patience with prayer.

We do not enter life consciously, and thereby, we receive the initial dispensation of respite's grace without realizing it. Gradually, over many years, we waken to mortal circumstances and either seek God or simply enjoy the finite benefits of this world. For those who seek Him, as Al'Qur'an teaches, God approaches them at a greater pace, surpassing any effort they might expend. When we begin this conscious collaboration with our Creator, He offers us additional Grace. Therefore, just as life itself is a gift of His Grace, so also are the additions of His favor. Those who not only believe but also seek Him, consciously receive these increments. But there are conditions for the receipt and utilization.

Contrary to the beloved doctrine of Christians, the grace of God's additional favor is not gratuitous and depends on continued obedience. In the finite world, the greatest manifestation of this additional grace is peace of mind; what some call dignity or (*gravitas*) in the face of all adversity. The reprobate may receive what appears to be favor but in reality is a temporary benefit that holds ultimate evil. Examples abound in the entertainment world or in business when men murder or suicide over losses or public embarrassments. But with sincere believers comes a binding contingency clause: along with more of God's favor comes greater accountability and the effects may appear more immediately in the earthly life. One observes this in the religious world when many a preacher or priest falls from the favor of God and men. In mercy does God judge them based on this contingency but still offers the eternal favor of Heaven upon sincere repentance. By contrast, the reprobate, hypocrite, or insincere believer goes merrily about their business 'till the Grim Reaper presents the final bill.

> "God has taken upon Himself to show mercy." [7: 12]

The Law of Grace is the only spiritual law whereby God imposed on Himself a reciprocal response according to man's effort. God obligated Himself to favor certain creatures by virtue of their faith and deeds; Paradise being the ultimate manifestation of the Law of Grace. Therefore, by grace we live; by grace do we experience mortal life; and by additional grace do we look forward to reward in Paradise. To the contrary, a ceaseless existence in hell cannot be called 'living' as it bears absolutely no freedom of will and is totally devoid of God's Grace, which is why it has been called the 'second death'. The soul is lost to eternal bondage, grace is removed, and the consequences of deeds performed during earthly respite are reaped, apparently without end; although scholars debate the matter. In this dreadful circumstance, we see that the Will of God is enacted *without* grace for the condemned creature.

Therefore, by faith and good works we work out our own salvation through degrees of God's Grace in order to inherit the promise of eternal benevolence, which holds the paramount deliverance of our soul to freedom. With this in mind, let us look at another aspect of God's grace.

WHO DESERVES THE GRACE OF GOD?

The question is actually moot, but I pose it for the sake of folks who reason in circles. No one *deserves* the grace of God. God's Grace simply *is*. It is offered as a real and increasing potential to everyone equally as incremental rewards for obedience. It is only the receptive knowledge or conscious taking of this grace that creates differential categories of additional benefit. Think of grace as an invitation to a wedding as analogized in the Gospels. For believers it is a given that we exist by grace and that any invitation to receive more grace depends solely upon the invitee's acceptance and preparation for the delightful event. We may choose to accept or decline the invitation, and there are those who pretend acceptance but give excuse later, or perhaps show up unprepared for the occasion. Those who consciously receive the invitation are humbled. Afterwards, they excitedly prepare by trimming the lamp of truth with the shears of Wisdom and then store enough oil (deeds) for the journey. All of this takes place during the sleep of mortal life.

What grace then remains for those who do not prepare for the final feast? The answer is 'none' because God's favor cannot be shared. It is specific for each individual. I cannot give you God's favor anymore than you can give me your spinal cord. Reprobates carry just enough oil of grace to complete their earthly lives. In the end, their lamp is empty because they refused the invitation and, by default, have declined additional oil for the festival in Paradise. All are weighed in the balance of God's justice. Those found light on the scale with empty oil lamps (i.e. insufficient good deeds) will have forfeited the invitation and discovered much too late that they are not welcome. These have only wronged themselves and there is no one else to blame.

What then? — must we be spotless in order to enter the garden? The answer is yes. Nevertheless, how can this be since we all continually sin? How is it that any man may trim his lamp and conserve sufficient oil and demonstrate a spotless and well preserved invitation card at the door? The answer is again by the grace of God's ever turning in mercy to forgive His servants. If sin equals one weight and repentance, prayer, a good deed or even its intention are equal to ten or a hundred weight, what excuse has any man? 'Ah then,' says the cunning hypocrite, "I may sin as I like as long as I balance my scale with prayers and good deeds!" "Not so my clever enemy of truth," says I. For if God weighs even the intention of a good deed in a man's favor, so also will He weigh a man's sinful intentions to his disfavor; so that a hypocrite's good deeds slip from the balance as grace given to those who received the benefit while he lived. This is because the intention is to justify sin and bargain with God:

> "Behold, the actions are but judged according to the *intentions*; and behold, *unto every man is due but what he intended*. Thence, whoso migrated for the sake of the world or to wed a woman, his migration is accounted for that unto which he migrated." - Hadith 1, Al'Bukhari

> "They (hypocrites) are worthless... They are the enemies, so beware of them. The curse of Allah is upon them! How are they deluded away from the truth! ... Allah will not forgive them. Truly Allah guides not rebellious transgressors." [63: 4-6]

Hypocrites are sincere liars who serve themselves and Iblis. Why would God accept the prayers of a liar or equate his eternal estate with truly obedient slaves of truth? So do not take God's Grace for granted or dare think to manipulate this law for earthly or eternal benefit.

The service of Iblis, father of deception, is incumbent upon those who indeed may believe but are without faith:

"... Satan and his legion keep a constant eye upon you.[24] You have no awareness of them. Their nature is to be the friends and guides of those who have no faith and no conviction."[7:27]

This verse establishes that Hypocrites are men who lack conviction by definition. What then is the nature of conviction with regard to belief in God? The answer lay in the antithetical example of Cain who believed in God but remained convinced he should murder his brother. Here we have a man of belief based on primary knowledge who placed his faith in a false promise from Satan rather than God.[25] He believed in God but doubted God's word. His deluded conviction was therefore one of belief in the word of a creature he associated with God. This classic illustration of shirk represents the impurity of worship that resulted in the prototypical religious murder or 'nascent crusade', which, in turn, separated this seed of Adam from both his family and God.

Cain had both conviction and belief but his faith in Satan misguided and misplaced his will and subsequent deed, despite his belief in and knowledge of God. He left the garden with nothing but the grace of respite, refusing first to acknowledge and secondly to repent of the foul deed when given opportunity. He then became the primal archetypical reprobate sectarian.

---

[24] A clear indication that Jinn rather than angels are the so-called 'Watchers' worshipped by the ancients and to this day by many.

[25] This is an archetypal pattern for all Secret Societies.

CONCLUSION

> "A philosopher is a dead poet and a dying theologian."
> - Will Durant, Historian -

It is appropriate here to comment on the nature of a science whose proponents put it forth as 'Theology'.[26] The term defines itself literally as 'the Study of God'. Yet pausing for a moment's reflection evokes the absurd imagination of men putting God under a microscope in order to define His existential nature and what makes Him tick. One may certainly study religion, wisdom, prophetic literature and scripture, creation, etc. but God Himself? I think it best not to concern ourselves with the paeans of dead poets or the gaunt piety of blind men of the cloth who claim reason while coining this confounding term.

> "And when they ask you concerning the Spirit, answer: 'The Spirit belongs to God. Given the little knowledge that you have, your minds must fall short of understanding its nature." [17:85]

> Writers and Philosophers have often exhausted themselves seeking evidence for God's immanence without avail, while others have sought to grasp the essence of the Creator Himself—all to no purpose.
>
> - Mohd. H. Hykal

To the contrary, Sufi-claimers and Hindus say that divine union-*with* and direct perception-*of* God is possible despite the fact that Al'Qur'an says it is impossible for man to even begin to comprehend the essence of His Spirit or 'Word of Command', let alone God Himself.

---

[26] "... In both Judaism and Islam, the codification of religious law (Talmud; Sharia) has been considered a separate discipline and has often taken precedence over theology. Both religions lay stress on the indivisible unity of God and his unknowability by humans, and their theologians were not therefore as exercised with the problem of God's nature as were Christian theologians. In Christianity, however, the interaction between ideas of essentially Jewish provenance and the Greco–Roman world, and the systematic attempts to define Jesus' relationship to God the Father and the Holy Spirit (Trinity), the relationship of divine and human nature in the person of Jesus, and the significance of his birth, crucifixion, and resurrection, have led to a long history of theological argument." - Oxford Encyclopedia, Tenth Ed.

Furthermore, if God were so readily available for human study there would neither be reason to test our faith nor any purpose for the dispensation of grace according to works of faith. It is difficult enough to define grace and agree on its existence yet the fact of the matter is that man's reason cannot go far enough to *prove* grace is even present, because reason can only *confirm* rather than *prove* that the grace of God exists, and such confirmation only stands in the affirmative for each individual and those who have the experience of the subjective cognizance.

Such is the case of a poor villager raised to Chief Minister who later retired in peace. He and those close to him are able to affirm and confirm the manifest nature of God's temporal grace in his life through direct observation and experience. As revered, successful, knowledgeable and wizened as he is, however, I doubt he would dare to describe or define God. But I'm certain he can attest to the effects of God's guidance and direction in his life and tell us exactly how he managed to receive his supplemental portions of grace.

Goethe had this to say about the limitation of man's reason:

> ... Let one phenomenon be traced to another. Let a definite sphere of knowledge be outlined. Let views lay claim to certainty and completeness ... Let everyone draw his own conclusions – they prove nothing, certainly no *isms* and *ologies*. Opinions on all things pertain to the individual, and we know only too well that conviction depends not so much on insight as on inclination, no one grasping but what is within his ken, and therefore acceptable to him. In knowledge as in action, prejudice casts the deciding vote - it is the spontaneous urge of our vital being towards truth as towards falsehood, towards all which we 'feel' in harmony.

Therefore, reason itself is the *subjective* advancement of the faculty of thought, which is a power bestowed by grace so that we may *acknowledge* the existence of grace and therefore also the existence of its Author. The corollary is that 'objective science' remains constrained by individual and collective biases that subjectively and collectively establish what is called a paradigm (consensus) rather than reality. An example of this is the famous 'Black Hole' theory which is currently being re-written and will no doubt be revised again in the not-too-distant future. Whereas, to deny grace is to deny God which therefore implies that the denier is devoid of sound reason, even less sensible than cattle, as the Qur'an so aptly puts it, or as Goethe says: 'whose prejudice is inclined towards the falsehood with which he feels harmony'.

How then can schismatics dare to define God or grace when they have repeatedly broken the law of Grace for millennia? The reality is that prior to the Christian Age there was no science of Theology outside of the pagan Mystery Religions. Monotheists studied the scriptures and if they lacked the grace of comprehension they either waited for more or kept silent. Others however, changed the Word of God then walked off to found another sect as did Cain in ancient Dravidia. The Revelation of Al'Qur'an ended all possibility of scriptural debate for the sane among us. Thus, its advent ushered in an era rife with new scholastic levels of conflict and schismatics from an even greater lack of grace because *its* Revelation was superior and final. These controversies eventually spawned *Atheism*, a phenomenon that had barely exchanged gases in former times. Can we therefore blame God for such foolishness? God forbid! His grace is available for all to come into the fold of comprehensive unity and thus end the debate. Nevertheless, man is contentious and 'seeks many devices', as said Prophet Da'ud in the Psalms.

The 'devices' Prophet Da'ud wrote of are, each and every one, apologies such as the cunning of Jesuit casuistry. These serve to preclude man's submission to God's Will and thereby justify the negative assertion of man's will towards sin. This is now called Humanism. Hence, Allah withholds the grace of Unity from His polity in the earth so that proud schismatics can crusade under private banners of dubious temporal respite, claiming all types of opinions rather than confirmations of what is indeed true. These people have used the grace-gift of reason's power to justify disobedience to the Giver of their sense of thought, and many are well versed in the science of Theology. What then is this madness; for to deny submission to God via His Prophets and their example is to deny God's absolute autonomy. How then can such demented men and women claim to know or study Him?

The truth is that we cannot study God but we can study what He created and what He related to us by His Prophets. Hence, the science of Theology is as ridiculous as the Oxford definition of the Trinity or the Sufi-claimer's 'mystic union' with God. We may study Creation and God's Revelatory Word because both reflect His grace in an astonishing manner for those who have not rejected His invitation to the festival of Paradise. Such a study, when not joined to *shirk* (idolatry), brings a unity of moral purpose inclined towards peace and intelligently responsible progress (*Hadhari*). To the contrary, those who have discarded the divine call to Paradise by calling *shirk* deviation or even worse, Islam, are proponents of disunity and will no doubt find fault with this text. Out of pity, I can only wish them a prolonged respite, for that is most likely the last of God's grace they shall ever know.[27]

---

[27] "God's curse is upon those who take graves for their mosque." — reportedly spoken by The Prophet during his final visit to the Madina Mosque, as recorded in *The Life of the Prophet* by Mohd H. Haykal – See also V 4:51, "the words "Jibt and Taghut" cover wide meanings: ... anything worshiped other than Allah i.e., all false deities, it may be an idol, satan, graves, stone, sun, star, angel, saints, or any human being. [see also Tafsir, Ibn Kathir]... and sometimes Taghut means a false judge who gives false judgment (V4:60)." *The Noble Qur'an*, ibid, page 117, also V 4:51 for Allah's curse.

The Law of Unity

To the extent that faith and works remain pure, Allah will bless men with the integrated unity of mind, body and soul and the fellowship of its likeness, and He will protect and preserve its incumbent power.

> The Faithful are like one man: if his eye suffers, the whole body suffers; and if his head suffers, his whole body suffers. You will recognize the Faithful by their mutual compassion, love, and sympathy. They are like one body: if one of its parts is ill, the whole body suffers from sleeplessness and fever.- The Prophet (wslm)[28]

HANIF OR NOT HANIF? THAT IS THE QUESTION

Impure religious doctrines may be readily discerned by identifying the pugnacious sectarians who support them.[29]

When reviewing a book on Islam I try to identify the sect or school of philosophy which the author claims. If stated, I set my guard against the bias and extract whatever truth is there. If I cannot identify the prejudice, I proceed cautiously, as was the case with my review of Mohd. Abduh, a Freemason whose occult credentials were unknown to me when I read one of his books. If an author claims other than essential Islam (i.e. just plain old ordinary unembellished 'Muslim'), one can rest assured that somewhere within the work divisiveness has been penned; even if he or she claims to be Sunni.

The Law of Unity's inverse corollary demands that we maintain the purity of core monotheist doctrine because truth cannot be joined to lies with divine sanction. Even so, my review of religious history reveals that just about all religious people (excepting a few indigenous creeds), and regardless of origin, have departed from their prophetic

---

[28] Al-Bukhari & Muslim, on auth. of Nu'man ibn Bashir

[29] pugnacity being a major symptom of Schizoidia, which describes the bearded lots of Islamists as a well as Marx and Engels. See footnote, #47

roots for the sake of sanctimonious fetishism whether material or not. This represents a kind of mass-psycho-pathological idolatry that involves a 'course of action [habit] to which one has an excessive and irrational commitment'.[30] The key words are 'obsessive' and 'irrational'. As we shall see later in this section, these activities are the direct result of political repression that coerces people to conform for the sake of safety rather than truth in order to preserve life and wealth to the repressor's advantage. To the contrary, the Prophets all said, in one way or another, that believers must lose his/her life in order to find it, referring to our temporal respite here on earth and eternal well being, respectively. The clear implication is that religiously preoccupied people are, for the most part, cowards:

> . . . it appears obvious that religious systems have also succumbed to ponerogenic processes and manifested the symptoms of a similar disease [pathocracy] . . . for example, the neocon-Bush administration is using Christianity as the ideology by which they mask pathocracy.[31]

Immediately on the death of the Prophet (wslm), the *Emigrants* and *Helpers* amongst his companions divided into sects that followed tribal leanings. Abu Bakr preserved their Unity by quoting the Qur'an, which managed to preserve the grace of Unity a while longer. This primal defense of Islam's Unity implies an inextricable union between 'Purity of Doctrine' and 'Political Unity' for the *theo-centric* system of governance espoused by essential Islam. Nevertheless, Satan incessantly suggests that sociopaths wed truth to lies in order to appeal and justify man's lower nature with higher faculties of fancy. Of course this inclines sectarian pools toward extrinsic activities beyond the pale of grace available from the prophetic stream of revealed

---

[30] fetish (from the Oxford Dictionary) **1** an inanimate object worshipped for its supposed magical powers or because it is considered to be inhabited by a spirit. **2** a form of sexual desire in which gratification is linked to an abnormal degree to a particular object, part of the body, or activity. **3** a course of action to which one has an excessive and irrational commitment. DERIVATIVES fetishism n. fetishist n. fetishistic adj. fetishization (also fetishisation) n. fetishize (also fetishise) v. – Origin: from Fr. *fétiche*, from Port. *feitiço* 'charm, sorcery'.

[31] Political Ponerology, op. cit. p. 270

knowledge. This tact inevitably gives rise to vain and dangerous imaginations:

> The religious idea then becomes both a justification for using force and sadism against nonbelievers, heretics, and sorcerers, and a conscience drug for people who put such inspirations into effect . . . swearing on the prophet's beard while using this for its doubletalk. Something which was to be originally an aid in the comprehension of God's truth now scourges nations with the sword of imperialism . . . [hence, in time] religious conflict assumes the character of political partitions, giving rise to warfare among various believers in the same God . . . [in addition] historically speaking, the ponerological process in [religious] groups runs its course in a much larger time frame. - ibid

Socio-Anthropology reveals that in an attempt to halt this straying and despoliation with pathological accretion and egocentric obsession, both scripture and most cultures hold the purity of marriage in high esteem because marital honor and fidelity reflect man's communion with divine law and best preserves social unity. But as we have seen, and as prophesied, Iblis and his Shaytans (human and not) professionally strive to destroy marital unity (purity) for their own gain and pleasure with the latter being a goal in itself. Today, it is, in fact, the ancient 'Way of the Romans' morphed to global cultural war (PSYOPS) prosecuted by the elite of the Judeo-Christian Occult Alliance in the West.

Manifest impurity, whether spiritual, moral or ethical is a strong indicator of individual or national disobedience to divine law and reveals its miasmic sway as various forms of patriotic tribalism, all of which are antithetical to Islam. Everywhere one travels there is pressure to tolerate impurity at all rungs of society. The reality here is that this permissiveness destroys the collective's 'Unity' (*elan vitae*) so that the grace of Divine Power and Protection are lost. What follows is this: God permits Satan's influence to advance the hysteria of heedless hegemony in favor of flag waving pride. Just about everyone has experienced this form of idiocy. Hence, wickedness gains currency as the finite power of civic strength waxes strong, all to the detriment of the weak and helpless and those who remain in steadfast harmony with truth. Both latter groups are marginalized and paid lip service.

> Whenever pathocracy emerges in an autonomous process, this means that the religious systems dominating that country were unable to prevent it in time . . . religious organizations have long tolerated and even uncritically inspired the development of pathocracy. - ibid (p. 275)

Purity in Islam is represented by the word *hanif* in reference to Ibrahim who Al-Qu'ran describes as a *pure* monotheist because he ascribed no partners to Allah (swt). To the extent one uses the term to identify oneself with Abraham within the context of the greater Islamic polity, use of the term '*hanif*' remains undefiled. However, to proudly distinguish one's self or group with this or any term other than 'Muslim' initiates forms of identitarian mischief. But before offering my distilled thoughts on the matter, we should discuss the meta-physical realities of Unity and Power.

UNITY & POWER

Since the safest measure of testimony is logical reasoning based on elementary truth, one should begin with Al-Qur'an and the scriptures it confidently confirms and/or completes. Unfortunately, most Muslims fail to access former scriptures and their points of departure for the latter rely on commentators or secondary and tertiary works where revelation is often quoted out of context or lacks gestalt correlation with the entirety of the book and relevant *hadith*—poor methods at best. To complicate matters, a majority of Muslims both pray and recite Al'Qur'an in a non-native tongue, which implies a shortfall of comprehension because most people cannot competently learn a second language and classical Arabic is no longer spoken. Classical Arabic is fine for religious purposes but woefully inadequate when it comes to practicing the faith as a way of life outside of the mosque. Furthermore, most Muslims lack knowledge of historical contexts outside the limited reach of the prophet and his companions. Making matters worse, many Muslims lack knowledge of their own leadership.

An example is that of Hasan Al'Bana whose family was steeped in Freemasonry as were his mentors. What benchmarks can then be established as to their interpretive validity, meaning and purpose in such dimmed light?

These problems fertilize the ponerogenesis of superstition and metaphysical speculations which appear to have infiltrated *hanif* doctrine with enough venom to cause the malaise of determinist lethargy that assists the pathocratic culture of elitist conceit. This same sloth and arrogance gave the Great Khan cause enough to hammer Muslim pride back to the 'Stoning Age' from which they have yet to recover Baghdad's divine intent and is not unlike penalties previously visited on their cousin, ancient Israel. The question is 'Why?' and the answer is 'the inverse product of disobedience to the Law of Unity as I will now attempt to explain.

The serial murders of the Righteous Caliphs of Islam began a chronic migraine from which the ummah still suffers. One look at most of today's Sultanates and political bugbears gives evidence for the prosecution. As an analogy, consider the ummah as a body, as did the prophet (wslm). A delicately filtered fluid surrounds the Central Nervous System (command and control center) which is a perfectly balanced solution that is pure in its constituents and well protected from incursions. Any insult to its composition *via* toxins, microbes, injury, fluid loss or increase, or chemical equilibrium will cause a malaise that leans both brain and body towards malfunction and often drives the patient to bedridden, inactive status.

Sociopaths of the Levant—many of whom were/are crypto-Jews like Ibn Maymun or Gemal Ataturk—carried on with homicidal traditions and usurped Muslim leadership while imposing adulterations such as the Fatimid *cum* Ishmai'ili dross, or Ataturk's Freemasonry and the present Wahabbi menace to peace on earth. Hence, what later became known as 'Islam' abroad does not compare in the least with the *élan vitae* of the Medina polity that permeated those who dwelt within its living memory. Consequently, due to habitual murder and

PART ONE: THE METAPHYSICS OF SPIRITUAL LAW
The Greater Maxims: UNITY

the foolishness of time-honored ignorance and superstition,[32] and although they increased in numbers, Muslims failed to assure the grace of God's protection as He promised to a unified polity. Under heaven's laws, any reliable scholar will confess that Muslim unity was irrevocably shattered and that the patient has, with few exceptions, since remained bedridden awaiting the remedies of *veritas*[33] [*haq*] and those virtues that naturally follow the actualization of truth in word and deed. In a nutshell, Mongol hordes scrupulously administered the divine intervention of God's judgment. This was followed by necrotic scholasticism and a culture of keeping-up-with-the-Khan sultanates, after which materialist 'Enlightenments' injected the polished poneros of the colonial zeitgeist while Imams compared harems and gold dinars instead of attending righteous accountability — all of which finally placed the *ummah* in its present coma.

It was very easy for sophisticated charlatans to usurp and divide what has become known as "Islam", especially beyond borders of the initial Semite dominion. Tell me, how can ordinary men and women (90% of the population) explain the Qur'an or come to any conviction that withstands apostasy if they study it in a language not their own? Under ideal conditions this may be possible for upwards of 5–10% of the general populace but the nose is readily slit for the remaining ninety percent. This significant linguistic factor is a major catalyst in the demise of both doctrinal purity and social cohesion. Any world class neurologist, educator, linguist, anthropologist and ethnographer will appreciate and endorse the reality. To the contrary however, the sanctimonious majority of religious folk lack this knowledge and consequently dig their heels further into linguistic ignorance which only aids the genesis of evil by ignorant pietists, the most dangerous of human creatures, such as those Malays who claim that 'Allah' is an ethnocentric term reserved for them alone and have outlawed its use

---

[32] Such as refusing to fight a decisive battle because the enemy suspended copies of the Koran from their lances.

[33] **Veritas,** latin meaning *truth*, was the goddess of truth, a daughter of Saturn and the mother of Virtue. Also the name given to the Roman virtue of truthfulness, which was considered one of the main virtues any good Roman should possess.

by non-Muslims—forgetting the term was used for centuries prior to Islam's incarnation. For the same cause of slitting the nose of the ninety percent cited above, albeit with a different twist, occult-driven shepherds of the Christian herd kept the original Judaic-Aramaic scriptures hidden while transcribing interpolations into a dead language (Latin) for more than a thousand years. This worked well for a time.[34] Muslims have inadvertently taken the same path.

Let me present some science on the acquisition of language skills, after which the reader will better understand what is meant when I wrote "under ideal conditions":

> We found that (1) early (before age 5) bilingual language exposure is optimal for dual language development and dual language mastery (Kovelman & Petitto, 2002). (2) Those bilingual children who are first raised monolingual from birth and who are then exposed to a *new* language between ages 2-9 years of age *can* achieve the morphological and syntactic fundamentals of the new language within their first year of exposure.
>
> > However, this rapid acquisition of new language fundamentals is possible only when extensive and systematic exposure to the *new* language occurs across multiple contexts, for example, in the community and home, with far less optimal dual language mastery

---

[34] Professional linguists are on the wrong track if they hypostatize a unity that does not function socially. For Gramsci, the problem of the lack of unity of the Italian language of his time was closely interwoven with another socio-political problem, one which originated in the fall of the centralized Roman empire, when a split arose between the written language of the intellectuals (Middle Latin) and the countless dialects spoken by the people (Gramsci (1979: 184; CW 168-171)).

From a cognitive linguistic perspective, meaning, rather than grammar, is unarguably the primary determinant of whether linguistic units can combine with each other (Lee 2001: 70)... Following the rise of sociolinguistics and of functionalism in theoretical linguistics (Halliday 1985), a great deal of attention was indeed being paid to the social and functional aspects of language use... It opposes the view that consciously learning the grammar of a language will result in an ability to use that language in social interaction... [hence] in line with Richards and Rodgers's (1986: 71) the primary function of language is for interaction and communication and the structure of language reflects its functional and communicative uses. - *The Oxford handbook of cognitive linguistics* / edited by Dirk Geeraertsand Hubert Cuyckens, 2007

being achieved if exposure comes exclusively within the classroom (Kovelman & Petitto, 2003; Petitto, Kovelman & Harasymowicz, 2003).

(3) Bilingual children exposed to two languages from birth achieve their linguistic milestones in each of their languages at the same time and, crucially, at the same time as monolinguals (Holowka, Brosseau-Lapré & Petitto, 2002; Kovelman & Petitto, 2002; Petitto & Kovelman, 2003; Petitto, Katerelos, et al., 2001).

Linguists have known for a long time that every person is a native speaker of at least one language and that by the time children reach the age of five or six, those children are proficient speakers of their native language. On the other hand, when a child or an adult learns a second language, they usually encounter some kind of problem, often with the phonology of the new language. [p 300] ...

... there is evidence from many contexts that certain social groups are in danger of being disadvantaged as a consequence of the language used in the legal system, since they may not understand the language and culture of the law. There is extensive documentation of miscommunication with indigenous minorities, children and second language speakers [p 334].

Indeed, a substantial proportion of the world's legal systems operate in a language that is for local lawyers a second language ... Given the complexity of legal language, teaching the language of the legal system to lawyers is an important and difficult matter. Solutions involve careful needs analysis of legal language and the development of tailored curricula [p 336].

... monolingual learner's dictionaries meet the practical challenge of providing language learners with the resources to meet their twin communicative needs: 'receptive' understanding and 'productive' use of a second language [p. 739].

Phonologically motivated sound substitutions are termed processes, morphophonemic alternations are called rules ... Processes are automatic [inherent, see Chomsky], rules are not. Processes interfere in second language phonology, rules do not. Further, processes, because they are natural, reflect inborn restrictions of the human articulation and/or perception and need not be learned and thus are restrictions the speaker imposes on his language, whereas rules are restrictions the language imposes on the speakers (Donegan and Stampe, 1979) and have to be learned in language acquisition.

A child's process of learning languages is different from an adult's process. A child can learn any language relatively effortlessly, while the same task becomes rather challenging for adults ... there is a period in the maturation of human organism, lasting from two years to puberty, in which nearly effortless and complete language acquisition is possible. Afterwards, this hypothesis notes, language learning requires more effort and motivation, largely because of a loss of brain plasticity resulting in the completion of the lateralization of the language function in the left hemisphere. Recent research claims have additionally shown that there are different critical periods for different grammatical structures of language. Since the accent (phonetics and phonology) of a second language is the most difficult to attain, the critical period for phonetics and phonology (approximately from five to seven years) is earlier than that for morphology and syntax. See Johnson and Newport (1991) and Bhatia and Ritchie (1999) for details [pp 1016-17].

Encyclopedia of Language & Linguistics, Sarah G. Thomason & William J. Gedney, Collegiate Professors of Linguistics (ed), University of Michigan, Ann Arbor, USA, 2007

I daresay leaders and educators in most non-Arabic speaking Muslim countries don't consider the complexities just cited as they ignorantly ruminate while denying the significance of the problem and force feed Arabic to the naturally inept student. Of course this is hardly scientific, most especially for the promoters of IOK. Rest assured, however, that ponerocratic hypocrites are indeed scientific, which is why they financially support the error and the ensuing chaos, ignorance, repression and economic stagnation that follows in its wake. Why the latter? Children waste enormous blocks of time on useless religious inculcation when they should be perfecting a trade, skill, or profession.

Linguistic science, therefore, allows us to deduce that, for example, if 'Classical Arabic' — the language of ritual prayer and Al'Qur'an — is not spoken in the home or on the street for practical usage, its acquisition is little more than 'Academic' at best and essentially useless for the man in the street, most especially for non-native Arabic speakers. Hence, this also indicates that learning *modern* Arabic or Mandarin is a much more profitable venture.

Considering that no one speaks classical Arabic in the home any longer, the realities of linguistic science present Muslims with a significant conundrum, especially for Islamists and IOK indentitarians. Of course this is a matter traditionally ignored by pugnacious defenders of fetish, as if ritualism for the masses is sufficient. Well, the latter sentiment is exactly what Mystery Religion ponerocrats think also.

There is indeed a priest-like class of scholars who maintain language liquidity behind white-towers like Catholic predecessors, but this on its own is counter-productive when governance remains both ignorant-of and divorced-from the Counsel of a *shura* that barely comprehends the legal contexts of its acquired tongue. This caste system lends itself to elitist isolation and furthers the arrogance of a demeanor that is anything but Islamic. Again, this is the very same attitude for which the Great Khan gave Muslims their long forgotten lesson. In support of this premise I offer the following:

> ... a diglossic situation [exists] when 'high' and 'low' language codes or dialects exist alongside each other in a community (e.g. classical Arabic vs. a regional form of Arabic). In a diglossic community, political, religious and educational views and values are established and perpetuated.
>
> THE LINGUISTICS ENCYCLOPEDIA, Second Edition (2002),
> Edited by Kirsten Malmkjær, Routledge, London, NY

This assessment would bear sweeter Islamic fruit were Muslim leaders and academics true Islamizers and properly oriented scientifically, but we have sufficiently articulated that this is not the case presently nor has it been for quite some time, although many "Islamizers" would disagree. Hence, diglossic elitists harbor high cultures of Classical Arabic minus the observance of Spiritual Law and most definitely have the legal and intellectual advantage of typical hypocrites over their respective polities as did their Latin forerunners. This is, dear reader, a natural recipe for Ponerocracy.

Furthermore, most Muslim leaders no longer speak 'Classical Arabic' except for recitations and ritual prayer. And if that's not sufficient to give a scientifically sensitive reader pause for concern, I personally found the tri-glossal crisis in Malaysia not only rampantly responsible for gross ignorance and religious arrogance but also accountable for professional exclusivity, closed minds and effete insult. Moreover, not one non-Academic Muslim I encountered during my initial years of conversion could relate, in their native tongue, the meaning of *Al'Fatiyah* let alone significant portions of their five-times-daily ritual recitations, excepting the *azan*. What is worse, is that as soon as most Muslim academicians learned that I knew no Arabic, I was shunned in many venues or pressured to learn it. Of course, as a scientist and non-native speaking late middle-aged well read adult, I knew this was a futile waste of time and effort.

At sixty-three years of age my left brained bias is concretely hard-wired but that scientific fact was of absolutely no concern to condescending 'learn-Arabic-or-else' reactionaries. I reasoned that I could learn far more about Islam by sticking to the language I knew well while learning enough Arabic to pray and politely say 'Alhamduillah' with a nod of deference to what many consider *adab*, although etiquette is not *adab* in the least; but that is subject for a different dissertation.

In summation, the bottom line is that if the early child doesn't obtain 'Classical Arabic' as a second language from the cradle and in multiple utilitarian contexts outside of the classroom or religious school, he/she will inevitably suffer degrees of linguistic dysfunction in the tongue which in turn causes not only religious knowledge deficits but also generates conflict (war) with the few who do manage Classical Arabic fluidly, as do traditional *qari*. As a demonstrative analogy of the immensity of the sacred language problem that Muslims deny, imagine a non-native speaker thinking they've mastered English well enough to teach a non-English speaker that the New York Yankees fought the Confederates in the American Civil War and you will get the drift of the reality here. This is not a small matter, especially for the young men who wasted time trying to learn the impossible and now lack enough practical skills to profitably work and get married—all for the sake of religion of course. These fellows also taught themselves to give the very same 'Alhamduillah nod' as I as a matter consequent to common sense survival skills. However, what I just described is part and parcel of the prevailing neo-patriarchal chauvinism that has little in common with Islam, and nothing whatsoever in common with Islamic Science except for identitarian desperation.

A matter of significance here must be emphasized and that is the inordinate amount of time spent by students trying to learn something that is academic at best but utterly futile with respect to earning a living. Little wonder then that young Muslim men cannot afford to marry in Muslim countries and are relegated to slavery and pious pretense and ranks of fornicating terrorist enemies of any state. The Ponerocrats who prosecute PSYOPS are well aware, however, and utilize the deficit to great advantage.

The better way to avoid this linguistic and unscientific morass of neo-patriarchal chauvinism is by making certain that religious instruction is carried out in native tongues and that only the 'gifted' are streamed towards mastery of 'Classical Arabic' under ideal conditions. Forcing the entire student body to do the impossible is foolish and has caused no-end of Muslim disaffection from the source of their faith, even if they remain nominal Muslims.

I invite you to read a brief exegesis as an example of the Judeo-Christian misguidance in this realm of linguistics before proceeding with Islam's lack of unity.

Isaiah 65:15 has something significant to say to God's servants about names:

'... AND YE SHALL LEAVE *YOUR NAME* FOR A CURSE UNTO MY CHOSEN: FOR THE LORD GOD SHALL SLAY THEE, AND CALL HIS SERVANTS BY ANOTHER NAME."

Christians think the new name is *Christians*. However, the word *Christian* is not Semitic nor is it the actual *name* of their man-god-prophet. The Hebrew word used in the original text is *shem*, the same as *Shem*: the proper name of the son of Noah who met Abraham in the wilderness as the King of *Salem* (Peace/*Shalom*) also called *Melchizedek*. The Hebrew

Nation was called *Israel*, or *God's Firstborn*! Israel literally translates: *he will rule as God*, and the prophecy clearly states that **this same name is now a curse** in the eyes of Allah's **chosen**! Charismatic Christians who like to call themselves 'Spiritual Israel' should actually experience some degree of chagrin, but as I said above, their method is eternally flawed. Furthermore, the King James translation is far from accurate. It should read:

> '... and **invite** or summon his servants by the ***next man of renown***, or authority.' or '***by another authority***'

In order to comprehend this prophecy and its application to the ummah as per Mohammad's reference, one must understand that Israel represented Jacob as 'One Man' or entity; specifically a *unified polity* through whom the Mesopotamian world was meant to be called to God by means of the twelve sons (tribes) which had failed to do so over the course of nearly 2,000 years, perhaps more.

Hence, the 'next man' or 'following authority' cannot be from Jacob's loins or Israel! This ***Next Man*** is also a man with a body politic. Again specifically:

> the next *'man of renown'* to replace Israel as Allah's political party of tribes or nations in the earth.

This and related prophecies are not discussed in Judeo-Christian and especially Zionist friendly forums for fairly obvious reasons. Here we see the scepter of authentic power and governance as prophesied by Jacob in Gen 49:10 (i.e. by Israel himself) passing away from Israel and confirmed by Isaiah.

The political entity cannot be Iesa (Jesus) because he is a Semite of Judah and represents the *same man*, Israel. Consequently, neither can the disciples of Jesus be the 'next man of renown' to form this political entity, which is why he rejected the scepter because he was not *authorized* for the mission.

— extracts from *Trinity, The Metamorphosis of Myth*, by the Author

The purpose, therefore, of Islam, was to replace Israel as 'One Man', i.e., a single body politic guided, governed and governing *vis-à-vis* pure monotheist doctrine in submission to Divine Law (i.e., Theo-centric rather than Theocratic). This lasted for about thirty odd years after which Muslims subjected themselves to failure as an inverse corollary to the Law of Unity. The body politic that confronted Genghis Khan was near death from dissipation. The propped up cadaver that followed the decimation may be likened to a trauma victim confronting their twin, Western Europe's incessant crusaders. Imagine both polities bandaged head to foot while beating each other with crutches and you'll crystallize a specter of befuddled fools. Therefore, it's no wonder present day Kabalists are given free scientific reign over believers who do not actualize their faith with unicity and thereby receive God's Grace, Protection and Divine Intervention—i.e. Power.

What to do? Let the Holy Qur'an guide us on the matter:

- Those who do not judge by what God has revealed-those indeed are the evildoers. [4:39]
- Whenever God and His Apostle have decided a matter, it is not for a faithful man or woman to follow another course of his or her own choice. [5:47]
- Obey God and obey the Apostle and those in authority from among you. [33:36]

The first surat dictates that an Islamic State cannot divorce Shari'ah from either Legislative or Executive instruments. The second directs obedience specifically to laws that remain valid only when not contravening the Prophetic Sunnah or Qur'an. The third *forbids* non-Muslims from wielding authority within the State.

I have outlined a brief scheme that fits the dictates of the first two Spiritual Laws as well as these surats. However, it is impossible to employ because the present secular World Order demands Islam's surrender to impiety (See: Endnote xxii). This abbreviated litany should convince men of discernment that the 'World-Class' cancer of liberalism has advanced beyond any cure save that of divine judgment, which is why Prophet Isa (wslm) is coming back. Adding the following four hadith only makes the task more daunting and confirms my thesis on several fronts:

1. A community in the midst of which sins are being committed which could be, but are not, corrected by it is most likely to be encompassed in its entirety by God's judgment. - The Prophet; Abu Da'ud on Authority of Abu Bakr.

2. By Him in whose hand I repose! You must enjoin right and forbid wrong, or else God will certainly send down chastisement upon you; then you will call to Him, but He will not respond to you." -The Prophet; At-Tirmidhi, on authority of Hudhayful

3. Nay by God, you must enjoin right and forbid wrong, and you must stay the hand of the wrongdoer, bend him to conformity with justice and force him to do justice-or else God will set the hearts of you all against one another. - ibid, Abu Da'ud, on authority of Abd ibn Mas'ud

4. If people see a wrongdoer but do not stay his hand, it is most likely that God will encompass them all with His punishment." - ibid, Abu Da'us, on authority of Abu Bakr

This enumeration is a far cry from the present gospel of 'Politically Correct' tolerance that undergirds the Jacobin Constitution of the USA and visiting Jesuit Scholars, but it does bear witness to Al'Qur'an, the Seerah, The Sunnah, al'Hadith, and the Law of Moses which Prophet Isa confirmed as divinely inspired. Therefore, the impossibility of establishing an Islamic State is readily apparent unless we resort to apocalyptic measures that would not only arrest the behaviors of the current Muslim majority, but also raise the militant ire of all other sin-bound nations.

THE MUSLIM POLITY AS ONE MAN: AN ANALOGY

The outer ritualistic form of the Islamic discipline of piety (*taqua*) requires ablution, prayer, fasting, and generosity in almsgiving. These are purification rites so that the grace of Unity with its inherent divine power may descend upon the polity. Ritual without knowledgeable conviction (certitude) and the implementation of virtue, however, must be understood as mere symbolism. It is akin to fetishism, especially when the polity wallows in quagmires of false doctrines, alien interpolations and practices, superstitions, or in partnerships with unbelievers and disobedience to divine law.[35] Consequences under such circumstances are devastating and the polity reaps what is sown according to the pre-determinants of divine law. There is no room for compromise in the matter, and no amount of scholarly discourse can change this fact.

When Prophet Elijah contended with the Idolatry of King Ahab and Queen Jezebel—who had given the entire nation over to the official worship of Baal & Ashstarte—there was a moment when he felt himself bereft and went so far as to wish for death. God admonished the venerable man and informed him there remained 7,000 righteous men in Israel whom He had preserved, *unknown to the prophet*. This represented a contemporary remnant of approximately 0.2% of the Hebrew population (about 1 in 500 people). This same fraction, or worse (1 in 1000), applies to the number of righteous souls today in keeping with predictions from al'Hadith.

Since the Law of Unity is implicit in man himself and follows the formative principles of anatomy and physiology, these may be applied as an analogy. Man has a head in which sits the brain awash in pure fluid through which information is conducted *via* sensory organs. The polity also has a head protected by the elite of its citizenry (*ulama*) and counseled by sensory organs (advisors with scientific expertise). The hands, feet, fingers and toes did not elect either the brain or its attendant sensibilities. God appointed (created) this central nervous

---

[35] E.g., the current use of 'crystal balls' or pagan gongs to open official ceremonies.

system (government) along with all of its organs of perception as 'companions'.

The brain itself has countless components that must interact in complete harmony in order to synthesize and analyze data before commanding the body. Moreover, an intrinsic guidance system within this complex organ (parasympathetic nervous system) remains fully independent of conscious action or thought. By God's grace, the latter system regulates all functions that maintain and protect vitality and consciousness, but only if it is not irreversibly damaged by impurities, infections or trauma (pathology). This parasympathetic system may be likened to the office of *hisbah* as described by the Hanbali Caliphate's extension of authority to the heads of families, villages, towns, cities and districts, which hardly represents any dictatorial central power. The latter is the socialist model of the new imperialism and represents pathocratic communes governed by elitist appointees with no relationship to the governed. This is not Islam.

As one lowers their gaze on our human template, one sees the same formative principles repeated within all major organs of the thorax and abdomen. The body implies, therefore, that the true polity of God (Kingdom of Allah) is one that is:

1. Created not *reformed*;
2. Appointed not *elected*;
3. Recognized and affirmed by reason and not *persuaded* by cunning propaganda imposed on the ignorant.

In any gathering of mature men they quickly determine exactly which fellows are superior and righteously or wickedly so. These cliques organize political parties that support the leader of their chosen bias. As I've already established, the bias of the majority is towards disobedience to divine law which implies that any democratic process wins the day by granting this innate pathocratic franchise the greater portion of power and dominion. These disobedient parties and coalitions then proceed to reform the polity according to the consensus of its biased imaginations and desires rather than God's decree. They use semiotic logos, slogans and icons that have nothing whatsoever to do with essential Islam. This democratic magic was a pregnant reality even prior to the Jacobin Revolution that made such facilities traditional in the guise of undefined liberty and equality. It is far better, therefore, for righteous men and women to avoid such confederacies and naturally form NGO polities as did Ibrahim and Mohammad; a supra-natural process that requires no political campaigns, slogans, banners and other foolishness.

After warning their errant brethren, righteous folks should excuse themselves and leave the fools to their chosen fate as did Pak Aziz in Malaysia. Men and women who do so, especially in today's plural societies, have no viable option other than exile or return to private life in order to consolidate their portion within the 0.2% remnant divinely assigned to them as a non-official, non-political fellowship. Otherwise, they waste their lives and energy in vain activities that only bring on more headaches and *fitna*.

A few men, much like Prophet Joseph, may find themselves in positions of power, however, which is a place that serves two purposes:

➢ To preserve and protect the remnant of God's servants (The Seed).
➢ To administer the charity of justice within the delimited frameworks of decadent pluralistic societies.

Should a righteous man or woman consciously remain in this office, he/she should limit their concerns to the purpose of God within these boundaries, making no effort to crusade for an autonomous Islamic State which they know is impossible. For this reason, the present gospel of tolerance is the only tenable option available until the iniquity of secular pluralism brings those adopting it to self-destructive judgment.

Leaders who excuse themselves from this fellowship of political tolerance should organize their companions according to the principles of the human body, doing whatever is necessary to promote rather than reform Islam within private domains and without challenging the extant secular government. Allah will honor and protect such organizations as long as they do not overstep boundaries by imposing themselves on others. Such NGOs must be prepared to die when the assault on the integrity of their unicity comes from the enemies of God, and come it will. They must never surrender, but should fight honorably as did Omar Mukhtar and Imams Hanbal and Shamil, against all odds until death or imprisonment is imposed.

There are those who posit that wickedness can be overcome with reasonable measures much as a Physician might assist his/her patient back to health. I disagree because the eschatology of revealed knowledge, when added to empirical evidence, insists that the only solution lay in the divinely appointed hands of the Messiah and Al'Mahdi, and neither have appeared on the scene as yet. To help the reader understand this perspective with greater clarity, I will now proceed with a discussion of real politics.

POWER

> Power should be in the hands of normal people. A ponerologist only demands that such authority be endowed with an appropriate understanding of less-than-normal people [sociopaths], and that the law be based upon such understanding.
>
> *Political Ponerology*, op.cit. p. 138

I happen to agree. The trouble is that, presently, the ulemma are endowed solely with their limited comprehension of Shairiah, little understanding for spiritual law (as espoused herein), and practically no psychological scientific training. If the latter were the case and empowered, most of our present leaders and ulemma would be disqualified from their positions due to one or another of several well defined and demonstrable psychopathies.

At his death, Dr. Kalim Siddiqui was working on a paper that presented several questions regarding the acquisition and use of power by the Prophet. I read his work with great interest and must say that it gave me the impulse to write this book. He naively but earnestly suggested that a study of the *Seerah* would unveil mysteries leading to yet another political system of government that *might* allow Islam to heal and rise from its present coma. Realists like myself acknowledge that political parties are little more than sects vying for the powers of imprisonment, capital punishment, and absolute censure. They are professional organizations devoted to different brands of sedition commonly called 'special interests'. These 'interests' most often suffice as apologies for disobedience to divine law. Nevertheless, all is in vain as Allah made it very clear how to obtain and maintain power by means that reject political partisanship.

"Allah has promised, to those among you who believe and work righteous deeds, that He will, of a surety,

- grant them in the land inheritance of power, as He granted it to those before them;
- that He will establish in authority their religion — the one which He has chosen for them;
- and that He will change their state, after the fear in which they lived, to one of security and peace.

And Furthermore:

They will worship Me alone and not associate aught with Me. If any do reject Faith after this, they are rebellious and wicked. [24: 55]

This should settle the matter for those with sound minds.

Since the Will of God is Power and the 'working of righteous deeds' is submission to His Will, what need have Believers of Political Parties when the answer is set plainly before them? To the contrary, it is non-believers, apologists and other disobedient fools who have a dire need for the politics of an idolatrous system of sectarian nationalism and secular humanism.

> The 'secret' of the Apostle's Power lay in the belief, commitment, and obedience of the men and women around him," said Professor Siddiqui, in answer to his own question!

But he went even further:

> It is possible that power is an all pervasive quality of Islam related to the belief and *taqua* of Muslims individually and collectively, whether or not they have control over a territory.

Taqua it is not a 'possible' requirement because it is, in fact, mandatory. This also indicates that secular analytics are futile because Righteous Power is one of God's *Mysteries*; one that naturally manifests through a polity's pious submission to divine law rather than political organization. In other words, it is a miraculous manifestation of divine grace.

'Authority' is divine permission to use Power, whether for good or for evil, which I discuss in the next section. It is therefore essential that any polity wishing to exercise divine power for good must submit itself to the divinely appointed Viceroy of Allah because power for the Good of all men proceeds to manifest solely by grace from God and is maintained *only by submission* to His Law. Persistent disobedience removes God's benevolent sovereignty and automatically replaces it with its inverse complement, whereby authority is granted to forces under the influence of Iblis and unrighteous tyranny. This is quite simple to grasp because any loss of Rightly Guided Power is directly proportional to the polity's loss of *taqua*.

LOVE, GOODNESS & THE CALIPHATE

Any Islamic movement based on *political reasoning* is therefore destined to fail because reasoning that neglects the guidance of God's Love cannot conduct the grace of unity. This is because love is a reciprocal phenomenon and God's Love for any Polity is dependent upon its submission to His Law. Mohammad's companions and their families amplified this reality as they continued the metaphysical atavism of the Prophetic stream that began with Adam. It is this unicity or 'group-soul' that formed one body with the headship of Muhammad's superior faculties by the Will and Grace of God. Hence, they were endowed with the Power of Unity for what is good and beneficial for mankind; specifically, the Kingdom of God as prophesied by Prophet Isa's gospel. They literally became the *'one man'* predicted by prophet Isaiah under Patriarchal command with a limited democracy, as were all governments established by Prophets throughout history. The prophet's companions brought their clans (families) rather than political parties into submission to Muhammad, and thus formed the body-politic of a true Caliphate.

We can judge, therefore, that corporate submission conducts corporate grace and guidance which then maintains the collective's power and dominion. This is only achieved via authority that is vested and supernaturally guided *vis-à-vis* the Patriarchal continuum of the authentic prophetic stream. None of this requires religious icons, idols, slogans, priestly hierarchy or political campaigns. It was more like the practice of a good doctor whose reputation precedes him and spreads purely by word of mouth throughout the community. There is no organization in the history of humanity that accomplished this politically[36] within moral boundaries as established by the Principles of God's Kingdom; albeit, during their sagely reigns, the Feudal Systems of China and Japan far surpassed Islam in civilized prosperity.

Hence, it is impossible to establish the Kingdom of God (Islamic State) politically without righteous Patriarchs and Matriarchs (such as Kahdijah) in authority, Now let us look at this image of 'God's Kingdom' in the earth and see what really happened to the Muslim regency.

---

[36] **adj.1** of or relating to the government or public affairs of a country. interested in or active in politics. **2 chiefly derogatory** *done or acting in the interests of status within an organization rather than on principle*. [Concise Oxford Dictionary]

ISLAM AS THE 'IMAGE' OR VICEGERENT OF GOD

The human body reflects an organization that:

1. Obtains and processes sustenance;
2. Distributes this sustenance;
3. Eliminates waste and toxins;
4. Provides mobility and structural support;
5. Protects from common insult, injury, deleterious substances or infectious agents;
6. Hormonally mediates a system of accountability (feedback) permitting executive constraint on the body;
7. Restores/Heals itself under optimal conditions.

The Nervous System (including the brain and peripheral sense organs) is the most metabolically inactive and 'helpless' of all organ systems and comes nigh unto useless paralysis or death with the slightest insult and then takes the body down with it because its property is to consciously and unconsciously mediate directives from an *'unknown'* power source (vitality). The systemic infrastructure (internal organs of the body) is devoid of inherent power which indicates that the mediated power of the polity does not lie in either the internal organs or the head. This 'Mediated Power' (i.e., the ability to activate, move or do something) has a dual nature in that (i) it originates as a gift (life force) from Allah SWT, and (ii) is a function of the polity's constituents as represented by the body's connective tissue systems which include bones, muscles and various fluids with complex macro and micro organizations.

Hence, common citizens recognize that their precious innards (respiratory/education, digestive/economic, circulatory/distribution and glands/regulatory) are given by God and, as a result of this common knowledge, do everything possible to protect these organs as well as those of mediation (CNS/governance). This includes self-sacrifice because their lives, power/autonomy and prosperity depend upon these organs. All depend upon a physical power source which is food, and this food is also dual in nature: (i) physical food; and (ii) metaphysical instruction: i.e. the Word of Allah (good food for the soul, what Jesus called the 'bread of life'), and worldly knowledge of creation (science). The anti-thesis of these is the word of Iblis (the 'Whispering' of jinn) which is bad food for the soul and causes negative consequences including premature demise for both individual and culture.

The tissue nearest the brain is the cerebrospinal fluid and may be considered a kind of Guard or 'Board of Censors'. Members of the connective tissue systems represent the coordinated cohesion of workers and men of means; and those of the peripheral nerves, blood and lymphatic systems represent a highly skilled military, intelligence network and constabulary. Internal organs such as heart, lungs, and those of the *viscera* represent different managerial, educational, industrial and distribution systems, etc.

THE BRAIN AS HEAD OR CALIPHATE

All systems are united integrally and wholly and all systems in some manner mimic or reflect this unity via the recapitulation of ontogenic restatements. Furthermore, all systems depend upon food for physical power. It is a grave mistake, therefore, for any man or governmental body to assume multiple functions as do tyrants or plutocratic oligarchies like our NWO Ponerocrats, because the tyranny of their reordering the natural government opposes divine design and belies a corruption of leadership that has rejected what is naturally miraculous. This is why leaders, and not just 'the people', must be subject to a Board of Censors (Spinal Fluid/*ulama*) that has absolute control over what enters or exits the Brain (Executive Government) as valid food (righteous commands for the good of the body). Hence, if this Spinal Fluid is poisoned, lost, or somehow imbalanced, an insult occurs followed by autonomous reactions that affect the entire body, which then ceases to vitally thrive in lieu of preserving a minimum of life functions.

It is now that the power to obtain food and the body's dominion over its limited autonomy comes to a halt after which the patient must be *nursed* if there is to be any hope of *recovery* (restitution of health).

If reformation occurs, it is usually of two types: (a) dysfunctional tumors or useless growths that are not subject to divinely intended formative forces that follow pristine patterns; or (b) degradation (lysis) occurs, depending on the quality of nursing care and the patient's constitution. Both processes exhibit morbidity; that is, imbalances that exceed the boundaries of sustainable life activities and subsequently cause further dysfunctions leading to death. Politically, these may be likened to reactionism and liberalism, respectively.

The 'blood-brain barrier' naturally and normally prevents any substance brought in by the blood stream from entering and contaminating brain tissue. Nevertheless, certain infectious agents and toxins under adverse conditions do enter. And although it is possible for the CNS to continue its functions in the presence of chronic infections, a slow dissipation occurs that manifests over time. Eventually, the patient is driven mad (as in the case with syphilis—Lenin is one such example), or remains cogent but disabled (as in Lou Gherig's Disease), or returns to worse than infantile imbecility (as is the case with Alzheimer's). All three dysfunctions may be seen in today's ummah. We have the mania of suicide bombing; a paralyzed, bloated bureaucracy; as well as self-serving senile academia and religious institutions dissociated from social realities and scientific methodology while miming their enemies.

We are also familiar with the problem of 'headaches', especially when leaders are habituated to toxins that eventually disable the body. Even the pill of Nationalism for the pain is failing while continuing the illusion of health. All of these stand in opposition to repentance (*tauba*) and true reform, the *halal* cures.

When a limb is infected and endangers the body with necrotizing sepsis it must be amputated to insure the body's survival. If the spinal column is severed below the second to fourth vertebrae, the body may survive but its becomes completely helpless and the patient requires total care. If the head is severely injured to include irreparable damage to the brain, the body dies; and if severely traumatized by concussion, febrile insult, chronic infection or serious chemical disequilibrium the patient will lapse unconscious and lay dormant in a coma.

In my opinion, this latter condition represents the reality of Islam's Unity as the 'New Man' prophesied by Isaiah. The body is intact spiritually as a perfected doctrinal system but the incarnate soul of the polity lies comatose without authentic leadership: i.e. a Central Nervous System enveloped in pure 'fluid of ulama' (*Calipha* and *Shura*). As did the Jews, Islam's usurpers murdered or failed to support their authentic Imams and then silenced their righteous ulama in deference to superstition, ritual fetishism and booty gathering. Therefore, until the advent of Hadrat Mahdi and Prophet Isa, the body sleeps while awaiting its divinely mediated restitution: its 'regeneration from above', what Christians call their 'Born Again' epiphany.

What appears on the world stage is a mannequin filled with dysfunctional tumors, artificial transplants and intelligence, and infected bionic limbs or internal organs in constant need of allopathic[37] interventions.

In summary, following the demise of the rightly guided Caliphs the perfected (pristine) body of Islam's polity began its journey towards the Khan's Hammer and ever since the concussion it has remained near comatose, though nursed by the 'few' of Ibn Khadun's 'faithful servants' who largely go unnoticed or are persecuted and marginalized in political venues. What subsequently appeared on the World Stage was a player—an actor mouthing words of truth while distorted imaginations ravaged the body. This is, unfortunately, the analogical reality. Authentic Islam's sleeps in a spiritually comatose body nursed tenderly by the obedient 0.2% of the general populace who have little or no voice in the charade; much like the humble 'nursing aide' in hospital wards as doctors submit faculties of reason to the half-

---

[37] Allopathy, n. the treatment of disease by conventional means, i.e. with drugs having effects that oppose the symptoms. Often contrasted with homeopathy. Homeopathy (also homoeopathy) n. a system of complementary medicine in which disease is treated by minute doses of natural substances that in a healthy person would produce symptoms of disease and thus stimulate a naturally mediated cure.

educated allopathic storm of the Twentieth Century that has caused more harm than good.[38]

Now it is a fact that some comatose patients are *aware* of their environment but lack the power to communicate. A few of these, if well nursed, may even re-emerge intact after several years. In my opinion, therefore, the authentic Muslim polity is aware but has no power to communicate or protect itself. Flim-flam sophists of the great pantomime march forward with a deluded *jihad* while Zionists, Jesuits and other Luciferians complete the task of organizing Dajjal's Beast for the devilish feast of Armageddon's vultures.

One day, Allah will certainly rouse the ummah to Unity and Power. In the meantime there is naught to do but assure the integrity of Islam's purity in our home and immediate community, to the best of our ability. In essence, those who understand are caregivers or chamberlains to a great hope that is helpless until a Prince of Allah stirs the mighty patient from its deep sleep. Perform your duties well therefore, but do not presume any authority to wake him, as did Hasan al'Bana, whose institution is now in the hands of Islam's enemies and racks the body with febrile convulsions.

---

[38] SEE: Eustice Mulins, *Murder by Injection*, National Council for Medical Research, 1998

The Companion Maxims

No Spiritual Law is a *lesser* edict. All Spiritual Law is united and integrated, but unlike the human body, one cannot discard a part or sever a 'jot or tiddle' of these laws. What follows is a roster of compressed definitions that are by no means complete and though I present the axioms in terms of negative corollaries, there is no hierarchy or purposeful order of importance intended.

The Law of Truth

- For any who deny God and His Prophets, God will dim their vision and deny them the fullness of truth and lasting benefits of His Wisdom.

Atheists beware.

The New Testament reports a moment when Isa (Jesus) stood in the Court of Pilate when the Roman governor asked him: "What is truth?" There is no recorded answer which, to my mind, casts doubt on the veracity of the text. There is only one answer and it begs all reason to expect a Prophet of God to let such a moment pass in mute response because *God* is truth. Mohammad answered this question in the *Night Vigil* prayer by reciting "You (Allah) are the Truth."[39] The re-discovery of truth is man's primal quest and since God is the author of all truth, He is *the* truth. In Him can be no falseness. Hence, all that is true proceeds from Him. This being so, to deny God and His Messengers is to deny truth and any act of disobedience to His commands equates with denial. Thus, all sectarians (deviants) partake in this denial to some degree and cannot possibly receive the pure fullness of the grace gift of knowledge of the truth except for the final unveiling at death.

---

[39] Sahih Al'Bukhari, 25: 558, Trans. by Dr. Zidan, A.S. Nordeen, KL, Maylasia, 2002

Consequently, efforts made by non-believers and those who willfully disobey Allah consistently fall short of the glory of truth which, in turn, frustrates whatever goal(s) they may set. This implies a deficit of wisdom with which man's efforts can only rebound with deleterious result. For example, since men deny or ignore the Law of Unity with its contingent adjunct of purity they cannot establish or enforce sexual morality or the *taqua* of marriage. Subsequently, licentious dishonor spreads to corrupt the most fundamental unit in society, which, in turn, destroys that society just as any unchecked infection eventually ravages the body.

"Wisdom is the cognition of Truth in matters not embraced by Revelation" [40] It was the Prayer of the Prophet for Ibn 'Abbas: "O God, teach Him Wisdom".[41] This grace gift of wisdom represents the 1/40th portion of the Prophethood given to those who 'rise in the night' and seek it in prayer and supplication—with a small 'p' of course. It is hence called 'Inspiration' and does indeed have a counterpart that is sourced from the whispers of the jinn. Nevertheless, this is the reality of the *'fullness'* of truth (guidance) and it can only be gleaned in the 'third part of the night' in which Allah 'descends' to bestow it. Therefore, how can worldly-minded sectarians or lethargic Muslims find and know this truth when they are actively blinded by denial and inattentiveness while, at the same time, they marginalize the *qari* and others who made efforts to possess the gift? Such folk remain morally, spiritually and virtuously stunted which equates with metaphysical dwarfism and thus, shortens their faculties of reasoning. This is why Isa said "the blind lead the blind"—the practice of *taqlid*, an art in which flag makers and wavers excel.

---

[40] Bukhari, *Sahih of Abu Dharr*, 'Abd al-Hamid' , vol V, 27

[41] Bukhari, section 27

The Law of Faithfulness

↳ If a people are unfaithful in prayer, or in sustaining the welfare of the poor and helpless, or in the enjoining of good and the forbidding of evil, God will substitute another people in their place.

This was the fate of Buddhist, Zoroastrian, Sabaean, Jew and Christian, and now threatens the Divine favor of Muslims as expressed in the following Surat:

> "If you turn your backs, God will substitute another people for you who will not be like you." [9: 38]

This is a dire consideration that is like stepping off a cliff or having the earth open a bottomless pit beneath your feet. Nevertheless, it happens in marriage, in business and professions so why not in religion? "Turning the back" is cowardice in the face of an enemy. We all admire the brave heathen who dies facing his enemy so what can be said for Muslims who neglect true *jihad* and even join the ranks of their enemy?

Generally speaking, Muslims are faithful to prayer but evidence for their attendance to social welfare by ensuring good and preventing evil is not readily admissible to courts of existential objectivity. You cannot assure the welfare of the poor by giving them a check for a paltry $100 once a year during Ramadan, as I have seen in Malaysia, or by covering usurious policies that aid inflation with equivalent bank fees, fractional reserve banking and money-management salaries that mimic Wall Street greed. Moreover, you certainly cannot assure justice by letting extrinsic (*kafr*) laws and cultural impositions control the streets and minds of your country's development. I posit, therefore, that God is the most serious of business partners and has no intention of backing the metaphysical usury of His contract with men, which is why He promises guidance only to the sincere of heart.

While you ponder the matter, do not think pro-forma ritual cuts a slice of grace or mercy out of the Divine pie. Look at the ever so faithful pro-forma Muslim dominoes in the Middle East as examples. Faithfulness has no substitute or compromise. Ask your wife or consider what would happen if the sun went lusting after planets in the next solar system.

The Law of Mercy

- Unless a man is amenable to self-reproach, empathy and compassion, he cannot receive God's mercy.

Jesus said it differently: "unless a man is *regenerated from above*, he cannot enter the Kingdom of Heaven' ... or ... 'love your neighbor as you love yourself."[42] Sociopaths who lead most Muslim nations are hereby indicted and condemned because they unequivocally lack the human qualities of their subservient minions. In essence, their perspective is one of 'executive privilege', one of exemption from the justice they insist on imposing on 'others'. Like Americans, they are convinced by jinn to believe they are 'exceptional':

> In the psychopath, a dream emerges like some Utopia of a "happy" world and a social system which does not reject them or force them to submit to laws and customs whose meaning is incomprehensible to them. They dream of a world in which their simple and radical way of experiencing and perceiving reality would dominate; where they would, of course, be assured safety and prosperity.
>
> In this Utopian dream, they imagine that those "others", different, but also more technically skillful than they are, should be put to work to achieve this goal for the psychopaths and others of their kin [perfectly describes Tamuludic Zionists]. "We", they say, "after all, will create a new government, one of justice". They are prepared to fight and to suffer for the sake of such a brave new world, and also, of course, to inflict suffering upon others.
>
> Such a vision justifies killing people, whose suffering does not move them to compassion because "they" are not quite con-specific. They do not

---

[42] 'Born-Again' is a common and popular *mistranslation* for 'regenerated from above'

realize that they will consequently meet with opposition which can last for generations.

Political Ponerology, op. cit. p.139

Mercy is the grace-gift of 'forgiveness and restoration (i.e., restitution)' as made manifest in the Parable of the Prodigal Son; but its receipt is contingent upon:

- a man's repentance or remorse for his error(s);
- a similar empathy towards his fellows;
- and reverence for his superiors.

Sin or error is referred to as man's 'gravitation to earth' in Al'Qur'an. This descent directly implies an abject immersion in materialism without the countering restraint of transcendent spiritual truth. The principle itself is manifest in the Law of Gravity: i.e. without the Spirit or God's 'Word of Command' as an opposing force, the entire Universe would collapse into a gigantic black hole. Physicists wrestled with the principle for three plus centuries after Newton said it existed and recently they have mathematically determined its veracity.[43] Even so, scientists are loathe to identify it as did the venerable Englishman.

In another analogy, children do not grow-up but rather grow down from the head. They begin with eyes closed then opened, followed by smiles and head movements, and slowly gain control of arms and torso. After a year, the little tykes begin to walk and cause no end of mischief. This process of incarnation is a manifestation of 'gravitating downwards'. Upon reaching the age of reason, man eventually looks to the stars and inclines himself to things beyond the confining principles of the dense material of his temporal prison, as did Ibrahim.[44] Nevertheless, without actualizing the spirit of remorse for either the

---

[43] It is now known as the 'Black Force': an energy field so huge it dwarfs all previously calculated energy in the physical universe, including the 'Big Bang'.

[44] Animals cannot and do not gaze at the stars.

loss of divine company, principles or memory of pre-incarnate existence, most either forget the stars or merely use them to apologize for ongoing error, and then continue to engage the pleasures of material gains under imagined auspices (myths).

To the contrary, non-pathological men of faith experience profound remorse for any lack of spiritual guidance and will begin a search for God. In response to this activation of faith, in mercy God runs to meet them in order to reveal Himself for the sole purpose of the man's restoration to His Kingdom. However, the experience of this chief desire and purpose of God's Mercy is a 'private' revelation. It is the real reason many men seek the company of other men *away* from urban distraction by fishing, walkabouts, or hunting in the mosque of pristine creation.

The man of faith continually and quickly turns in repentance after every error or sin, upon which God forgives and restores the man to His Grace in mercy, according to sincerity. Each time a person turns in repentance to seek God's forgiveness and mercy they seek the restoration of lost grace. Moreover, if a man is not in sin but lacks understanding, each time he turns his query to God with a sincere heart God will turn to Him in mercy and grant an answer according to the man's ability to receive it. This is why the Qur'an is called a Mercy from God given to the Prophet. The practice of daily prayers is the discipline that should help us to acquire mercy continually, but because of hypocrisy (insincerity) and ignorance (prayer without understanding), it often and sadly fails.

Therefore, without faithful repentance, men cannot enter the Mercy of Restoration to God's Kingdom; neither here nor in the hereafter, because no other provision is made for their rehabilitation. Without the sincere repentance that conforms one's behavior to the moral imperatives of divine law men cannot obtain God's Mercy. Without it, we can only continue in subjugation to the Law of Gravity and collapse to singular black holes of infinitely dense futility. Such is the Law of Mercy.

There are also contingency clauses: (a) if man does not forgive his companions; and (b) if he does not faithfully submit himself to his betters *he* will not be forgiven no-matter the pro-forma petitions. Why? This is because both 'un-forgiveness and 'pride' are benchmarks of pathological insincerity and mark one as a member or supporter of the psychopathic tribe(s) described above. The Grace of God descends only as a Mercy and Guidance to those who are earnest. So be careful.

The Law of Communion

- If a man does not communicate with God, God will not communicate with him.

    communion: the sharing or exchanging of intimate thoughts and feelings. - Oxford Dictionary

Communion has absolutely nothing to do with the eating of sun-god wafers that derive from decadent anthropophagus Mystery Religions and everything to do with intimate exchange. Communication is essential for every aspect of life but the concept of communion refers to a particular intimacy that resides at the core of social unity, whether for good or for evil. Secret Societies engender and guard this rapport with vile oaths; religious groups think they express it through vain rituals; but it is faithful spouses who experience it at its zenith in undefiled marriage. Marriage is actually the best human analogy for Communion with God and is often referred to throughout Judeo-Christian Scripture by the term 'Know' — e.g. 'And Adam *knew* his wife'. This 'knowing' is an integral component of man's growing conviction and increasing faith, whereby he consciously encounters the guidance of God as discussed previously in the Law of Grace.

Religious ritual is not—I repeat—is not communion with God. It is nothing more than a coin placed in the slot of a metaphysical phone box that allows us to place a call to heaven. It is pure protocol; a discipline performed for community and self but certainly not for God—Who requires it of us for these reasons but certainly doesn't need it. It is 'we' who need to both talk to and listen to His response. After placing the call it is time to talk, to enquire, to make entreaty, to request help, and to ask for forgiveness.

During intimate converse there is always an exchange and what we most seek from God in exchange for our worship is His Mercy and Guidance. But God's answers are not as readily available as are sound waves vibrating from phones or the sweetened lauds that follow a lover's embrace, which is why 'prayer and patience' are married in both Bible and 'Al'Qur'an', for without a period of conscious and patient 'waiting upon the Lord' we return to affairs of the world and miss His response. For this reason, the Prophet said that 'the 'remembrance of God *is better than* solat' (ritual prayer) or the mumbo-jumbo of tedious recitations like good monks.

In remembering God, we practice an active ongoing communion and some people 'talk' to Him as if He were sitting on their shoulder. Indeed, Al'Qur'an says He is 'closer than our jugular vein'. I, for one, accept this as reality and care not to know the mechanism. I often go about in continual conversation with Him, lost in the pre-occupied expectation of His answers. Is this piety? Heavens no! It is 'my' own approach to the active remembrance of God that has come to be a regular and natural expression of my faith as habit. Without this intimate communication with God, I have nothing of value to share when talking or writing.

The question that remains, however, is this: 'How *does* God answer? The answer is what makes life exciting and stimulating for genuine God-Seekers. Actually, it is an excellent mystery-adventure-drama in which *you* happen to be the star. God's responses are immediate at times, but most often they are delayed. They come in a myriad of forms, at the strangest of times, and very often are complete surprises and may even present as answers to forgotten prayers. Often, they oppose what one expects and desires in life or are of a nature that is not readily comprehended at first, and may even be far greater than what one may have asked for.

Dreams and visions are certainly encountered along the way but it is more likely that one meets the divine response through relationships with other people. These include challenges, unexpected circumstances, disappointments, a good book, the wise counsel of an elder or spouse, the innocent response of a child, an observation from nature, the remarks or deeds of an enemy, perhaps calamity, or even the behavior of a pet. All require patience, fortitude and conscious observation with personal discipline if one is to discern God's various modes of rejoinder. Otherwise, one is tossed to and fro on the high seas of life without a pilot's license or compass, or perhaps reduced to reading omens like sincere animists and astrologers.

This topic of communion with the Almighty brings us to the Islamic concept of *Taqua* (piety), without which we cannot perceive the divine response to prayer and thereby follow God's guidance. Picture this metaphysical reality with the imagination of walking a tightrope suspended above hell: The only aid available is the rope, your strength and the balance beam in your hand. In order to complete the walk safely and securely, one must be constantly on guard and balance each step. The expanse that is crossed represents our earthly life; the rope represents scripture and the many examples of God's messengers; your strength represents personal discipline and faith according to what is written; and the balance beam represents God's intervention and/or response to prayer. In order to utilize the balance beam, one must be morally strong and sensitive to any loss of balance in order to adjust the beam and maintain the equilibrium that stabilizes each step. This requires consciousness and conscience, the two guardians against the perils of evil. What man or nation can discharge such a feat without God's help?

Since our individual and collective powers of discernment constantly fall short, many pitch themselves to flammable infamy rather than call upon God in the manner of His Prophets. Without *Taqua* it is impossible to reach the divine ear let alone hear God and obey Him well enough to fulfill the destiny of our service to Him; which, by the way, is to our benefit, not His. Without *Taqua* we are doomed: many fall and do not know it till the flames engulf them. That is why service to a Rightly Guided Imam is essential because most people have lost their inclination to develop *Taqua*. Those who do have discovered a secret that many a mystic has perverted: the discipline of quiet meditation (*taffakur*) which is contemplation in remembrance of Allah.

The modern world corrupts and exploits the purpose of this time by calling it *holiday* instead of *Holy Day*. However, it is divinely commanded to be a period of withdrawal from the world and not a head strong plunge into its delusion of pleasure. It is a specified interval intentionally reserved for interfacing with God in order to discern His Will through the many signs He gives, both collectively and individually. It is a time set aside to listen to the 'wee small voice' within each of us, closer than our jugular and more potent than any pineal 'third eye' of New Age shamans, or the denser gray matter of humanists. But how can a man hear and obey this voice when he is constantly inundated by the press of earthy life in a modern world full of vain distractions?

When most pedestrians sleep, men and women of *taffakur* rise to pray and seek God's counsel; patiently seeking the wisdom inferred by our collective cognomen (homo-sapiens-sapiens or 'wise-wise man') along with the divine guidance needed to adjust the balance beam. They do this fully expecting an answer and have no doubt it will come in due season.

I caution you, therefore, not to be swayed by lesser minds who may think that ritual, good deeds or even charity are sufficient activities for the communion of divine guidance. On another note, if you lack the will or desire to actually communicate with God as did the Israelites at the foot of Mt. Sinai, I suggest you submit your service to a person who has it. But be careful not to worship him or her as do sectarian hero mongers. Authentic imams with such character make no pretense to the office and, generally speaking, go about unnoticed. So leave them in peace but follow his/her example to the best of your ability. Obey their counsel with the assurance of God's blessing, as did the men of Ibrahim and the Companions of Mohammad.

Without intimate communion with God, men can neither validate their faith nor experience the reality of righteous guidance as discussed previously in the section on obedience. For this reason, many succumb to false doctrines along with the sectarian kahunas whom Satan transforms to dimmer lights that temporarily eclipse truth for the brief respite of man's life on earth. In the Book of Genesis,

Moses (pbh) called this source of delusion the 'lesser', or, literally translated, the 'insignificant' light. It is not the moon as is commonly conceived. Most people succumb to what sociopathic elitists have termed the 'Right Hand Path' of Satan, referring to popular religious formats that are easily managed and policed by Ponerocrats. These jinn inspired encouragements are accepted forms of repression that make it easy to 'gravitate to earth' under the pretense of serving God in the safety net of collective egocentrism, which, in essence, is the praise craving tribalism of people with underlying inferiority complexes and perhaps brain damage as a result of modern and post-modern influences — in other words, flag-waving patriots who drop bombs on innocents and thank God for the crime; or knife wielding madman who take heads bearing beards just like their own. Idiots, all.

You can spot the wolves of this game by the extreme emphasis they place on ritual protocols and long wigs and robes rather than comprehension, practical education and consequent justice. Here, a corollary-caveat must be mentioned:

The greater the pageantry (ritual) *the lesser the divine communion and guidance.*

This is an occult principle of propaganda and is exhibited commonly under symbols (idols & icons) of nationalist hero worship. Unfortunately this includes the celebration of Mohammad's birthday as initiated by Jew-inspired Fatimids, and the Shi'ite apotheosis of Hadrats Ali and Hussein. It is for this reason that symbols (icons), idols and hero worship are expressly forbidden in Islam and images of the Prophet (pbh) are shunned.

As it is with one's spouse, communion with God is a private matter not to be subjected to the immodest exhibitionism of those who recite exceptionally long prayers. Remember also, that when sanctimony fails, envoys of Satan place grandiose displays of tribal power and retirement plans as 'safety nets' under life's tightrope walk as a substitute for genuine *taqua* and authentic communion with reality. These ancient ploys are part of a pretense that never fails to enlarge hell. Hence, I suggest that sincere believers revert their holidays to Holy Days and gravely reconsider the fact that if we do not genuinely communicate with God rather than iconic substitutes and bodiless beards, there is indeed a rather unholy spirit eagerly awaiting our intimate conversation.

The Law of Worship

➥ If a man does not worship God alone, he will perish.

Worship means many things to many people, but to God it means slavery to His Will for our everlasting benefit. The derivation of the term in English comes from the 'recognition of worthiness'. And in ancient Hebrew it literally means "to bow down' or 'prostrate' oneself before a king; or 'to grovel like a dog and lick the master's hand' — not a particularly acceptable image to proud, egocentric eyes, which is why Jews rejected and/or murdered their prophets in deference to Chaldean and Philistine magi. Nevertheless, I think it best to grovel than become part of Hell's ongoing expansion program.

It is worth the effort to review the Judaic commandment from the King James Translation of the Torat; Deut. 5: 6-10:

> I am the Lord thy God, Which brought thee out of Egypt, from the house of bondage. Thou shalt have none other Gods before me. Thou shalt not make thee any graven image, or any likeness of anything that is in heaven above, or that is in the earth beneath, or that is in the waters beneath the earth: Thou shalt not bow down thyself unto them, nor serve them: for I the Lord thy God am a jealous God, visiting the iniquity of the fathers upon the children unto the third generation of them that hate me, and showing mercy unto thousands of them that love Me and keep My commandments.

On review of this passage, we understand why Protestants abbreviated the original version and Catholic authorities, especially, discouraged and even forbade its reading. The command also confirms my several remarks on the use of symbols and icons. The latter use, i.e., semiotics, is a major party to all sectarian divergence, and most especially those of occult fellowships. Symbolism, when referenced to the metaphysics of cosmogony and theology constitutes forms of subliminal idolatry. To excuse this and continue using of the Star and Crescent of ancient Chaldea to represent Islam is a position that cannot be defended on the Day of Judgment.

'Idolatry' in the Hebrew is the word, *hebal*, which means 'vanity' or 'worthlessness', particularly the latter. This extremely meaningful word brings us full circle to the definition of Worship, which is *the conscious acknowledgement of that which is more worthy or superior*. One must ask, therefore, to who or what do sectarians bow when they prostrate under symbols or photos placed on a parade ground or within prayer and meditation rooms? This is a straightforward matter; for which there is, unfortunately, no excuse, especially on the day of judgment.

The Law of Worship, therefore, like all Spiritual Laws, brooks no compromise and carries a distinct warning. It is a law that bears within it the concepts of honor and love. If a man breaks this law, he inadvertently pays honor and respect to an enemy of truth no matter how high his deluded aspiration attempts to ascend. God will not accept his prayer or deed no matter how wonderful or glorious it appears in the eyes of men. Keeping this in mind, and as a practical exercise in the political science of ponerology, raise the matter of symbolism (iconography) in any religious or political forum and sectarian deviants (the skirtoid type, see footnote #44) will surge in its defense with threats to marginalize (or worse) all who do not agree with their apologies for the crime against heaven. Another ostensibly non-pugnacious lot—mostly hypocrites and elitists whose positions depend on idolatry—will politely excuse you as not 'worthy' of membership in their respective cliques and country clubs; this includes most politicians, business CEOs, bankers, and academics; all of whom will immediately return to the pretense of politically correct punditry like so many roosters.

One should not underestimate the power of symbols or the duplicity of institutions that effectively wield them; including the Church and its derivatives of Humanism, Socialism and Communism and other institutionalized fetishisms. Essentially, they are sigils that work a form of magic on the general populace as illustrated by the slides below:

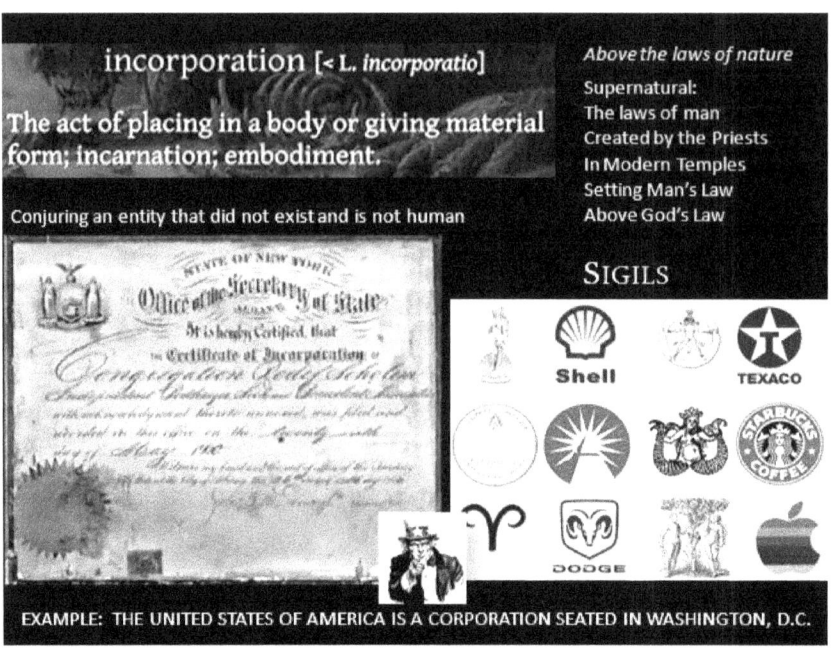

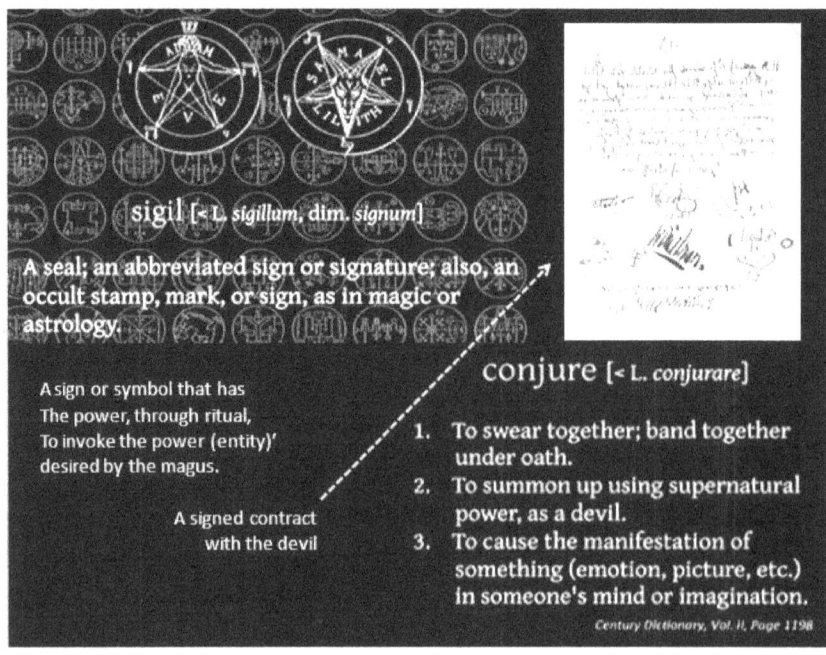

PART ONE: THE METAPHYSICS OF SPIRITUAL LAW
The Companion Maxims

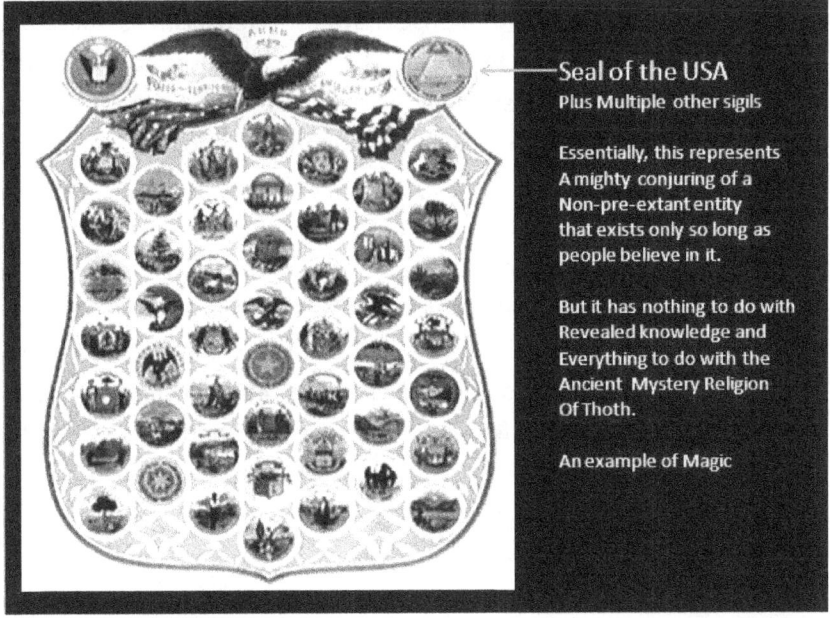

The first recorded Muslim example of such an exercise was that of Mu'awiyah who raised the Qur'an as an icon which then altered the course of history in his temporal favor. At that particular moment he otherwise would have been defeated, but the results of his action were so powerful and immediate that troops of Hadrat Ali succumbed to superstitious fear rather than obey the legal command of God's authentic Viceroy. This cunning exploitation of man's superstitious nature is called *pragmatics* in the science of *semiotics*:

> The process of interaction within the triadic unity of sign–designatum–interpretant is called *semiosis*. Morris decomposed this process into the three dyadic relationships-processes:
>
> a) syntactic studies relations among signs,
>
> b) semantics studies relations between signs and their designata,
>
> c) pragmatics studies relations between sign-vehicles and their interpreters.[45]

The power of symbolic idolatry is such that it causes men to ignore divine guidance. In the case just cited, divine guidance was Hadrat Ali's command to attack. The immense power of fetishism is therefore demonstrated as a type of PSYOP conditioning tool used to silence the mob's better judgment, especially in public venues. In this instance, the result was an act of obedience to an inanimate object, the written Koran, which, in all truth was mere ink and paper material, whereby the essence of the Koran was completely ignored to the public's immense harm, which then allowed the ponerogenic usurpation of Islam by lines of typically sociopathic dynasts. This is a misplaced form of veneration that is historically rampant as practiced also by Catholics, Hindus and Buddhists, among other fetishists, and was prophesied by the Prophet (wslm) who referred to the manufacture of 'gilded Korans' whose content would never pass beyond vocal chords to enter the ark of the human heart. Hadrat Ali's defeat, therefore, was the result of sociopathic cunning. Someone in Mu'awiyah's camp, most likely a Kabbalist Jew, had psychological expertise enough to manipulate the

---

[45] *Neural networks and Intellect: using model-based concepts* / Leonid I. Perlovsky; 2001, Oxford University Press, Inc.

Skirtoids [46] in Ali's army by using superstition as a fulcrum and the Koran as an idol.

In paying honor to an idol, one expresses love, veneration, reverence and obedience to something other than God, His prophets or their representatives. And since 'God' is a term that literally means 'He who decides', it is better to grovel on the dirt floor of an icon-idol free shed than the finest marble floor of a Mosque displaying the Star of Isis & Crescent Moon of Baal (SIn).[47]

The Law of Knowledge

→ Seek after all available knowledge and honor authentic, eclectic scholars [not just the religiously preoccupied]. If not, be easily misled.

The consequences of going astray are dreadful, which is why Al'Qur'an places considerable import on continual study in all areas of knowledge and states that 'rightly guided' scholars are of the highest value among its disciples. But the latter group has been replaced by politicians, assorted gainsayers and average ignoramuses commonly called mullahs (alternatively, 'imams'). Unfortunately, this 'knowledge maxim' is commonly steered towards useless forms of theology with

---

[46] Vital, egotistical, and thick-skinned individuals who make good soldiers because of their endurance and psychological resistance. In peacetime, however, they are incapable of understanding life's subtler matters or rearing children prudently. They are happy in primitive surroundings; a comfortable environment easily causes hysterization within them. They are rigidly conservative in all areas and supportive of governments that rule with a heavy hand. - Political Ponerology, op. cit. p. 136

[47] This symbol actually represents the horns of a bull worn as a head-dress by Nimrud, grandson of Noah and King of Babel who contended with Ibrahim. It is a constant feature of both Mithraic and Baal Worship from ancient antiquity through to modern derivatives. In ancient Haran, the moon-god cultus referred to him as *Sin*, a term that is traced through Acadia to the Dravidian Culture of the Hindus Valley of present day Pakistan. The star represents Isis or the ancient Chaldean goddess Ishtar. See appendix. They idolatrous icons were elevated for use in Islam by the Ottoman Turks during the 16th century.

an over emphasis on the religious study of jots and tiddles, especially in Muslim communities. The result has led to a loss of balanced perspective and social cohesion, as well as cultural and scientific decline. Imam Ibn Khaldun and others documented the phenomenon quite extensively:

> . . . Great historical diseases have taught historians to distinguish two phases [of degeneration]. The first is represented by a period of spiritual crisis in a society, which historiography associates with exhausting of the ideational, moral, and religious values heretofore nourishing the society in question. Egoism among individuals and social groups increases, and the links of moral duty and social networks are felt to be loosening. Trifling matters thereupon [the legalism of 'jots & tiddles'] dominate human minds to such an extent that there is no room left for thinking about public matters or a feeling of commitment to the future. An atrophy of the hierarchy of values within the thinking of individuals and societies is an indication thereof; it has been described both in historiographic monographs and in psychiatric papers. The country's government is finally paralyzed, helpless in the face of problems which could be solved without great difficulty under other circumstances. Let us associate such periods of crisis with the familiar phase in social hysterization.
>
> *Political Ponerology*, op cit, p. 192

The post-Mongolian, post-Ghazali epoch of the Muslim religious zeitgeist fell into this error by seeking knowledge of God and human service to His cause entirely through religious training; not to mention the piling up of booty. I might add that the impractical aspects of being 'pre-occupied-with-religion' is a form of misguidance that has been encouraged by Islam's enemies and elitists who generously support useless religious education. [48] The reason for this is that one of the

---

[48] SCHIZOIDIA: Here, we cannot help but think of Karl Rove, Dick Cheney, and Donald Rumsfeld, protégés of the neo-con philosopher, Leo Strauss. Strauss [a Zionist Jew, as were many of his students] evidences typical schizoidal doctrinaire characteristics . . . The combination of religion and nationalism is the elixir that Strauss advocates as the way to turn natural, relaxed, hedonistic men into devout nationalists willing to fight and die for their God and country."

principles of satanic governance is to keep religiously minded people ignorant and thereby prevent their progress by permitting shizoidal sociopaths full reign.[49] This makes them far easier to exploit and is part and parcel of the Babylonian system which Maltese Knights of Romanism have successfully brought forward to the 21st century under Jesuit guidance for select portions of earth bound slaves.

In its entirety or gestalt unity, the 'knowledge of God' made available to men implies 'all that exists', which is why the contingent word 'all' is in the Law. Hence, for example, when materialists make a discovery in science but discount spiritual laws their contemplations lack communion with the Divine and cannot lead to divinely approved moral utilization of the knowledge. Such is the case with nuclear energy. The contrary is also true but represents a far worse scenario because religious extremists who wallow in ignorance are amongst the most arrogantly pugnacious and dangerous factions of human facsimiles. These fellows commit simultaneous suicide and mass

---

- Shadia Drury, Professor of Political theory,
University of Regina, Saskatchewan, Ontario, Canada

The point here is that Straus was not the first to join hedonism, Nationalism and Religious fixation. This is an ancient ploy, and is used by enemy infiltrators to seduce ignorant youth into sacrificing their nation's integrity. - oz

Schizoid characters aim to impose their own conceptual world upon other people or social groups [Christian Evangelists for eample], using relatively controlled pathological egotism and the exceptional tenacity derived from their persistent nature. They are thus eventually able to overpower another individual's personality, which causes the latter's behavior to turn desperately illogical. Examples: Karl Marx and Engels. The quantitative frequency of this anomaly varies among races and nations: low among Blacks, the highest among Jews (3%). Estimates of this frequency range from negligible up to 3%. In Poland it may be estimated as 0.7% of population. My observations suggest this anomaly is autosomally hereditary.

- *Political Ponerology*, op. cit, p. 138

[49] Schizoidals are psychological loners who then begin to feel better in some human organization, wherein they become zealots for some ideology, religious bigots, materialists, or adherents of an ideology with satanic features. Karl Marx is an eminent example, along with Engels and others who may be considered "bearded schizoidal fanatics" *ala* Peter Jacob Frostig (1896-1959), Professor of King John Kasimir University in Lwow, (now Ukraine) - ibid. pp 185-6

murder, deliver severed cow and pigs heads as insults, and otherwise repress women and children in the name of God like the neo-patriarchs of old fashioned Catholicism minus the alcoholic penchant. The elite of such mobs become so uselessly effete they open wide gates for cunning Machiavellians and actually roll out the red carpets for them. I have witnessed this in Malaysian academic forums and can attest that many alim had no idea who they were hosting.

When religiously minded folk emphasize metaphysics over the inspection and utilization of Creation's manifold secrets (science) they fall into a grave imbalance that has caused the neo-patriarchy of the profoundly bearded, long-robed and chesty chauvinism that plagues the ummah. These primates have caused and continue Islam's demise for the lack of true reform due to the marginalization of qari Sheikhs, who are actually excluded from top shelf Islamic Universities, as discussed previously. This writer gives sufficient explanations for the indictment. As a result, such unbalanced communities of zealous sanctimony are easily misled by anyone as cunning as Mu'awiyah's advisors whose disciples of the occult govern the West; men such as the guru of the Bush Brigade: Leo Strauss, a Talmudic Jew, Zionist, and perhaps Kabbalist to boot.

The Old Testament declared somewhere that "Without knowledge My people are destroyed," which is as plain as a maxim can be. Hence, for Islam's complete fruition, the revelations of God—which are wholly moral—must be married to the revelations of science. But what is more important is that the synthesis of this knowledge must be joined to wisdom and incorporated at all levels of education. Ostensibly this is the purpose of the IOK movement. However, there is a caveat:

> This synthesis must suitably match the scientifically determined abilities of every graded state of comprehension so as to attend each type of intelligence and not just the famous 'Three Rs' of the Anglo-American mandate.

The thirst and/or respect for gestalt knowledge must be reinforced in every child and established as a life-long enterprise because its desire is part of inherent *fitrah*. Otherwise, and as it is now, those who are led astray become multitudes of misguided beggars wanting both truth and the means for sustenance.

The Law of Community

- To the degree a man withdraws from community, God withdraws His divine guidance.

It has been written and accepted by many that God created Eve because "It is not good for man to be alone". I dare say the reverse is also true and further implies that it is 'bad' to go without the companionship of a mate and/or fellow human creatures. These are facts that medical science has since confirmed in many realms of research. I posit therefore that going forth to 'multiply and subdue the earth' is a joint venture that requires families as opposed to the surrogate pathocracies of socialism. Furthermore, I also posit that it is simply not an acceptable option to excuse oneself permanently in order to seek God and escape the responsibility of being your family's keeper — which is an obligation that extends to the community.

Accordingly, God delimits His presence and that of His ministering spirits (angels) which then permits permanently assigned Marabout God-seekers to better communicate and commune with reprobate jinn. Hence, communities of such anchorites who wish to escape the responsibilities of 'family keeping', easily mistake the companionship of jinn for angels according to the spiritual law of inverse proportion. They even marry them; this is on record. However, such a pathological application reflects how crucial and deeply ingrained the instinctive drive for family keeping and generation has been implanted in man by the Almighty.

Nevertheless, the purpose for communal living is not to seek God, but rather to do God's Will by means of the divinely imposed trial of being accountable to one's fellow creatures, beginning, of course, with the family unit. Without the challenge of this restraint, man's imagination runs wild with disordered fancies magnified by jinn who love to inhabit the isolated domains of monks or the cults of life's alleyways, underworlds and byways of modern urban anonymity; not to mention mortuaries like Westminster Abbey. Such colonies, especially those called 'Catholic', incessantly seek exclusion from civil laws with tax exemptions and from sexual norms in particular; the latter being an inveterate form of peculiar exceptionalism. When given a free hand, they often foment sedition and even seduce children from the faith of their parents because they consider themselves above the natural law of parenthood due to an advanced state of piety. I'm not referring to the 'Mother Theresas' of the world, though it may stand true for those who've assumed their mantles.

Holiness is a term that literally means 'reserved for God' and it is highly unlikely that men and women who avoid civil accountability—which is the normative social basis for the challenge of faith—can be considered God's reserves. The recent revelations of enormous insults to pediatric constituencies by the clergy—including institutionalized murder and coverup—bears witness to the truth of this thesis. After all, reserves are forces called upon in times of distress and not a cause of trans-generational deprecation and hardened depravity.

Accountability, however, especially within the community of Islam, is a requirement of life membership and fellowship because without it man inevitably loses the balance of *taqua* due to a number of *jinn-tonics* brewed in metaphysical distilleries. Muslims have also traditionally failed the requirement of being their brothers' and sisters' keepers in authentic social settings; a venue that is purposely filled with God's trials of both faith and intention.

I posit that the environments that so-called 'ascetics' establish are artificial constructs apologized for on the basis of an unhealthy 'self-denial' that allegedly brings them closer to God. But if that were God's intention he would have left Adam a randy bachelor or perhaps made Catholic celibacy with a side-dish of perversion a requirement for his prophets. Nothing could be further from the truth when one considers the commands given to Eve and Adam or the lives of His many messengers, all of whom were intimately involved with the world at large and most of whom were polygamists—especially the Major Prophets like Jesus. The 'Essene' mentality, therefore, is a religious absurdity that runs amok among those who delight in effete devotee seduction. It is a potent libation filled with symbolic doctrines, allegories, myths and the romantic fancies that alluringly lead men and women towards 'Lord of the Ring' carnivals of overcompensation for deviant imaginations; far from the common sense of Divine Guidance.[50]

MENNONITES, HUTTERITES & AMISH

The longest standing and truly Christian Communities are the rural havens of the Mennonite, Hutterite and Amish clans of North America. These are agrarian communes of patriarchal families committed to fundamental Christian principles and earth-husbandry in its many forms. Harvard University's Sociology Department commissioned a study some years ago to determine the 'whys' and hows' they withstood the onslaught of Materialism for three Centuries while maintaining autonomy, integrity and longevity when all other utopian ventures failed. [51]

---

[50] . . . The most frequently indicated and long-known of these is the asthenic psychopathy, which appears in every conceivable intensity, from barely perceptible to an obvious pathologic deficiency. These people, asthenic and hypersensitive, do not indicate the same glaring deficit in moral feeling and ability to sense a psychological situation as do essential psychopaths. They are somewhat idealistic and tend to have superficial pangs of conscience as a result of their faulty behavior. On the average, they are also less intelligent than normal people, and their mind avoids consistency and accuracy in reasoning. Their psychological worldview is clearly falsified, so their options about people can never be trusted. A kind of mask cloaks the world of their personal aspirations, which is at variance with what they are actually capable of doing. Their behavior towards people who do not notice their faults is urbane, even friendly; however, the same people manifest a preemptive hostility and aggression against persons who have a talent for psychology, or demonstrate knowledge in this field. The asthenic psychopath is relatively less vital sexually and is therefore amenable to accepting celibacy; that is why some Catholic monks and priests often represent lesser or minor cases of this anomaly. Such individuals may very likely have inspired the anti-psychological attitude traditional in Church thinking. - *Political Ponerology*, op. cit. p. 134

[51] See: *Heavens on Earth: Utopian Communities in America, 1680-1880,* by Mark Holloway.

They determined that the deciding factor was not doctrine but rather the continuum of concerted efforts these communities exerted to guarantee the following benefits:

1. That none of its members were in need of basic human amenities;
2. That all were educated;
3. That their methods of husbandry remained current but did not disturb or destroy the natural environment (= sustainability).
4. That everybody actually worked for individual and community welfare.

In other words, there were no shirkers or pot-bellied intellectuals or imams collecting tithes or inflated salaries for discussing heavenly matters of no earthly significance. Actually, religion was the least significant factor excepting that its fundamental principles of social import were actually expressed by deeds. Leadership was also low on the totem pole of their success because almost any community member was capable of taking up where another left off *without* nomination.

Of interest was that, except for commerce, each commune's leadership kept the community isolated-from rather than integrated-with the secular world; which speaks some good for apartheid policies; something Zionists rally against intellectually and legally[52] but practice by deed in Israel, as do Middle East Arabs in the Gulf States. They also prevented usurious expansion and proselytizing, although sons and daughters did migrate to establish new communes. The movement's leaders protected the integrity of the community by maintaining borders of 'self'- and 'other'-hood via religious indoctrination and the prevention of evil (secular) intrusions. Thus, they forbade evil and ensured good which are Islamic mandates.

Secular communities wanted no part of Mennonite Hutterite or Amish discipline and generally left them in peace. At the same time, respect and admiration for the clans did develop but took several generations of tenacity with increasing prosperity in the face of all

---

[52] AIPAC Lobby, Southern Poverty Law Center and ADL are typical examples.

odds and the lack of modern conveniences. Most of their communities refused public utilities and modern modes of transportation until recently, and even now it is done on the basis of necessity without ostentatious abuse. They also forbade/forbid TV, which is not an insignificant *non-influence* leading to their robustly established track record.

The success of this economy of equitable fellowship continually prospers for 8-10 generations (400 years plus), despite the onslaught of modernist and post-modernist futility. Again, the key is not religion but rather common-sense fellowship that required the entire community to be each other's keepers [53] in clear contradistinction to the pathological attitude of the biblical character of Cain, whom many admirers of Western culture and subcultures imitate.

The Harvard study was secular (i.e. religiously non-aligned) and the results speak for themselves. That Mennonites and Amish followed moral codes of conduct goes without speaking but when sociologists evaluated their data, this was not *the* major cause of success because many other failed utopian communes also behaved morally. The chief qualifier for success was this: the individual members of these communities actually helped each other on a continuum and enjoyed doing so. In addition:

1. they did not practice usury;
2. the men did not abandon women and children to their own devices;
3. they made equitable distributions of profit;
4. they practiced an economy best described by the phrase: 'waste not want not', which included time and labor.

They were commonly known as the 'Plain People' at first because their lifestyle was and remains completely unembellished (no jewelry: sorry ladies).

---

[53] The sociologists determined that the most important activity that secured the longevity of these communes was the singular fact that each community held weekly meetings in order to determine and provide for the needs of its members. This singular factor segregated them from all other failed groups subjected to scrutiny.

Clearly, God did not withdraw His Guidance from these people. This cannot be said for most other communities I've encountered, including Muslims. Am I implying that Muslims are deluded ascetics who've withdrawn from the society of the responsible? In a sense, yes, because they withdrew from the practical responsibilities of fellowship, education, industry and commerce and cannot meet their own needs let alone those of their neighbors. Muslim pre-occupation with religious fetish rather than practicum has created a global community of consumers addicted to form rather than substance, indicating also that survival came to depend on booty (charity?), subterfuge, and traditional Ali Baba hypocrisy. This quite bluntly is pathological fetishism-in-action, which Harvard sociologists suggested was the major causative factor for the failure of all other utopian communes in their study. There is a lesson here.

The leaders and citizens of every 'failed' utopian effort spent time and resources on the discussion and dissemination of dogma, hypothesis and ideas rather than on the deeds of practical application. Ritual and sophistry became paramount while the real work of maintaining the community went unattended. Basic needs were provided for as long as charitable booty held out, but personal responsibility was cast upon unspecified waters ('society at large') without consequent provision-for and administration-of networks requiring personal accountability; much like the now failing American Government. When loot proffered by philanthropists ran dry, dogma mattered little to utopian seeking sheep, who then wandered off to greener pastures. This sounds a lot like today's liberals (the flower children of the 1960s), or desert Arabs moving on to Iraq, Iran, India, the Magrib and Granada after exhausting the tithes of Egypt and their own God-given peninsula. The trouble for most Semites, however, is that there are no more 'greener pastures'. This certainly leaves their majorities wallowing in a squandered backwater heritage: the failure to sustainably exploit and responsibly utilize God-given wealth.

The closest thing to successful Islam I have yet to see on the face of the earth are North American Mennonite, Hutterite and Amish Communities. Here is why I say this:

- they live in peace;
- command the respect of neighboring unbelievers;
- have little or no crime or immorality;
- survive in the midst of a materialist society without assimilating moral, social or economic chaos;
- are financially independent and prosperous without reliance upon the government;
- have little to no poverty;
- are autonomous communes with an impressive and unassailable individual/collective integrity.
- are clean; nowhere do you see rubbish or slap-dash hovels utilized for anything.
- The men are fit, virile, long-lived and without vice.
- The women are icons of modesty and home-spun industry.
- Their character and history is almost universally unimpeachable, except for the few bad apples that fall from every tree.

These good people outpaced all other Christian sects as well as Islam for the following reasons:

- They are not an aberrant sect. They are as pure to the doctrine of Prophet Isa (Jesus) as can be expected in light of Christian history and have no vestiges of idolatry in their worship; not even the Cross.
- They put the Spiritual Laws into actual practice: they are not *talkers* but *doers* of faith.

With the exception of the Trinitarian Doctrine and their mode of worship, all other differences between their religion and important Islamic Doctrines are trivial. I fully expect (pray) that when the judgment of God falls upon America, most of these communities will be spared the horseman's wrath.

After giving you this living example, there's little more to say about the Law of Community except to admonish all readers to stop talking and start doing. It is more than possible for Muslims to establish enclaves of Islam in a similar manner, and I have seen a few initiatives of great promise moving in this direction; including Imran Hosein's initiative, the 'Muslim Village'. May Allah guide Muslims away from the neo-patriarchy of accepted social noxiousness and pretense towards continual success in authentic communion with the Divine Purpose for community.

The Law of Humility or Law of Opposites

- If a man/nation does not humble himself/itself, he/it will commit sins associated with prideful arrogance on a continuum.

This is the 'Law of Opposites' and is found in one form or other throughout the entire spectrum of scientific study as the principle of polarity or opposing forces: whether in subatomic spheres, the earth's magnetic poles, in chemistry and electricity, in dynamic physiologic processes, or in mathematical derivatives. Occult Sabeans of the 'Authentic Traditions of Magic' [54] posit this principle as 'Dualism' and attribute it to characteristics of God as Good and Evil. Specifically, this describes the psychotically projected fantasy of an hermaphroditic *primal cause* or Supreme Deity, as illustrated by the Gnostic Baphomet.[55] Nevertheless, attributing valid observations of polarity in the created world as being inherent within Allah swt is a grievous pathological construct of anthropomorphic theology. Indeed, it is an egregious error to presume we can analyze and explain the nature of The Almighty in narcissistic terms.

---

[54] "And they learned what harmed them, not what profited them. And they knew that the buyers of magic would have no share in the happiness of the Hereafter. And vile was the price for which they did sell their souls, if they but knew!" (2:102)

[55] "Sabeans refers to the people of Harran who had a religion in which stars [Fallen Angels' or 'Watchers'] played a major role. Moreover, they were a repository of Hermetic [now Freemasonic] and neo-Pythagorean philosophy. They played a major role in the transmission to Islam of the more esoteric schools of Hellenistic philosophy as well as astronomy, astrology, and mathematics. They became extinct during the first few centuries of Islamic history and must not be confused with the Sabaeans or Mandeans of Southern Iraq and Persia who still survive." *Shia*, ibid, page 85, note 6.

In the human quest for knowledge, psychologically balanced souls are constantly humbled by life's mysteries much like Prophets Musa and Ibrahim (pbt). In the Taurat, God is recorded to have called Moses the 'meekest' of men and if we examine the Hebrew word for *meek* we find that its root means *teachable*. But many among us, especially leaders, choose to reject criticism [56] and are, as was Lenin, not among the teachable. These cannot be guided by the Word of God—which is His Holy Spirit in its many forms. Whether this pathology is primary or secondary (brain damage vs. spiritual reprobation) remains a matter for professional and scholarly investigation and debate. Nonetheless, believers should take defensive heed of the proud (sociopath or pure narcissist) or else fall prey to oppression, censure and exploitation along with a complete lack of compassionate empathy:

> Love, for the psychopath, is an ephemeral phenomenon aimed at sexual adventure. Many psychopathic Don Juans are able to play the lover's role well enough for their partners to accept it in good faith. After the wedding, feelings which really never existed are replaced by egoism, egotism, and hedonism. Religion, which teaches love for one's neighbor, also strikes them as a similar fairytale, good only for children and those different "others".[57]

> The psychopath feels little, if any, guilt. He can commit the most appalling acts, yet view them without remorse. The Psychopath has a warped capacity for love. His emotional relationships, when they exist, are meager, fleeting, and designed to satisfy his own desires. These last two

---

[56] In a group in the process of ponerization, spellbinders [charismatic sophists politicians] take care of "ideological purity". The leader's position is relatively secure. Individuals manifesting doubt or criticism are subject to para-moral condemnation [marginalization]. Maintaining the utmost dignity and style, leadership discusses opinions and intentions which are psychologically and morally pathological. Any intellectual connections which might reveal them as such are eliminated, thanks to the substitution of premises operating in the proper subconscious process on the basis of prior conditioned reflexes [PSYOPS mind control]. - Political Ponerology, op. cit. p. 172

[57] *ibid.* p. 131

traits, guiltlessness and lovelessness, conspicuously mark the psychopath as different from other men. [58]

Hence, proud sociopaths unavoidably subject themselves to misguidance, as do those who submit to them and mold their lifeways accordingly by not rocking boats of pathocracy; behaviors that are completely un-Islamic. This all too common human condition is the unavoidable consequence of implicit inverse determinants that metaphysically emanate from all Spiritual Law, most especially the Law of Humility. For to willingly submit to and defend the proud egocentric pathocrat is to partake in the crime. This is what happened to the Baath Party in Iraq, which subsequently and systematically exposed the entire nation (innocent and guilty) to God's judgment. As it is written, the sunnah of Allah swt does not change.

To the contrary, when we humble ourselves before God we do not become some kind of negative 'pole' but consciously rid ourselves of pride, even if momentarily. This creates a kind of spiritual vacuum through which communications from an uninhibited *fitrah* [59] and/or a Spirit of God (angel) may enter our sphere of cognizance and lead us to the liberty of truth in order to correct thought, word, deed and attitude in any given circumstance. This is not accomplished at the foot of Benny Hinn gurus with hallelujah choirs, mindless mantras or bearded conformity. Quite the opposite, it is achieved through the ordinary processes of regular prayer followed by the communion of contemplation as described previously. After all, God grants his wisdom and grace to whomever He chooses. Hence, no one group has

---

[58] McCord, W. & McCord, J., *Psychopathy and Delinquency*. New York: Grune & Stratton, 1956.

[59] Subordinating a normal person to psychologically abnormal individuals has severe and deforming effects on his or her personality: it engenders trauma and neurosis. This is accomplished in a manner which generally evades conscious controls. Such a situation deprives the person of his natural rights: to practice his own mental hygiene, develop a sufficiently autonomous personality, and utilize his common sense. In the light of natural law, it thus constitutes a kind of crime. - Political Ponerology, op. cit. p. 139.

exclusive claim to either Divine guidance or grace. Be careful if you deem otherwise as it could be the divisive crime of sectarian pride.

Remembering also that when man puffs himself up with the Sabean ideations born of Nimrud's long haired, long bearded, and long robed Babylon, the ideations that enter one's heart are leavened with the jinn-inspired yeast of falsehood. These whisperers, as the Qur'an instructs us, have indeed stolen some truth from the ether's angelic conversations, but they are mixed with lies that magi, priests, psychics and shaman amplify and *re*-present as absolute truth. Over time, these ideations (mostly identitarian myths) are repackaged by gainsaying spellbinders as semiotic guidance and packaged as slogans, catechisms, reforms, icons, protocols, idols, games (Olympiads), and sundry forms of rote travesties for the front-pages of consensus building literature, school books and media. This is the naturally manufactured, *modis vivendi* of the hysteroidal cycle [60] for all PSYOPS departments in the employ of sociopaths since the Sumerian dance with Cain's posterity. The only way to escape this cycle is to remain humbly teachable yet psychologically strong enough to overcome evil 'with the help of Allah', which was, after all, Mohammad's ensign.

Ascetic sectarians and sundry cult leaders, especially hero and saint worshippers, cannot be divinely guided due to the fact that they oppose Allah's social cause with pride by considering themselves masters of 'Self'—what the Qur'an calls the delusion of "self-sufficiency" (see: 92: 5-10). This malediction reflects doctrines that accompany the many forms of Luciferian Humanism. It is one pole of a continuum that historically leads ponerogenic hedonists towards fascist reasoning. For examples, the latter approach to occult ascendency is used by Kabalists, Talmudists, Whahabis and Maltese Knights of the fanciful masquerade, to categorize and thus, dehumanize others—non-Neocons, non-Jews, non-Whites, non-

---

[60] Hysteria is a diagnostic label applied to a state of mind, one of unmanageable fear or emotional excesses. Here it is being used to describe "fear of truth" or fear of thinking about unpleasant things so as to not "rock the boat" of current contentment.

- Political Ponerology, op. cit. p. 86.

Whahabis and others of the majority of saner but common rabble—as profane animals led to sheep pens for sheering or slaughter:

<u>The Hysteroidal Cycle</u>

. . . Man enlisted the natural power of animals in order to make his dreams come true, and when this did not meet his needs, he turned to his own kind for this purpose, in part depriving other humans of their humanity simply because he was more powerful. Dreams of a happy and peaceful life thus gave rise to force over others, a force which depraves the mind of its user. That is why man's dreams of happiness have not come true throughout history. This hedonistic view of "happiness" contains the seeds of misery and feeds the eternal cycle whereby good times give birth to bad times, which in turn cause the suffering and mental effort which produce experience, good sense, moderation, and a certain amount of psychological knowledge, all virtues which serve to rebuild more felicitous conditions of existence.

- Political Ponerology, op.cit. p. 85.

<u>All Secret Societies and circles of power are associated with icon bearing religions that endorse the grievous sin of pride</u>, no matter the outer guise of self-made attributions or claims, or even remarkable achievements. When they finally reach the end of their self-taught walk on the earth, they will find that Satan, with God's permission, holds the rope on which they crossed the chasm. Such is the Law of Humility and the horrid end of its inverse determinant.

The Law of Guidance

- God's divinely ordered cosmos guides us according to the choices we make.

As established previously, our entire life is a trial of faith and the husbandry of its inherent trust (*amana*) that God will provide us promised eternal reward(s) in the hereafter. Furthermore, there is no indication, other than the death of the body, that we do not have some form(s) of eternal existence and all evidence that does exist is in the affirmative. Consequently, the cultivation of trust and faith according to divine law, or its neglect, determines both individual and collective destiny whether for good or evil, success or failure. Unfortunately, cognizance of the unalterable determinants of Spiritual Law has been reduced to dogmatic ritual fetish and mythic speculation among obdurate sects of mystification, many of which are bound by the pugnacious tenacity and abject material hedonism that possess the successful domains of politically correct worship. Nevertheless, it is important to understand that the results consequent to the determinants of metaphysical law are no more than positive or negative aggregates of a personal and collective continuum with both pre-existence and the hereafter: i.e. of instinctive cognition (acknowledged, ignored or denied) and the record we accrue by means of intention and deed throughout the span of our earthly lives and then carry to the grave. Furthermore, gravitation towards the sub-human pole of sociopathic habits can only be opposed by God's grace via efforts made to achieve what is good; which, in turn, obtains greater favor (grace) with God as described previously in the essay on the Law of Grace. This reality is clearly stated in the Qur'an as follows:

> So for him who gives of his wealth, guards against evil, and confirms goodness, We make good easy for him; but for him who is niggardly, thinks he is self-sufficient, and gives the lie to goodness, We make evil easy for him. [92: 5-10]

Hence, revealed knowledge makes it clear that metaphysical impulses for good or evil inherently comprise man's created constitution. But what is more significant and made plain in this verse is that God also provides external forces as adjuncts. Specifically, these are (i) the cited spiritual determinants which exist as a trans-dimensional code of justice; and (ii) angelic or demonic helpers who are created powers (aliens?) extant in the multiverse and extrinsic to man's existential constitution and daywalker consciousness. Both of these force collectives, i.e., intrinsic and extrinsic, oppose or pull us towards evil or good, respectively, according to choices we make that are directly related to desires entertained and deeds committed or intended. All the above comprise a kind of inter-gallactic multi-dimensional code of unalterable ethics and justice that mimics but far exceeds the famous Code of the West or Twighlight Zone imaginations.

These influences substantially enhance our efforts as we pave our own road of destiny and, in all truth, actually represent divine guidance, whether for good or evil. With each thought, word and deed, these forces initially oppose us, either to test our 'strength of conviction' for good, or checkmate us if we are bound for evil. In the event of a moral incompetent subsequent to brain damage, for example, as was the case with Stalin,[61] society is naturally meant to be the ever conscious policeman (al'hisbah) that halts such a defective man's evil. Eventually, much like a rocket, our internal inclinations—collectively or individually and according to established habit (culture and customs)—escape any external opposition to evil/good and reach the comparative ease of a 'weightless' condition in a fixed orbit that is not easily altered; again, whether for good or for evil. A wise father does the same for his children. He will oppose their inclination towards narcissistic evil by his guidance and trial until they mature, whereupon he releases them to their individually chosen orbits of habit. If they have chosen evil, he prays and awaits their return by God's grace, as was described in the parable of the Prodigal Son.

The Law of Guidance is, therefore, an initial restraining force that eventually becomes a dispassionate liberating guide that eases man's journey towards doom or eternal joy. Like all spiritual law, it stands as a maxim for individual, family, culture, and nation. To say more on the matter is not really necessary.

The Law of Love (*agape*)

- When a man or woman does not pursue and endorse God's honor with their life, they cannot love God nor be loved by God.

---

[61] "Stalin was not a psychopath. He was a case of frontal characteropathy due to the damage of frontal centers (10A&B) caused be a disease he suffered as a newborn. This produces dramatically dangerous characters." - *Political Ponerology*, op. cit. p. 191

Contrary to a deluge of Sufi-claimer and other love-gurus, the love of man towards God has nothing to do with affection and everything to do with obedience. The scripture does not say that 'the love of God is the beginning of all wisdom' but rather that 'the fear-of' or 'reverence-for God' is. Prophet Isa also commanded that a man should love God and love his neighbor as he loves himself,[62] reiterating the Golden Rule of Buddha, and then added the caveat that all of the law was found in two commandments.

The actual words used for love in the New Testament Greek are *Agape*, *Fileo*, and *Eros*. But either carelessly or purposefully, Christian scholars have indiscriminately translated all three words to the now famous Rastafarian, "One Love", which is grossly misleading because each word in the Greek text distinctly refers to different aspects of the human experience having to do with desire, need and devotion. These are (a) erogenous desire, (b) endearing attachment, and (c) honorable esteem, respectively. What is commonly accepted as love in Western materialist societies is the affectionate emotion of a beguiling human fancy called 'Romance'. Love Gurus maintain that this is the 'love' that must be shared injudiciously with all people—and whether or not they deserve it—in order to achieve 'peace on earth'. As described above by the psychopath's take on love, such a notion is further from truth than Hell is from cool water and may be ascribed to the false constructs of Jacobin philosophy, namely: Freedom, Liberty and Equality, not to mention Rousseau's noble savage.

A critical review of the scriptures reveals that almost every reference to the 'Love of God' is in the context of the Greek word, *agapeo*, which means to 'bow in reverential obedience to the King'. This is the noble act that represents Submission to Divine Law or Lao Tse's 'Mandate of Heaven'—nothing more and nothing less—and it has everything to do with the conscious knowledge of our helplessness before the King of All the Worlds, Allah (swt). No other being deserves

---

[62] Muhammad said "unless a man desires for his neighbor what he desires for himself, he cannot be a Muslim".

this act of honor. Isa (Jesus) went even further to define the love of God (*agapeo*) by saying:

> "Herein is *agapeo*: that you keep my commandments," and again: "If you *agapeo* me, keep my word."

This clearly has nothing to do with sentimental affection and is most certainly divorced from the erotic sphere. To the contrary, it has everything to do with the concept of what normal people instinctively consider Noble and Righteous, which are apperceptions drawn from an un-earthly preexistence.

Thus far, therefore, we may conclude the following from our discussion of spiritual law:

- there can be no true nobility of soul without virtue and
- since there is no virtue without grace
- there cannot be any lasting affection (*fileo*) or brotherhood among men without honor or *Agapeo* towards God.

This is so because the grace gifts of *fileo* and *eros* [63] are faithfully maintained in trust and solely so by the principle of *agapeo*. If this were not the case then Paradise would have no reason to exist, even if only imagined. But because it is so, war is inevitable while men remain in a state of disobedient heedlessness, which is to say a state of *non-agapeo* towards God, and consequently, towards each other. In other words, there is no real 'fear factor' directly related to final judgment, the real terror, because God is forgotten or simply dismissed from human affairs, even if they pray. Therefore, since brotherhood and sexual intimacy are secondary and tertiary expressions of love — both being subordinate to the noble love of obedient reverence towards God and His Law — to teach that the latter affinities are the foremost expressions of what men call 'love' is a pathogenic travesty of man's intellect and moral core—or at best, a gross distortion of scripture.

---

[63] *eros* being the more intense expression of physical and emotional affection between man and wife.

It follows that man cannot love himself or his neighbor sufficiently without expressing reverent cognizance towards God and Divine Law. Hence, what commonly passes as love between brethren or lovers is little more than childish doting that, more often than not, unfortunately fails to develop virtuous nobility. America presently stands as witness for the last statement, along with others who claim Divine grace. For this reason, men are wont to be swayed by unripe passions rather than reason because justice is perfectly served only by the dispassionately seasoned heart —a dish best served cold. Thus, the zealous ardor of bias disaffects men from divine favor as *agapeo* wanes because such hearts can only embrace fond attachments (feelings) for deviant doctrine and those who attend the communion. This state of biased ignorance, as we have established previously, cannot possibly endear them to God, but it is grand enough glue for pathocratic mobs bent on the imbalance that favors the fall from final grace.

"Shall we then treat the People of Faith like the People of Sin? What is the matter with you? How judge ye? Or have ye a book through which ye learn ye shall have, through it, whatever ye choose? Or have ye covenants with Us [God] on oath, reaching to the day of Judgment, providing that ye shall have whatever ye demand? Ask thou of them, which of them will stand surety for that!" [68: 35–40]

The Moral Imperative[64]

> Unless a man is regenerated from above, he cannot enter the Kingdom of Heaven. - Hadrat Isa (Jesus)

Restating this in light of this study: 'Unless a man is morally conformed to virtue by God's grace, he cannot enter the Rest or Peace of Allah' (*as-Sakinnah*). Without the acquisition of moral virtue, man remains in his 'natural' state, which is but a step above lower kingdoms in as much as all of creation follows the imprint of inherent forces (instincts), characteristic qualities, and thermo-dynamic principles. Nevertheless, even the exercise of morality is insufficient for entry to the 'Kingdom of God' because morality is not *spiritualized* until virtue consciously serves activities that promote 'The Cause of God' as the sole focus of behavior. This was ideally intended to be the 'Way' of the Chinese Mandarin under divine guidance as per Lao Tse and Confucius.

In his natural state of consciousness, man's thoughts and activities focus on himself (egotism) and those whom he favors for his benefit.[65] This is hardly moral in light of tribal bias[66] no matter how handsomely

---

[64] The definitive text on this law is *The Philosophy of the Teachings of Islam* by Mirza Ghulam Ahmad, first published in Lahore, India, 1896. I will merely attempt to give a précis of that noble work for it cannot be stated in better terms. I urge the reader to study his book thoroughly despite his obvious mania.

[65] Experience teaches us, first of all, that [man's] natural world view has permanent and characteristic tendencies toward deformation dictated by our instinctive and emotional features [egotism] . . . we often meet with sensible people endowed with a well-developed natural world view as regards psychological, societal, and moral aspects, frequently refined via literary influences, religious deliberations, and philosophical reflections. Such persons have a pronounced tendency to overrate the values of their world view, behaving as though it were an objective basis for judging other people. They do not take into account the fact that such a system of apprehending human matters can also be erroneous, since it is insufficiently objective. Let us call such an attitude the "egotism of the natural world view".

- Political Ponerology, op. cit. p. 53

[66] This 'natural' state typifies the racial bias of Arabs, Jews, and Malays for example. It is the essence of apartheid.

the group is dressed. Furthermore, even when morality is achieved through excellent discipline it is often pressed into the service of human glory in defiance of Divine Command and in favor of some form of chauvinism. For example, many Roman and British Patricians were exemplary moral men among their own fellows while simultaneously serving powers and principalities dedicated to false gods and the merciless exploitation of the weak.[67]

To the contrary, the spiritualized, truly virtuous human delights only in serving God's Cause rather than the preferment of worldly desire and tribal delight. Wealth, family, medals and reputation mean nothing to such people other than responsibilities and/or tools in the service of God. Such folk enter the rest of God here on earth by means of divine communion as described previously. They do not go through the motions of ritual or merely practice morality because they have learned the requirements like practiced psychopaths and sycophants; they do these things because they embody morality in every sphere of thought and deed. These are the 'Salt of the Earth' 'Peacemakers' Prophet Isa (Jesus) spoke of on the Mount of Olives; which is to say that they are men and women who have actually made peace with God and kept it because they delight in it more than any other pleasure.

This consciously moral position also reflects the difference between natural and what is unscientifically and commonly called supernatural. Many people confuse the 'paranormal' with the supra-natural (supra-mundane) and from thence easily regress to idolatry and confusion. However, it is better to discard the term supernatural in favor of supra-natural or what is 'above' our comprehension of the natural material realm. This is because all that exists, except for God, is created and is, therefore, also natural, including things that go 'bump in the night'. All phenomena called paranormal or supernatural result from various influences derived from creatures or scientific principles that are not yet fully grasped. Therefore, the acquisition of additional divine Grace in the process of man's moral transformation is a *supra-*

---

[67] Most British Nobles are Freemasons of upper rank, at which degrees they secretly but knowingly worship Lucifer.

natural (ultra-mundane) and truly metaphysical event causing the regeneration of his heart in conformity with divine law.

When a man's conformity to morality is mere facile plastic surgery, such as that adopted by sociopaths and other creatures, the 'Peace of God' cannot be attained because communion with God is impossible. When confronted with their impersonation of a true human they decompose like hydrogen peroxide in water. This is another reason for the massive demonstration of 'major sin' recycling by the so-called 'faithful', because most human mimics have never truly repented with sincere and fully-informed conviction. The majority, unfortunately, are ordinary decent folks going through motions that avoid rocking various boats of the pathocracy to which they have become accustomed.

> In the social sciences, conventional terminology eliminates critical standards and puts ethics on ice; in the political sciences, it leads to an underrated evaluation of factors which describe the essence of political situations when evil is at the core. - Political Ponerology, op. cit. p. 41

They are uncritical thinkers comprising nations that do not carry the 'Peace of God' because they have never known it inwardly via the conscious reception of Allah's supra-natural grace. If the generally accepted excuse for collective moral activation is that the entire concept is an abstracted and unattainable ideal, then, how on earth can they enter the Kingdom of Heaven which Jesus quite frankly said was 'within them' and also 'at hand'? The entire world presently bears the burden of this conundrum as presented by nations like pseudo-"*Judeo-Christian*" America.

You can recognize the Spiritually Mature person because he or she bears a powerful dignity with a joyous childlike demeanor and yet will dispassionately cut off the head of a pedophile or pederast, or shoot a murderous intruder without batting an eye then have lunch blessing the names of God and make love to their spouse—a bit like Sala'u'din I imagine. I pray the reader can now better appreciate the 0.2 % factor mentioned in the Law of Unity.

Here is the Qur'an's representation of this simple reality:

> For him who fears to stand before his Lord and is in awe of His Greatness and Majesty, there are two gardens, one in this world and the other in the hereafter. [55:47]
>
> Those who are wholly devoted to God will be given a drink that will purify their hearts and their thoughts and their designs.[76:22]
>
> The virtuous shall be given a drink which is tempered with camphor, from a spring wherefrom the servants of Allah drink. They cause it to gush forth through their own efforts. [76:6-7]

Explanation:

The 'earthly trees' are good deeds and intentions sent forth to establish gardens in the hereafter. The 'drink' is God's Grace of Communion representing the wisdom that follows the conscious knowledge of receiving divine guidance. The 'camphor' is an extraordinary grace gift from God that overcomes worldly passions. The 'effort' comprises prayer, study, honest work and patience.

The moral virtues cannot be acquired or perfected without effort or God's Camphor as an active supra-natural force that helps us to subdue worldly passion in favor of virtuous restraint in deference to appropriate action. If it were possible, self-reliance would be the reality and God superfluous, not discounting, of course, that the Satanic illusion is, indeed, possible and quite common. An example of this genuine grace is the reservation of passionate sexual delight to marriage, whether monogamous or polygamous. As artificial camphor never works (the pretense of ritual religious fetishism), we often see men who affect such virtue suddenly run amuck, commit suicide, drop dead of heart attacks, frequent brothels, or cross borders for secret liaisons, etc.

The 'Rest' or Peace of God is manifest as the call of holiness in normal social settings, not just the Mosque, Church, Temple or political parade. It is the conscious reserving of one's self for God's Cause in the earth. Here is meant the stage of maturity where authentic Unity with God's will is attained in thought, word and deed; as Isa said: 'I and my Originator are one' – or as stated in the Koran:

Allah's hand is above their hands. (48:11) It was not thou who didst throw, but it was Allah who threw. (8:18)

Virtue, therefore, is the highest elevation of the moral qualities whereby the middle path of *taqua's* balance is maintained via direct communion with the divine Word of Command in harmony with Spiritual Law. It is not achieved by maintaining a balance between good and evil as Magi or Freemasons like Albert Pike taught. Virtue is keeping the exact middle path between two major insults to self and heaven: excess or niggardliness in all thought word and deed. Do not turn the other cheek to someone who is about to murder you and your family or should you succeed in subduing him, do not forgo justice if it allows him to harm someone else. Do not give alms to a man or nation of sloth, and do not give so much you impoverish yourself or tempt the recipient to excess. Do not cover the crimes of thieves if it permits them to steal again. In other words, be appropriate in your judgments according to God's Law and not dubious interpretations made by unconscious Divines who eat jinn-crisp semiotics, fetishist ritual wafers, or scriptural interpolations instead of truth.

This being the reality of the Moral Law, it is imperative that parents nurture children towards the acquisition of the camphorated grace of Allah, otherwise, their efforts will fall short of the mark. The Straight Path is actually quite easy; the difficulty lay in sectarian and especially, governmental influences that readily distract natural instincts which must be guided towards moral imperatives with conscious sincerity. This requires not only education but also example, which is where Muslims have miserably failed as have all others. What to do? Simple: Obey God's Laws.

> "O ye who believe! Why say ye that which ye do not? Grievously hateful is it in the sight of Allah that ye say that which ye do not." (61:2-3)

THE RIGHTS TO SIN & WAR

FREE-WILL'S RELATIONSHIP TO JUSTICE
AND EQUANIMITY

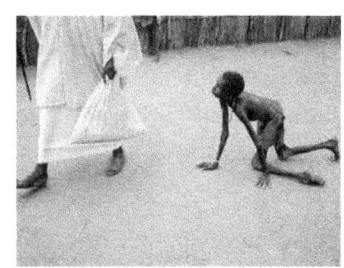

→ Until men honor the rights of their neighbors, and until commerce is joined to truth, there will be sin and war.

The chief purpose of Divine Justice is to ultimately establish that God's 'rule of law' must be obeyed so that individual and collective human rights are consistently honored. Albeit, the reality is that this ideal estate cannot be achieved until *after* the Day of Judgment. Discussions that avoid these conditional relationships circumvent the core of Islam's purpose and traditional dialogue as I will attempt to explain.

The chief human right among men is that of our inherent free-will to chose whether or not to obey Divine Directives, which are primal concepts that begin to gel in man's consciousness with the fitrah of common sense. All human rights, therefore, hang on this prerogative because God purposely subjected them to this primal freedom. Accordingly, this means that humans have the temporal 'right to sin'; a right that is removed from the individual on death, and from the collective at the final judgment.

This right is the legal basis for non-compunction in religion and also why Muslims have no right to dispose the affairs of non-believers unless the latter freely submit to 'authentic' Muslim dominion rather than the current charade being propagated by sociopathic, Islamist mobs.[68] Nevertheless, within an Islamic polity and those submitted to its protection, Shari'ah should be enforced among people who publicly confess their willful submission to God's Kingdom. But even if Muslims do 'change their mind' and convert to another religion, please don't murder them; just mark them and let them go in peace. Most likely,

---

[68] Muslim do however, have a right to set non-believing, non-submissive communities outside of their domestic boundaries, or otherwise relocate (flee from oppression).

the community has mismanaged Islam's way of Life and, God willing, they will repent. Hence, this elemental free-will option indicates that a limited and extremely discriminatory degree of social apartheid is, in fact, 'Islamic' when it comes to protecting those who choose Islam's way of life, and for other communities that submit to Islamic sovereignty.

When leaders obey Spiritual Law, Muslim or not, all subsidiary human rights are distributed as a matter of course like waterfalls. But when leaders choose disobedience, the inverse consequences of Spiritual Law are autonomously initiated. Essentially, the unalterable Word of God's curse is thrown at them and those under their hand from the universal ether. Hence, any shower of human rights consequently decreases per degree(s) of communal sin in harmony with the elevation of wicked tyranny. This fact further implies that those who knowingly submit to such tyranny partake in the crime(s) and accordingly reap the harvest of harm. Hence, the quality of leadership is extremely important for the wellbeing and benefit of mankind. Presently, harm is universally, liberally and wantonly flowing upon the entire earth by means of this ponerogenesis. It is the unalterable sunnah of the Divine Word.

'Free Will' is singularly independent and its exercise has no possibility other than to provoke outcomes that follow pre-defined metaphysical determinants for good or evil. And, mind you, even if you're a neutral apologist, 'no harm' is actually a benefit. Hence, man's' Free Will' stands alone like a prince over the release of good and evil, benefit or harm. This implies that all human rights are absolutely and ever contingent upon man's free-will, which also indicates that human rights go begging their due when choices are made that counter inherent common sense.

Internationally, especially under the NWO's pathocratic fascism, human rights will unreservedly go 'wanting' until mankind's leaders exercise the option to 'hear and obey' the Word of God; which, unfortunately, is not going to occur until sociopathic leaders and their attendants are removed from the ummah. According to Islamic eschatology, this will occur when Hadrat Isa (Jesus, the son of Mary) and Imam Mahdi (pbt) arrive on the scene. This being the case, the question of human rights is simply a trial of man's faith in God rather than the state, most especially for polities that do not throw off sociopathic parasites. If mankind truly believed in God's Word, all would fear our inevitable judgment and consequently choose what is best and then act on it. Nonetheless, it seems that most people do not actually take the prophets seriously and subconsciously convince themselves that hell is a myth and that paradise is an earthly realm for the hedonism of exceptionalists.[69]

As for equity or justice: this is a matter that is too often subject to mediocre thinking and philosophical fancy. The misapplication of this construct (justice) even helped create an undeserving welfare-state in nascent Islam, one that caused a 'gang' mentality that directly contributed to civil war. How so? What right did every Muslim in Medina have to tithes that were brought in from out of their realm? Like spoiled children, the distribution of unearned wealth fostered an offensive militancy, even bigotry, that heralded industrial sloth and the exogenous envy of other barbarians. I'm afraid our righteous imams erred.

The proofs for this assertion are seen in (a) Hadrat Umar's favoritism (nepotism) which opened the doors of civil war; and (b) that Arabs failed to properly manage nearly every piece of arable real estate acquired from judiciously exiled Jews. These Semite cousins of the rejected 'chosen' irresponsibly let livestock overgraze—mostly goats who eat every plant and its root—which then turned bountiful orchards and tillable lands into sand.[70] Later on, a similar desertification analogously happened to an *imperialized* rather than *Islamized* approach to governance, most especially in India; not to mention the insults that invited the 'Hammer of God' to ruin Baghdad. This abbreviated litany does not reflect responsible husbandry.

---

[69] Hedonism is not just sexual incontinence, it is also the pursuit of pleasure as a matter of ethical principle and an ethical system that evaluates the pursuit of pleasure as the highest good. Ibn Khaldun described this as the estate of a civilization steeped in the materialism that relaxes morals and discipline and thus, invites dissolution.

[70] See Prof. A. Hourainy's *History of the Arabs*

Equity (what Jacobin collectivists call egalitarianism), is a principle that distributes wealth and justice, not according to the availability of booty and man's desire, but rather allows the largess of heaven to flow in harmony with (i) human need, (ii) human ability, (iii) human efforts, and (iv) requirements for sustainable development. The latter reality implies limits rather than industrial sprawls of monetized greed and unrestrained anonymous consumerism. However, (a) unripe minds, when given the franchise, tend to think that all distributions should be made in equal fractions of confiscated pies; or (b) according to the popular patriotic adoration of Machiavellian pathocrats and government employee sycophants. This is a bit like dispensing jelly beans to children; a sort of thinking that falls afoul of Islam right into the troughs of Zionism's Bolshevik mafia and Jesuit friendly socialism.

It is of note to remind readers that the spiritually mature among Medina's Muslims refused their share of the 'takings' because they had no real need of it, which implies that they consciously (with a mature spirit) claimed no 'right' to the wealth of others. Hence, one of the many lessons drawn from this conveniently overlooked fact is this: the man who does not work needs to be kicked in the seat of wisdom sufficiently enough to cause him to do so in order to preserve his and the community's dignity, integrity, equity, and hence also, equanimity. This is one of the forms of justice that prevents traditional socialist usury.

Unfortunately, Muslim leaders presently and at the time sought mob placation through a policy of appeasement rather than civil discipline. As 'Rightly Guided' as they were in numerous matters, serious errors were made in this realm of elementary human affairs (Sociology-Psychology 101). What right does a man who doesn't work have to anything he has not earned save that of his patrimony or gifts? The Prophet Suleiman put it differently in his *Book of Proverbs*: "The [able bodied] man who does not work does not eat." I happen to like that particular *'by the sweat of thy brow*" law.

As an analogy for justice and equity, consider a man with two wives, one who is educated and the other a happy unlettered domestic. Does he give the latest upgraded computer to both women just because some pot-bellied mullah says so? If I educate two children, one to an M.D. degree and the other to carpentry according to their respective capabilities, have I been unjust in my spending? Preposterous injudiciousness has crept into Islamic jurisprudence and its resultant social policies are impertinent intrusions into private affairs. This has become a kind of waving of some else's largess, much like that of American and British pathocrats of the Jacobin Conspiracy. Among Muslims, this has even become part and parcel of those who administer *zakat* (charity funds). For example, in Malaysia, so-called 'administrators' retain more than sixty per cent of contributions, ostensibly for 'admin costs' while the majority of collected funds remain undistributed or otherwise unutilized.[71]

As for commerce and industry: if the cost of living is $1000/month but employees receive only $500, the owners of the business as well as the governors of the state who allow the injustice are thieves. The scripture is clear that thieves are not permitted to enter Paradise, especially leaders who deny the fact till they meet the grave. If you buy from the farmer for $1 and sell for $10 what he has produced by *his* labor but your costs are only $2.50, you're a double thief and excellent shylock, having stolen from both farmer and consumer. All of which (and more) indicates that if Muslims were to conduct themselves equitably and honestly—not to mention intelligently—in their business affairs, more of mankind would wish to do business with them and the faith would spread by means of commercial benefit, as it once did.

As it is now, however, war and sin reign and now you know why. Please make certain, therefore, that you consciously refrain from the right to sin.

---

[71] I have edited recent university papers by top Malay professors on the subject.

In Conclusion

The Body Politic of Islam is a 'Living Organism' created and established by God, not men. Therefore, it cannot be imposed upon men as a conventional political institution any more than democracy can be foisted on a herd of elephants or monogamy on a Lion. It simply is or isn't. It prospers in health or withers in illness according to the obedience of its constituencies to the instinctive righteousness of divine law. When sick, it cannot be treated artificially with programs, new laws or reform. The only curative medicine is that which is administered through the grace of submission. We can study its components and come to an understanding of its inherent qualities and mechanisms and, on occasion, apply the surgeon's knife or the balm of admonishment. But Islam cannot be artificially inseminated, cloned, or bionically restored to sentient potency by human effort alone because it absolutely requires the contingencies of God's grace that attend the beneficial (positive) aspects of the spiritual determinants described above.

Muslim political viability and authority as Godly nations or vicegerents can only be so established and subsequently inherited by the next generation with the prayer that they will remain obedient. Alas, 'if the salt loses its savor' the potency needed for healthy reproduction depends upon salubrious habits, and the vigor of God's Polity depends solely upon submission to God's Will—His Law—His Holy Spirit—His Word—and not the chauvinist opinions of pot-bellied mullahs of psycho-pathology.

There are certainly more spiritual maxims but I've exhausted my impetus to write on the theme so that further effort would be in vain. Perhaps a later edition or another writer will advance the task. I've been as honest and spirited as possible for the sake of what seems to me the veracity and incontrovertible position of mankind in the earth. Muslim or no, the principles of God's Kingdom stand before us all as a challenge to the disposition of our present (temporal) and future (everlasting) estates. After all, what's a human lifespan compared to forever?

It is my hope the reader is better enabled to consider the enormity of any reform movement before raising sails for republics of Islamization Utopia. Beware of pirates and their flags. A vessel called 'hope' is easily launched and maintained well enough to reach the Isle of Peace and Prosperity but only 'with the help of Allah' rather than ensigns who mimic His enemies, as does the iconic flag of Malaysia. Communal effort requires unanimous agreement in submission to divine law. If you join such a crew, remember: you're only a privileged brick in the house of God: a crew member of a much larger body politic.

Finally, bear in mind that when the last rank of souls has incarnated, both sides of God's Laws will be fulfilled—for good or evil. It really is that simple.

PART TWO

Essays on Islamization and Islamic Science

Prologue:

Mankind's Fallen Estate:
The Two Hands of the Satanic Worldview

The concept of 'Islamic Science' in the current milieu of polemics, modernity, moral neglect and "terrorism" seems as foreign and un-embraceable to many an academician as quantum physics is to a circus barker. Consequently, those who support and foster the concept as a valid worldview and extant reality should strive to express it in terms that are clear and readily acceptable to the humblest faculties of reasoning; an effort that requires plain definition rather than intellectual gymnastics.

The concept and religion called 'Islam' denote components of creation that inherently and naturally and/or consciously acknowledge their submission to Allah as the sole Creator and Possessor of the worlds in congruence with the principles of Spiritual Law as described in Part One. And since children are born believers, theoretically this should not present much of a problem:

> Dr Justin Barrett, a senior researcher at the University of Oxford's Centre for Anthropology and Mind, claims that young people have a predisposition to believe in a supreme being because they assume that everything in the world was created *with a purpose*. He says that young children have faith even when they have not been taught about it by family or at school, and argues that even those raised alone on a desert island would come to believe in God.
>
> 'The preponderance of scientific evidence for the past 10 years or so has shown that a lot more seems to be built into the natural development of children's minds than we once thought, including a

PART TWO: ESSAYS ON ISLAMIZATION & ISLAMIC SCIENCE
Prologue

predisposition to see the natural world as designed and purposeful and that some kind of intelligent being is behind that purpose', he told BBC Radio 4's *Today* programme.

'If we threw a handful on an island and they raised themselves, I think they would believe in God.'

Martin Beckford, Religious Affairs Correspondent,
BBC (24 Nov 2008)

The BBC failed to mention that Al'Qur'an revealed the very same scientific phenomenon quite some time ago. Nevertheless, for a genus that begins life by believing in God, something's gone awry when ladies and gentlemen pay and praise their children for dropping bombs on fellow creatures they've never met. Let's see if we can learn why that is.

When considering 'creation' and 'creature' we can attest that inanimate, elemental components of Creation submit naturally and scientifically to Allah according to their natures. Excepting for man and jinn, we may also admit that sentient (animals) and sub-sentient creatures (plants) inherently, by virtue of their created natures, also submit to God Almighty. However, on considering the polities of men and jinn, a practical dichotomy emerges. We can admit that only portions of either group have actualized their inherent knowledge (*fitrah*)—as described by Dr Justin Barrett—of Allah through cogent remembrance and sincerely submit to divine guidance.

Furthermore, we can also admit that the latter are diminutive fractions of rational earth-bound entities who not only recognize but also remember Allah's signature in the wondrous unity of Creation according to the several universal Revelations of God's numerous Messengers ("strength of evidence"). The majority balance, however, rejects this insight or fails to act accordingly in its support. Hence, my thesis is that these lots of creatures develop or adapt to spiritual blindness according to the inverse determinants of spiritual law. These phenomena are expressed as either anti-social behaviors or pathologically passive support.

Admitting, therefore, that 'diminutive fractions' of creatures both perceive creation's *tawhid* and consequently submit to Allah by virtue of the grace of 'divine guidance' that permits them to establish principles of moral imperatives as an habitual practicum, we may conclude the following:

1. There are those who perceive *tawhid* and act in concert with the revelation;

2. There are those who do not by means of carelessness and/or the ignorance of material preoccupation;

3. There are those who perceive *tawhid* but actively deny the perception for selfish gain; the majority of whom are subsequently subject to reprobation (spiritual blindness).

Fortunately, for those who contemplate in light of *tawhid*, Al'Quran confirms the existence of all three classes of rational creatures and is particularly concerned with the third category (27: 13–14; 74: 23–24; 54: 1–3; 25: 21):

- And they denied them, though their souls acknowledged them, for spite and arrogance.

- They turned away in pride and said: 'this is naught else than magic from the old.

- They denied the truth and followed their own lusts.

- And those who expect not a Meeting with Us … Indeed they think too highly of themselves, and are scornful with great pride.

This well defined fellowship of high minded sub-humans has unilaterally activated truth's denial by virtue of the pride and desire (arrogance) that fertilize the metaphysical soil of reprobation. Their accompanying estate of defective reasoning therefore lasts until the awakening of death, a period of time which Al'Qur'an calls 'respite'. In turn, the arrogance of this reigning majority of flawed thinkers fosters the same error in their children so that (a) Deism (ritual without relationship is enacted to cloak cognitive dissonance for the majority of religious fetishists [Muslims included]; and (b) Materialism (the idolatry of monism) becomes the inevitable worldview construct adopted by the next generation of Ibn Khaldun's "many". With few exceptions and under this auspice, mankind has been widely governed during the so-called civilized ascent of the recent deca-millennia-plus since the last ice age. This entire epoch represents the devolution of Cain's Creed and has inevitably led to the fascism that presently confronts us globally in light of the 'New Imperialism' of the neo-conned world of men.

This satanically inspired worldview holds forth two systems of management (governance). One is extrinsically operable and the other is hidden:

1. <u>The Right Hand Path of Satanism</u> through which men are herded into repressive folds of left-brained conformity to icon ridden sects such as Catholicism, Islamism and modern Buddhism, democratic-philia and various pagan permutations whereby men self-govern according to constructs that pay lip-service but deny in practicum the diktats of inborn knowledge and the revelations of their respective prophets, which have long since devolved to religious myth.

2. <u>The Left Hand Path of Satanism</u>: a system reserved for elite initiates of the occult sciences who knowingly govern the 'Right Hand Path' of popular religion and nationalism, etc. This is a libertine fold of narcissists riddled with high functioning sociopaths who are completely self-serving and devoid of compassionate concern for the governed. They represent the psychopathically reprobated 1% against which 'Ninety-Nine Percenters', most of whom are subject the Right Hand Path, presently attempt to rally.

Hence, you may thus better appreciate the current world conundrum. In effect, the Deism espoused presently by the latter group(s) leads to Materialism, Monetization of resources (Mercantilism), and the religions of Atheism and Secular Humanism (belief systems), all united under auspices of the purposely undefined democracy of collectivism that utilizes 'the people's this and that' as Leninist slogans. In addition to others, such constructs comprise a facade for the plutocrats of Global Fascism to preach toleration and pluralism while pillaging the world's religious folk—dissertations made elsewhere.[xxiii] Those who embrace these notions—both Right & Left Hand Paths—accordingly discount, reject or even arrogantly amend Prophetic Revelations and God's ongoing interests and interventions in Creation and Creature. They prosecute psychological warfare by metaphysically murdering or twisting the child of Allah's *fitrah* with mind-bending ideations that inevitably dominate all societal levels and institutions. Unfortunately, this includes ignorant Islamist zealots and the dense mullahs who unscientifically activate the default determinants of spiritual laws as described previously.

> . . . [Evil] leadership discusses opinions and intentions which are psychologically and morally pathological. Any intellectual connections which might reveal them as such are eliminated, thanks to the substitution of premises operating in the proper subconscious process on the basis of prior conditioned reflexes [conditioned customs become the collective's ritual fetish]. An objective observer might wish to compare this state to one in which the inmates of an asylum take over the running of the institution. The association enters the state wherein the whole [community] has donned the mask of ostensible normality [political correctness].
>
> *Political Ponerology*, op. cit. pp. 171,172

Such behavior(s) denies Allah's existential immanence, his many warnings, and the consequences we all face after the first death. Presently, Muslim examples are the several 'forbidden' alliances made with the One Percent's leadership *ala* NATO's Knights of Malta or Washington D.C.'s neo-con pathocracy that have wrought the scourge of Islamist enthusiasm [via Saudi Whahabism and finances] on the Muslim world under the guise of a fictitious Al'Qaeda created by those

PART TWO: ESSAYS ON ISLAMIZATION & ISLAMIC SCIENCE
Prologue

who worship the governance of lies.[72] Such weighty errors cause the grace of divine inspiration, guidance and protection to withdraw completely from those who most adamantly and pugnaciouslu claim it. Factions that attend this misrule subsequently rely upon diminished faculties that further their constituency's dependence on both 'superpowers' and 'superstition'. The latter realm of misguidance is cunningly allotted to deviant shamans and the exalted sophists of politically-correct rhetoric as well as idolatrous monks, priests and quasi-Muslim (usually pot-bellied) counterparts. In addition we mention here the greater demigods of pluralism's cultus as portrayed by the Apotheosis of George Washington on the dome of Washington D.C.'s Capitol as reflected by the Freemasonic George Washington University and Jesuit Georgetown University mobs; and let us not forget the quasi-deification of Ali's family by Ishmai'ili simpletons and the contemporary promotion of their identitarian myth.

These endemic crimes of humanist hero-worship also promote something called Universalism amongst Muslim intellectuals who have aligned themselves with the sinister (Left Hand) doctrines of Frithjof Schuon and his disciples. To my knowledge, such men are not *Qari"* and, hence, they can only qualify as interpolators. In their transient ascendance, these chiefs of deviance have managed to hold and marginalize genuine *Qari"* as 'Sheikhs of Backwardness' as they subsume, and thus, subvert, divine doctrine with non-prophetic interpositions and speculations. The unsullied portions of *Al'Kitab* calls their art of accretion a cacophony or mixed wine.[xxiv] The Talmud is a perfect example of mixed wine, for example. But unshaken students of spiritual sobriety rightfully call it blasphemy.

Once the theosophy of Deism and Materialism take hold of human hearts, the ability to judge right from wrong is dramatically reduced and eventually develops an auto-immune response to absolute truth. This weakened reasoning estranges logic from the

---

[72] Here, we cannot help but think of Karl Rove, Dick Cheney, and Donald Rumsfeld, protégés of the neo-con philosopher [Zionist, B'nai B'rithian Freemason], Leo Strauss. Strauss evidences typical schizoidal doctrinaire characteristics. - *Political Ponerology*, op. cit. p. 191.

'Cause of Allah' in the earth and, hence also, from the inherent rights of men. Reasoning becomes crippled and bent towards what is amoral or immoral and unethical or unjust with respect to the discernment of man's authentic purpose in what human faculties perceive and execute.

The Deification(Apotheosis) of George Washington

By means of pre-determined inverse defaults of metaphysical law (divine guidance), this cited domain of defective reckoning becomes readily aligned with the vanities and vices described in several Quranic passages and other respected texts. Hence, when such a dysfunctional majority of men estrange reason from their true purpose, traditionally acceptable (i.e. politically correct) incompetence assaults the throne and often usurps it. The present result is the collectivism that is shrewdly termed democracy, which is, in fact, denial of any rule of law in conformity with the misrule that presently enthrones moral relativism, situational ethics, tribal partisanship and sectarianism (special interests) rather than the clearly defined and absolute moral responsibility of the offices and officers of *al'hisbah*.

ALLAH SWT mentioned in the Holy Qur'an in surah al-Imran, verse 104:

PART TWO: ESSAYS ON ISLAMIZATION & ISLAMIC SCIENCE
Prologue

> "Let there arise from you a group calling to all that is good, enjoining what is right and forbidding what is wrong. It is these who are successful"

When justice is not enforced the result is circus venues for sophist colleges of idiot savants such as the Council on Foreign Relations or the Comintern Think-Tanks of the UN and Cecil Rhodesean Round Tables so relished by the World Parliament of Churches, or the absurdity of Jesuits aligned with Islamization of Knowledge and Islamic Science dialogues and movements, not to mention the Rothschild consortium that has managed the papal purse since Napoleon and now holds global wealth extraction facilities that heartlessly oppress 80 – 90 percent of humanity.

In summary, this fallen estate is not any civilized ascension of humanity, but to the contrary, it is a transhuman linear collapse towards the hellishness that accompanies misguidance where anything but righteous leadership is placed on the table as fair game for governance. A perfect example is illustrated in the film: "The Act of Killing", which shows just how repulsive the contemporary Muslim governance of Indonesia has become in the present context of the global collective. Except, therefore, for miraculous intervention, how in the mighty names of God can the Islamization of any human institution take place under such auspices? — especially when Muslim factions assist their enemies in the dropping of bombs on innocents?

Luciferian Wall Tapestry of the United Nations

CHAPTER ONE
Universal vs. Authentic

I vehemently take issue with (i) the alleged "traditional" approaches that support the perusal of unseen worlds objectively; and (ii) the philosophically entertained quiddities of "Active Intellects", sometimes called Ibn Sina's *noumena*—which Imam Ghazali soundly refuted. I suggest these claims are superfluous at best or gross misguidance at worse. If the latter, they constitute a soundly deliberated satanic delusion. In either case, these supposed crowns of Sufi-claimer metaphysical speculation have surely failed the trials of Real Politics, unless, of course, they are/were employed for the purpose of delusion, in which case they have succeeded. After all, the genuine temporal issue—which is presently nowhere in evidence—was and remains the divinely stamped dominion that was bequeathed to the Prophet's immediate disciples, whom, he said, "were the best", and whom many contemporary pundits of religious superiority are wont to idealize.

This abject loss of Islam's autonomy to Universalists, i.e. Christians and others in league with Jews] of the Jesuit led New World Order (NWO) mold,[73] was succinctly prophesied in Al Qur'an. This should give us sufficient cause to ponder if *quiddity* infested Islamists or Sufi-claimers with projections into subtle jinn-infested dimensions accompanied by effete definitions truly represent the Traditional Islamic Discourse and/or divine guidance. After all, when poems are read and speeches are made, and the IOK presses are stopped, it seems to me that God has abandoned all such Islamizing mania to the fury and wiles of Iblissian globalists. Neither am I alone in the assertion that fans of peculiar *tasawwuf* [xxv] artisans are innovators who defy principles of iman[74] by probing the 'unseen' in spite of Al'Qur'an's multiple injunctions.

---

[73] *Catholic* means Universal

[74] Some evil actions can nullify Imaan e.g. practicing magic, reading palms, supplicating to other than Allah, allying with disbelievers. This last qualification applies in the above implication, as many of the alliances made are with non-believers and

These fellows claim a crown that subsumes all doctrines and law with subjective "cognitions" called 'Unity with God-ism' or the Universalism of *Religio Perennialism*. I've no recollection of these manufactured concepts from my reading of hadith or Al'Qur'an's several English translations. What's worse, according to some of these fellows, is that I have absolutely no desire to know what they're talking about—which qualifies me as a 'profane' human. I experienced this same identitarian-*imaginaire* labeling of suitably marginalized 'others'[75] during my years of occult studies, especially in Freemasonry and Anthroposophy, both of which are children of Kabbalism's Holy Grail, itself the legacy of the ancient Serpent Cult of Cain's Gnosticism. If you do not know about these cults and their well hidden influences on world historical events, it is best hold both tongue and pen.

Nevertheless, the elevated status of such Gnostics is understandable, especially when one willfully holds commerce with a princely "Divine Principle", whatever that is. Furthermore, our edification advances by the report by Professor Osman Bakar on Abu 'Sa'id,[xxvi] an adept who projected 'powers of the soul' like a first-class Tibetan Lama or sorcerer's apprentice by performing the typical poltergeist tomfoolery so beloved by martial arts manics as well as *Lord of the Rings* and *Harry Potter* minions; not to mention Catholic exorcists:

---

even sworn enemies of Islam, such as the Jesuits. In addition, none of the 60 branches of Imaan involve perusing the unseen, unless you wish to qualify this by admitting seeking after forbidden knowledge.

[75] The earlier phase of a ponerogenic union's activity is usually dominated by characteropathic, particularly paranoid, individuals, who often play an inspirational or spellbinding role in the ponerization process. The power of the paranoid characteropath lies in the fact that they easily enslave less critical minds, e.g. people with other kinds of psychological deficiencies, or who have been victims of individuals with character disorders, and, in particular, a large segment of young people. At this point in time, the union still exhibits certain romantic features and is not yet characterized by excessively brutal behavior. *Soon, however, the more normal members are pushed into fringe functions and excluded from organizational secrets;* some of them thereupon leave such a union. - *Political Ponerology, op.cit.* pp. 161-2

PART TWO: ESSAYS ON ISLAMIZATION & ISLAMIC SCIENCE
Chap. 1: Unversal vs. Authentic

> Abu'Sa'id took up his metal vase and threw it into the air, whereupon instead of falling down it stayed up in the air. "What is the reason for this?" he asked…"What is the violent force?" "Your soul!" replied Ibn Sina, "Which acts upon this."
>
> *Tawhid and Science*, Osman Bakar, 2009, p. 97, in reference to S.H. Nasr's, *Islamic Cosmological Doctrines*, p. 194.

I doubt this juggling trick is an example of *Karamah*.[76] I suspect, however, that David Copperfield would take issue and side with Professor Bakar's endorsement of the event as a genuine Islamic moment.

On the other hand there are down-to-earth Sufis who don't waste time inspecting or speculating on the unseen while enemies of the ummah develop and utilize weapons of mass destruction. These fellows, much like Imams Shamil al-Daghestani or Omar Mukhtar, actually do something about clear and present dangers. Common pedestrian pietists know that Allah only helps those who prepare in unity to defend their autonomy, as did these men; both of whom lost after decades of struggle due to traitors and "brothers in faith" who failed to aid them as commanded by Shariah—which reminds me of OIC's and the Arab Little League's failure to censure NATO recently—reason enough for Allah to withdraw such capable and learned men from the earth as prophesied.

> "But seek with that (wealth) which Allah has bestowed on you, the home of the Hereafter, and forget not your portion of legal enjoyment in this world…" [al-Qasas, 28:77] … "And make ready against them all that you can of power…" [al-Anfaal, 8:60]

---

[76] This is a supernatural occurrence granted to a "waliy" (a highly righteous man/woman that practices what is Islamically obligatory and performs additional acts). This form is also found in the Qur'an. Scholars have said that the "karamah" of a "waliy" is a miracle to the Prophet. This supernatural happening testifies that this man is a truthful follower of the Prophet peace be upon him. Many such "karamahs" have been documented by mainstream scholars. A "karamah" is a Prophetic association and not a satanic form. – Shk. Mustapha Karalli in a critique of this treatise, Nov 2010, ISTAC, KL, Malaysia.

Furthermore, those like myself whom Allah graciously rescued from metaphysical mischief, know firsthand that Universalist-cosmology reflects doctrines common to the Hermeticism embraced by several species of Deists, Romanists, sundry pagans and Kabblist/Persian magi. These Universalist doctrines do bear the Inquisitorial endorsement of the elite Jesuit task force, which is the most ominous of mankind's foes ever to tread the face of the earth in the name of religion. And while it is true that Perennialist dogmas are universal, the pertinent questions are these: (i) 'Do they qualify as authentic components of Islam's already perfected *deen*? or (ii) what is now called Islamic Science? or (iii) as sciences of the forbidden arts disguised as authentic components of both?'

Taking Ocham's razor in hand rather than a "maze of elaborations" (as per Prof S.N. Al-Attas);[77] to my limited ken the Perennialist approach contradicts all prophetic example. The preserved sunnah of the prophets repeatedly demonstrates that it is Allah swt Who opens the heavens for His angels to descend and manifest themselves to select individuals. This is what occurred to Prophets Mohammad (mirage) and Jacob (Jacob's ladder at Bethel) as they slept, and to Prophet Daniel while captive in Babylon (pbt), and Mary, the mother of Prophet Isa (pbut). To the contrary, aside from antithetical accounts of sorcery, there are no scriptural records of homo-sapien-sapiens *tasawwuffing* through inter-dimensional time warps in pursuit of Allah's unseen knowledge in the name of *hanif* Monotheism. Certainly transcendence occurred following reasonable ascetic approaches such as fasting and prayer, but these accounts of 'transcendence' unanimously describe a 'subscendence' on the part of heaven into our dense domain rather than willful human incursions into the *samawat* and beyond.

Nevertheless, aside from the crossing of forbidden interdimensional bounds, I seriously doubt that 'suspending lamps in mid-air' in order to prove a point is the prophetic *sunnah*. Furthermore, the 'scientific principle' supposedly demonstrated by such levitation should

---

[77] *Some Aspects of Sufism as understood and practiced among the Malays*, S.N. Al-Attas, Malaysian Sociological Research Institute, Singapore, 1963., p. 19.

have been empirically delineated and generally applied for the ummah's benefit on condition that both sunnah and Shari'ah permitted it. To the contrary, the Sufi-claimer's "gaining of power" (*jabarut*) is a singularly private "scientific" step towards *gnosis* (*marifah*) on the way to *haqqiah* in order to win a glimpse of immortality, or so I've read.[78] But 'what's the point? I emphatically posit to the contrary that such efforts manifest a lack of iman (faith), as did Jesus, who is reported to have said: ". . . an evil and adulterous generation seeketh after a sign . . ." (Matt 12:39). Furthermore, Al'Qur'an alludes to this forbidden knowledge with reference to the sacred calf of Egypt (*Apis*), an idol that represents the entirety of forbidden Gnostic initiation which included magi-centered, self-engendered journeys into unseen worlds: "There came to you Moses with clear signs (i.e. karamah); yet ye worshipped the calf[79] (even) after that, and ye did behave wrongfully." [Surah, *The Calf*: 92]

Again, "What's the Point?" of this wanderlust for the unseen when I or other sober slaves can perceive immortality within our hearts by simply contemplating a tree and then return to real work?

> Say those without knowledge: "Why speaketh not Allah unto us? or why cometh not unto us a Sign?" So said the people before them words of similar import. Their hearts are alike. We have indeed made clear the Signs unto any people who hold firmly to Faith (in their hearts). [ibid: 118]

Hence, if this "gaining of power" (*jabarut*) is an ideal goal of Mystic Sufi-claimers and is being honored by "many" imans of parochial Muslim cultures, it becomes easy to understand why Muslims have little time or inclination for the real work of excelling at living in our rather solid *dunya*. To be blunt, in schools of Occidental Psychology, such people give evidence of magical thinking[80] with more than a

---

[78] *Ibid*. p. 35.

[79] Inferring the complete system of Egyptian magic.

[80] <u>Magical Thinking</u>: The sense that the paranoid individual can use his or her thoughts to influence other people's thoughts and actions; a symptom of paranoia. A sign indicating the Schizotypal personality disorder: These individuals may be

'touch' of religiously oriented paranoia (fear). I suspect this is why some Muslim jurists adjudged the pitiful Hallaj fellow as temporarily insane—though I doubt his case was temporary.[81]

In addition to these premises, those of us who have practiced magic or dealt with jinni impositions and/or attended accomplished shamans, know empirically that it is jinn rather than human 'soul forces' that account for poltergeist phenomenon. I would think this settles the matter unless shamans, bomohs and their defenders wish to contend on equal terms with Prophet Solomon on Judgment Day.

On the Matter of Tasawwuf

As a layman, and as I understand it, *Tasawwuf* has many proponents, opponents and critics. Voices from both camps strongly object to these "journeys through and beyond the cosmos to the Divine Presence" as per Prof. Osman Bakar's recording of Ibn Sina's "Realized Knowing of Truth", which is something Prof. Bakar calls a "traditional Islamic Scientific fact." [82] Prof. Bakar writes as if Imam Ghazali hadn't rebuked Ibn Sina and further infers that the latter's 'subjective-objective' and extremely personal experience of "reality" was/is not only *halal* but an empirical fact of Islamic Science. Another scholar, the eminent Prof. S.N. al-Attas, also fostered Perennialist sympathies by calling this suspect pilgrimage a journey "back to God" or to a "Permanent Reality". Granted, he wrote this before changing course in his

---

superstitious or preoccupied with the paranormal . . . distorted and magical thinking dominates his/her thought process. - *Gale Enc. Of Mental Health*, 2008

[81] Classical scholars executed Hallaj because he committed an act of blasphemy by stating that he was "al-haqq" (a name of God). If contemporary scholars believed that he was momentarily or permanently insane, they would not have executed him. – M. Karalli, op. cit. // Grandiose delusion: An individual exaggerates his other sense of self-importance and is convinced that he or she has special powers, talents, or abilities. Sometimes, the individual may actually believe that he or she is a famous person (for example, a rock star or Christ). More commonly, a person with this delusion believes he or she has accomplished some great achievement for which he or she has not received sufficient recognition. - Gale's Enc. of Mental Health (2010)

[82] *Tawhid and Science*, op. cit. p. 68.

remarkable development by describing it as the 'unobservable' act of becoming "one with the One" — again: whatever that means.[83]

But despite those who claim orthodoxy and yet favor the congregation a nebulous unification with God, Muslim observers of human behavior who are hardcore scientists and ex-hardcore occultists have trouble accepting the qualifiers 'empirical' and 'Islamic' for what appears to be highly subjective experiences held in common with the very real science of raising-lamps-in-the-air sorcery; which, by the way, is scientifically established as fact by unbelievers.

Phenomena such as astral travel with inter-dimensional journeys are established scientific facts in secluded government labs which cater to the proclivity for purposes of "national security" and plain old curiosity. These are not issues worthy of denial, especially since modern science has perhaps reached the end of its materialist quest in sub-atomic never-ever land.[xxvii] Rather, the points of contention are the method, temporal context, and the supposed "Divine Presence" at the end of the sojourner's rather subjective tunnel vision. These matters trouble those of us who've settled for ordinary faith; i.e. the universally confirmable empiricism that will be provided on Judgment Day's prophesied appointment with human destiny's ultimate end because the prophet(s) have said so (pbut).

Nevertheless, the premises taken up by apologists for the enigmatic "journey" are heterodox and border on brainsick escapism or pathological brain-damage,[84] especially so when efforts of cognition

---

[83] *Some Aspects of Sufism*, S.N. Al-Attas, op.cit., p. 20.

[84] Current Western medical opinion states: Endogenous toxins include heavy metals, pesticides, food additives, and industrial and household chemicals can damage the liver and kidneys; they can also cross the blood-brain barrier and damage brain cells. Workers exposed to high levels of inhaled manganese showed concentrated levels in the basal ganglia, and exhibited Parkinson's-like syndrome. Observational studies have also shown increased levels of aluminum, mercury, copper, and iron in the cerebral spinal fluid (CSF) of Parkinson's patients. It is not fully determined whether these minerals found in the brain have any clinical significance. (Mitchell J. Ghen, D.O., Ph.D., and Maureen Melindrez, N.D. and others) — NB: Many of these insults are purposely carried abroad by vaccine programs, as the vaccine are consciously contaminated for this purpose. - oz

are applied towards the unseen—something Allah specifically stated is reserved for Him alone. However, the graver matter is that of governance (guidance), because the superior spiritualist is always a bit of a pope in that he/she inevitably lays claim to the throne of man's guidance; which is why, I imagine, many leaders amongst so-called Islamic nation-states routinely consult shamans and bomohs instead of sunnah and shari'ah.

As for authentic *tasawwuf*, the best definitions of I've come across so far are these:

> Tasawwuf, in its most pure and pristine form, only means the rectification of the heart from all the deficiencies and filth that occasionally overcome it due to the abundance of sins and shortcomings committed by the heart internally and by the organs externally, and the beautifying of the heart through pleasant qualities and grand exhilaration in the love of Allah which are desired by Sharia'a as well. The highest rank of that is 'al-Ihsaan'.[xxviii]

> The early Sufis differed from later Sufis who spread *bid'ah* (innovation) to a greater extent and made shirk in both minor and major forms commonplace among the people, as well as the innovations against which the Messenger (peace and blessings of Allaah be upon him) warned us when he said, "Beware of newly-invented things, for every newly-invented thing is an innovation and every innovation is a going-astray." (Reported by al-Tirmidhi, who said it is *saheeh hasan*) . . . The Sufis claim that they take knowledge directly from Allah without the mediation of the Prophet (pbh) and in a conscious state (as opposed to dreams). So are they better than the Sahaabah?? They say, "Haddathani qalbi 'an Rabbi (My heart told me from my Lord)."[xxix]

Here again, Mustapha Karallii deflated my ignorance and bias by taking issue with the above endnote. He remarked:

> In the Hadith about innovation, Wahhabis misinterpret the word "*kull*" to mean "every" innovation is bad. It should read "most" innovations are bad. The wrong translation stated here as it has been said is "Beware of newly-invented things, for [every] (should be most) newly-invented thing is an innovation and every innovation is a going-astray".
>
> The Arabic word used in the Hadith is "*kull*" which generally means either "most of" or "all". The scholars, in accordance with this Hadith,

stated that the meaning here is "most innovations are astray", and they said this in compliance with another Hadith which means "whoever innovates in Islam a good innovation has its reward and a reward similar to those who practice with it after him without lessening any of their rewards".

Furthermore, in classical Sunni texts we can find that the scholars have divided *"bid`ah"* (innovation) into two types; a good innovation and a bad innovation. Fringe sects refuse to accept that there is a good innovation. As to note 'xx' we can see that the quotation attacks the mentioning of the name of God as in Allah, Allah or Ya (Oh) Allah, Ya Allah. This again is a Wahhabi creed, which contradicts mainstream tradition. In a nutshell, Wahhabis attack all Sufis, while mainstream Sunnis differentiate between true Sufis and Sufi-claimers. Sufi-claimers, for example, repeat the words *Ah* or *Uh* as names of God, this is refused surely. But this does not mean that a Muslim cannot repeat in remembrance of God the name of God "Allah".

The website mentioned in note 'xx' is clearly a Wahhabi fringe source. Further, this source falsely states that "different *tareeqahs*" (Sufi ways) attack others in a sectarian fashion; this is a fabrication. The source also uses verses about the *"mushrikin"* (disbelievers) such as Al-Room 30:31-32 and turns them against Muslims. Wahhabis are notoriously known for doing this. Another deviant statement which lumps its attack on all Sufis linking them to devils states: "With regard to the question of the whether the Sufi shaykhs have some kind of [spiritual] contact, this is true, but their contact is with the shayaateen, not with Allaah", this reflects the degree of hatred that Wahhabis have for true men of "tasawwuf".

While Nasr, Bakr & Co do not qualify as Sufis, this does not discredit *"tasawwuf"* because these fraudsters have claimed its name. The wording in the above statement is biased, and yes, true Sufis have spiritual abilities such as the *"karamah"* mentioned earlier and as sanctioned in the Qur'an.

In 1996, Shaykh Nuh Ha Mim Keller also took issue with *Perennialism* and was explicitly critical of a view that:

> ... has waited for fourteen centuries of Islamic scholarship down to the present century to be first promulgated in Cairo in the 1930s by the French convert to Islam, Rene Guenon, and later by his student, Frithjof Schuon, and writers under him. Who else said it before? And if no one

did, and everyone else considers it *kufr*, on what basis should it be accepted?[85]

As you see, I'm not alone with my queries and concerns. The lack of mystical connotations in the definitions of *tasawwuf* as offered and the opposition of Shaykhs Keller and Karallii are apparent. As I pursued this vein towards mother lodes of orthodoxy, I found an absolute vacuum of 'Batinite' claims of 'Unity with the One' or 'direct perceptions of God' or 'Divine Principles' or 'Universal Souls' and whatever else Universalists imagine these highly romanticized abstractions are.

If one objects to the descriptive, 'romanticized', I suggest you take a few hours to read mystic 'Sufi-Claimer' poetry. But don't be fooled by claims of cryptography in order to prevent profane masses from knowing their secrets.[xxx] The very same claim is made, from time immemorial by minions of all Hermeticists, beginning with the sons of Cain onwards towards King Thoth (Hermes) and especially among higher degrees of the rarified gas that sustains Kabbalist-cum-Jesuit-run Freemasonic Boy-Scout clubs — traditional havens for damnable occult pederasty and other fetishes. An example of the latter is found, once again, in Freemasonic Egypt, the land of Toth:

> Baden-Powell [British founder of the Boy Scouts] embedded in his movement a delicate balance between local deference and global ambition. Within England, the physical activity of Scouting would provide a safe outlet for the otherwise volatile energies of youth, but on a global stage, the very same training would strengthen and embolden a generation of mighty young men ready to defend the glory of the Empire. In Egypt, this same dualistic understanding of physical activity generally and of Scouting, more specifically rested at the heart of royal projects in the realm of youth culture.[xxxi]
>
> *Extracurricular Nationalism: Youth Culture in the Age of Egypt's Parliamentary Monarchy*[86]

---

[85] "On the validity of all religions in the thought of ibn Al-'Arabi and Emir 'Abd al-Qadir: A letter to `Abd al-Matin."

If you visit endnote 'xxxi', you will see a brief account of typical occult relationships that students are guided away from by wizened mentors of the 'Left Hand Path'.

Hence, and quite to the contrary, I've come to appreciate authentic *tasawwuf* as the straightforward discipline of apprenticeship to spiritually mature personages grounded in the practical affairs of religion and the mundane businesses of living on the ground as opposed to speculative excursions to universal studios of the unseen. In other words, genuine Sufis are people who keep their mind, body and soul on earthly 'benches' where Allah placed their backsides until the seat's removal—a rather unromantic definition of Sufism?

What is more is that some apologists for Sufi-Claimers do not like ordinary, first generation Sufi benches. Their reports imply that Sufism experienced an evolution *cum* metamorphosis that produced superior fruitcakes. Quoting from R.A. Nicholson's review of an early work, a renowned Malay professor actually went so far as to gently diminish the memory of Seventh Century *Quietists* or 'Bench People' described as the first Sufis:

> they] … loved God, but they feared Him more, and the end of their love was apathetic submission to His Will, not perfect knowledge of His Being. They stand midway between asceticism and theosophy or gnosis. The word that best describes their attitudes is quietism.
>
> [citation withheld out of respect for the contemporary author as advised by Bro. Karallii]

Well now, praise Allah the writer reversed a rather youthful and impassioned position. However, as a lesson in reality, and for the sake of the argument's 'imperfect knowledge of Allah's Being', I'll continue with the example of the intoxicated thought process subjected to growing pains to which many are prone. The trouble with such developments is that many of us don't make it to post-maturation materials and may adopt as firm positions the youthful errors, which,

---

[86] Aaron Jakes; Ms. Phil. Thesis in Modern Middle Eastern Studies, St. Antony's College, University of Oxford, May 2005.

in this case, are "apathy" and "perfect knowledge of His being" — as if the latter was possible or even worth consideration. I suppose the best thing is a book-burning rite of passage, something I once did with a manuscript justifying the Trinitarian faith —a two year effort— of which I don't even have a soft copy left.

It is 'bad enough business' to use ideations born of Orientalism but to ascribe apathy to first generation defenders of the faith and actually infer that the "Middle Path" of Islam is in error suggests reasoning that prefers the maze of reckoning that befuddles genius all too readily. I later came across Perrenialist praises for an Egyptian Mystic said to have lauded King Thoth (Hermes) as the first Sufi and Originator of the Gnosticism that followed. What is troubling here is that no correction crossed the path of my literature survey until Brother Mustapha Karallii, once again, soberly intervened where academic superiors failed and many scholars dare not tread:

> There are references to Dhun-Nun Al-Misri, who like Ibn `Arabi, has been attacked by the Jews (forefathers of European Orientalists) who adulterated his writings in order to give currency to the old Alexandrian schools of mysticism [Gnostics]. Dhun-Nun Al-Misri was a classical "`alim" whose statements on the creed of *Tawhid* are as clear as the sun. In fact, like Ibn `Arabi who had the Cordoban cabalist cum talmudist Jews on him, Dhun-Nun was a recognized traditional scholar who developed the school of *tasawwuf* in line with shari`ah despite the envy of Jews who posthumously attacked him by manipulating his books through commissioned copyists.
>
> Some of your comments are: "This obscure man of the late third Century was a mister Dhu'l-Nun al-Misri", and again in note 'xxxvii', which states "It is not mere coincidence that the doctrine of *Gnosis* was first worked out in detail by the Egyptian Sufi, Dhu-L Nun (d. A. D. 859), for Sufiism, on its theosophical side, was largely a product of Alexandrian speculation" [Encyclopaedia Britannica, 14th Edition].
>
> In response to these remarks and as a defense from the traditional camp, I say to the editors of the Encyclopedia Britannica and its commissioned cabalist Orientalists "state your sources and let us peruse them." If we ourselves undergo this exercise as many scholars have done (and do), we will find that these Orientalist claims do not hold even to the most basic elements of academic veracity, as they are blatant lies.

Dhun-Nun never stated what is claimed about him by and in the West. One way of verifying this is to refer to contemporary scholarly works that quote Dhun-Nun, or to cross-reference the different works of this scholar, only to find that, in fact, his books (in their genuine manuscript forms) state the complete opposite of what Orientalist sources have and are putting forward.

Without such correction(s), students and generic readers are readily led to believe that Imam al-Misri opened doors which Rosicrucian Alchemists, Jesuits and Freemasons later learned to admire well enough to enter the abyss of Gnosticism. Many Sufi-claimers who profess orthodox Sunni perspectives have apparently raised this 'middle path' bench of 'quietism' to Gnosticism's exhilarating journey to the impossible realms of knowing God via 'loving' Allah rather than 'fearing' Allah'[87] — never minding prophetic admonitions that the fear of Allah is a fundamental principle of both wisdom and *iman*. Here we must note that an unbalanced 'loving of God' is a fundamental principle of Christian cum pagan deceptions that have cast many sectarians into histrionic conniptions for centuries. This Theomania [xxxii] is recorded throughout the Occidental saga, and is presently seen among many Western 'Born Again' Christians. But once again, I must turn to Brother Karallii for authentic Islamic clarification:

> Muslims, according to scholarly traditions, are asked to both love God and to fear God. The love of God does not abolish the fear of God, nor does the fear of God do away with the love of God. If people of other religions claim to promote the love of God, then their claims with their mouths do not make the Muslim principle of loving God an innovation or a "contradistinction" to the fear of God. Muslims are asked to be between hope (*raja'*) and fear (*khawf*). The hope is for God's mercy and the fear is of God's punishment, and this is irrespective of what disbelievers utter with their mouths on this issue.

---

[87] Ibid., p. 7.

The Christian word for the love of God is *Agapeo,* a Greek term that literally has roots that better define it as "to bow in obedient submission to the king."

I am satisfied at this juncture that I have put a large enough dent in the armor of *Perrenialism's* pretense to move on to more significant matters. Nevertheless, we will return to poltergeists and the magi forum later.

Queen Semiramis, the wife of King Nimrud

CHAPTER TWO

Islamic Science & Muslim Humiliation

Definitions, Apologetics, Consequences, Admonitions

The significance of Goethe's objection to mathematical concepts of natural science is that he wished to forestall biased thinking so that science would remain free of pedagogical extremism. Conclusions drawn solely from statistical analyses are examples that represent the downside of materialism with its narrowed reductionist approach to problem solving. Goethe hoped that men would hold on to insight imbued with moral realism drawn from direct scientifically ordered observations such as offered by Nicola Tesla's empirical genius. He hoped men would chose to discern what is beneficial and true while rejecting abstractions that bring harmful applications and misconceptions steeped in the myopic cerebration of amoral-immoral sociopaths and other egotistically inclined members of the selfish clan identified in the Prologue. Instead, the world is burdened with a 'big pharma' oriented medical system, for example, that denies the public access to proven cures for cancer, etc.

> Physics must be sharply distinguished from mathematics. The former must stand in clear independence, penetrating into the sacred life of nature in common with all forces of love, veneration and devotion. The latter, on the other hand, must declare its independence of all externality, go its own grand spiritual way, and develop itself more purely than is possible so long as it tries to deal with actuality, seeking to adapt itself to things as they really are. [88]

For the most part, 'Love, veneration and devotion' have gone the way of indentured ritual servitude to a post-modern Babylonian Papacy, [89]

---

[88] *Proceedings*, op.cit. p. 148

[89] This has its basis in *pre-* and *Babylonian* as well as *Dravidian* cultures that gave rise to Vestal Virgins *et alia.*, and upon which the Roman system of ritual 'religious'

and 'adapting to things as they really are' will remain in contention till Judgment day. Furthermore, while traditional Islamic approaches to science more than exceeded Goethe's pristine position in the past, presently, and with few exceptions such as Dr. Maurice Bucaille, we cannot say the same for the majority of contemporary Muslim dilettantes. The fact is that orthodox Islamic scientists of Islam's 'Golden Age' never even entertained the term, 'Islamic Science'. It simply was not a concern to men and women who worked for a living.

The subject of 'Islamic Science appears to be both bane and boon perhaps because the idiom defies definition. For some it is a redundant superfluity while for others, such as die-hard Positivists, it approaches oxymoron status. Nevertheless, that advocates of 'Islamic Science' represent it as an ideal is modestly justifiable:

> Fazlur Rahman Ansari presented and advocated Islam as the last and final way of solution for ultimate and immediate problems ... He wrote that Islam means conformity to natural laws and that the Islamic Principles are so rational and valuable that modern science is actually based on them.
> - Mujeeb Ahmad [xxxiii]

> The term "Islamization of Science" has been a confusing, or to a certain extent, even an unpopular term. It is confusing since its proponents have different versions, understandings and methods; and unpopular since it implies the relativity of science which so far has been universal, although this assumption is not fully correct. - Mulyadhi Kartanegara [90]

Conventionally, Islamic Science describes scrupulous disciplines of the tenth Century (BCE) Muslim world of orthodox *Fiqh*, *Tafsir*, *Hadith* and *Kalam*, etc. However, post-Modern supporters appear to be stretching the second term 'science' to subsume modern sciences. For rigorously disciplined hard scientists of the world this represents a generous broadening of the imagination since standard definitions of Modern Science disallow it as 'fanciful'. Hence, the term invites confrontation.

---

fetishism is based. See my books, *Trinity*, *The Hand of Iblis*, and *Cain's Creed* for more details.

[90] *Secularization of Science and Its Islamic Answer*, ibid,, p. 157

As a rule, Modern Science is defined as:

> ... a branch of knowledge conducted on objective principles involving the systematized observation-of and experiment with phenomena, especially concerned with the material and functions of the physical universe. [91]

This near universally accepted definition specifically indicates the study of the material universe *via* rigorous methods including trials and systematic examinations leading to independently *replicable* results, hopefully upon which discernible principles of cause and effect relationships are established as objectively as possible. Nevertheless, the presently accepted scientific method remains a reductionist challenge because it precludes the synthesis demanded by Goethe and the current suffering world. Furthermore, most reduced materialists who have monetized their thought processes are not the least bit concerned about any search-for or definition-of ultimate purpose or the transcendent truths that apply to all phenomena under the scrutiny of bottom-line oriented microscopes, military budgets and managerial criminals—although scientists incessantly pose for such efforts after politically-correct articles are chosen for publication. Of course, all of this means that any gestalt approach to philosophy (the love of wisdom) is dismissed as foolhardy by utilitarian sociopaths such as Dick Cheney, the Rockefellers, Pol Pot and the Bush clan. Such deliberators and dismissals hold the reins of power within most circles of Islamizing ventures and similarly ignore synthesis.

> A Century that has relied solely on analysis and is almost afraid of synthesis is not on the right road." ... Nothing occurs in nature that is not in relationship to the whole. When experience appears solely as isolated, and experiments are regarded as isolated facts, nothing within them indicates their isolation. There is only one question: "How do we find the relationship of these phenomena, of these occurrences?" [92] - J.W. Goethe

---

[91] Oxford Dictionary, 10th Ed.

[92] Goethe's *Color Theory*, p. 61.

That was written 200-plus years ago and the situation has only worsened.

Although Islam's *tawhid* is approached in some quarters of God's earth as a matter of indigenous instinct, in the West, knowledge synthesis is generally viewed in mercantile deist terms of New Age "holism". These designs are, however, generally divorced from the sound moral footing of essential monotheism and its revealed knowledge. Sadly enough, this obscurity, and hence also the rejection of Goethe's and traditional Islam's surpra-Goethean transcendence, is partly due to the ummah's loss of the *élan vitae* of its once glorious autonomy. This is in direct reference to the *group feeling* that accompanied Islam's initial success, which was directly consequent to the metaphysical determinism outlined in Part One of this tome.

Nevertheless, the term 'holism' or 'wholism' is yet another piece of evidence that confirms linguistic worldview assimilation on the part of conquered Muslims—a kind of Stockholm Syndrome considered acceptable subsistence fodder. Another cause may be attributed to Fabian-Socialist Darwinists such as G.B. Shaw and the Yale Bonesman, John Dewy of the Chicago School. The latter adept almost single-handedly Fabianized 20th Century Education parlors in America based on the London School's modifications of the Prussian system. This concerted occult effort included policies and brainwashing textbooks sufficient to produce fragmented work forces of deliberately dumbed-downed servants amenable to elitist fleecing by those who stand behind world collectivism and (i) the One World Government; (ii) the immensely successful 9/11-PSYOP-treason; (iii) global finance and industry; and (iv) serial murders of idealists like the Kennedy brothers or John Jr. and his wife, or Malcolm X and anyone else pseudo-scholars fail to support while seeking after tenure's pickings.[93]

The fact is that that although Muslims rigorously established the rules and fundamentals of today's scientific method that saved the West from the Dark Age of Papist Tyranny, Muslim leaders

---

[93] For details and history, see *The Hand of Iblis* by the author, A. S. Noordeen, Kl, Malaysia, 2008.

subsequently failed to carry them through well enough politically and metaphysically to preserve Muslim dignity and dominion. Hence, in the eyes of compartmentalized non-Muslim reductionist scientists the world over, Islam is a 'Has Been' religion while for ill informed pundits who burn Korans and urinate on dead Muslims for a living, it never was a legitimate concern.

Consequently, contemporary knights of global Islamia hardly qualify as world-champion advocates of anything in academic and other international cartel arenas for monopolists; especially when punch drunk from boxing the shadows of (i) philosophical imponderables, or (ii) dismal socio-political failures like Pakistan, or (iii) doltish Middle East sectarian neo-patriarchs, along with (iv) neo-Arabian phallus wielders reclining on (v) daunting dais of disconcerting propaganda, whose (vi) moguls and reprobate collaborators (Salafs and MB) re-conduct crusades (Libyan and Syrian fiascos) for the forbidden (vii) Occult Judeo-Christian Alliance whose vanguard comprises (vii) Black-water monks of St. Collateral-Damage. So much for the term 'science' and its application to present day Islamia: hard, soft, social and political.

As regards the term 'Islam', it readily relates to 'soft science' and deals with metaphysics as a revealed philosophy (*hikmah*) or 'Way of Life' espoused by its sacred literature, traditions and history. As such, using the abstracted adjective 'Islamic' is indeed a noble attempt to mate metaphysical (soft sciences) with the physical (hard sciences) and surely such a union is commendable and no doubt much needed. However, in the face of tsunamic reductionism, [xxxiv] one is forced to concede that the commendation is, of necessity, reserved for believers. Yet even for believers the term requires additional criteria that qualify its agents as imbued with the *tawhidic* perspective that preserves *fitrah* along with a continuity of inductions drawn from the knowledge of *akhira*, and this by virtue of inspiration, intuition, and polymath study added to Confucian action. It is, however, the latter three requirements that have been abandoned by the ranks of prayer mongering academics thanks to the endemic Muslim preoccupation with ritual servitude and its attendant waste of time and cerebral talent; not to mention the linguistic conundrum we described in the *Law of Unity*, Part One.

The most worthy of worldviews (i.e. Islam's *Tawhid*) is acquired by degrees of contemplative intuition, rigorous discipline and ceaseless learning of far more than the unbalanced mastering of 'soft-science-only' degrees in religious fetishism. The worldview of Islamic Tawhid actually represents the near Renaissance-polyglot status of a warrior prince: one might say "a 'nobody's-fool' *tasawwufian*" flanked by an incorruptible vanguard every bit as capable as the OAS, Navy Seals or personal guard of Ivan the Terrible. Obviously there are not many around and one should ponder 'why' in order to solve the issue conclusively in the name of Islamic Science, which, I imagine, is subject for a very gritty PhD thesis if you can get it past the padded shoulders of 'soft-science-only' tenured chairs.

In any case, the balance between religious and secular knowledge is necessary (most especially for leaders), lest one sprouts the wings of Icarius on magic carpets of politically correct fervor to produce ritually fixated constituencies such as found in Malaysia and Indonesia. As long as the oil holds out, Malay Muslims are capable of importing 70-80% of their food supply while non-Muslims build their roads, transportation, communications, defense and distribution systems and generally dig the earth to extract the wealth that affords and assures that this near-total dependence qualifies them for more prayer time, back-door 'Ali Baba' doles and the cronyism of traditional nepotism. One could just as easily, however, cite the more appropriate example of the princely mafia that runs Saudi Arabia, minus the prayer time of course.

In the light of these realities, the concept of Islamic Science and/or "Scientists" presents even more obstacles for non-Muslims given the fact that Muslims cannot agree on their scripture and metaphysical commentaries well enough to present a common political and professionally institutionalized front, as have their occult Occidental counterparts. Not that I praise the latter group of felons, but I do propose it is far more criminal that Muslims—primarily due to the cited disunity—failed to protect mankind from the dragon cult's trans-millennial bequests of institutionalized evil. Consider merely the Sunni-

Shia divide that equates with the Catholic-Protestant contest or that the great Madhabs have their share of pugnacious munchkins who've also succumbed to sectarian devolution. The present Syrian tragedy is evidence enough that religious exhibitionism and fetish is readily exploited by the Machiavellians of Cain's posterity.

If this is thus far an insufficient brief, I can add that Muslims generally do not repeat—other than prayer and ritual ablution—or present their so called 'observations', deductions, inductions and inspired innovations in any manner that would universally qualify the term 'Science' as an empirical descriptive for Modern and Post-Modernist executives of thought. Not that this is necessary, mind you, but it might improve the earthly status of doleful congregations spread across several arcs of crises were it achieved in concert. Sadly however, and contrary to the Western Scholiast model of 16th Century occult genius, genesis and Jesuit cultivation, Muslims have failed to protect and nurture their once exquisitely scientific institutions via the office of *al'hisbah;* which is to say 'by the enforcement of good and the forbidding of ponerogenesis', especially in government houses. But such an institutional effort requires righteous intellectual musclemen rather than the back-door Ali Baba leaders of two-hundred-odd million barely literate Malay-Indonesians, or the dim-witted Mussulmen of Islamist mania, or the ignoramuses of the nearly universal neo-patriarchal repression that presently afflicts a flailing ummah filled to the brim with befuddling and obsessively compelled religiosity that appears to be of little earthly worth. But perhaps, in their minds, that is the goal.

It seems that simple principles of Psych and Sociology 101 were employed to deploy active potentials that exacerbate the substantial influences of sectarianism:

> This [Arabic neo-patriarchy] differs dramatically from most preindustrial societies, where family based groups typically performed the functions of the firm and often those of the school, the political party, the welfare agency, the police, and the army. Where families are managed as production systems—and often as political parties, police forces, and so on—emotional ties take on a different character from those built as pure

relationships: personal feelings of affection and animosity merge with calculations of resource deployment and strategic alliance. Many important life choices—including one's vocation and spouse—may be made by family elders, a situation that requires everyone to adopt broadly "collectivistic" values rather than "individualistic" ones.

The Middle East, A CULTURAL PSYCHOLOGY
by Gary Gregg, Oxf. U Press, 2005, 47.

Being mindful that 'collectivism' is neither communalism nor cosmopolitan, I'd say nature took its course without divine guidance in true deist style. And if you didn't catch the pun you have some serious catching up to do. Furthermore, if the latter passage didn't complete the brief for jury and judge, perhaps the following Freemasonic British gentlemen will add to the burden of proof:

We must put an end to anything which brings about any Islamic unity between the sons of the Muslims. As we have already succeeded in finishing off the Caliphate, so we must ensure that there will never arise again unity for the Muslims, whether it be intellectual or cultural unity.

Lord Curzon, Brit. Foreign Minister, 1924

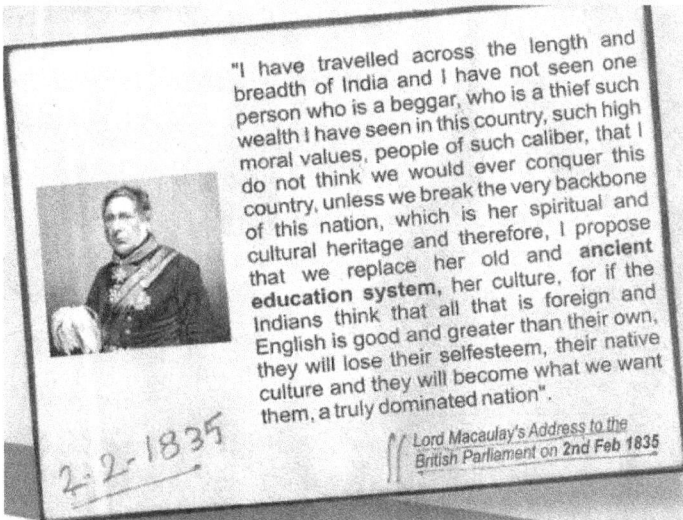

"I have travelled across the length and breadth of India and I have not seen one person who is a beggar, who is a thief such wealth I have seen in this country, such high moral values, people of such caliber, that I do not think we would ever conquer this country, unless we break the very backbone of this nation, which is her spiritual and cultural heritage and therefore, I propose that we replace her old and **ancient education system**, her culture, for if the Indians think that all that is foreign and English is good and greater than their own, they will lose their selfesteem, their native culture and they will become what we want them, a truly dominated nation".

Lord Macaulay's Address to the British Parliament on **2nd Feb 1835**

PART TWO: ESSAYS ON ISLAMIZATION & ISLAMIC SCIENCE
Chap. 2: Islamic Science & Muslim Humiliation

This is plain evidence that monotheist ponerocrats from the West systematically exploited the immature emotionalism[94] Muslims were meant to avoid. They easily spread their occult governments [xxxv] globally with the cunning genius that genuine Islamic leaders would have readily withstood and dominated by Divine Design had Muslims been the least bit inclined towards the sciences of human behavior and governance according to principles of spiritual law. Of course this would have required the assistance of additional grace and the oft prayed-for but rarely-achieved guidance and protection of Allah SWT as discussed in the first portion of this tome.

To the contrary, and again, sadly so, it appears that Muslims universally adopted inducements that conformed them to mediocrity, which hardly qualifies as Islamic let alone science. Consider the following realities, again, in light of sixty years of IOK leadership:

- Rote memorization of a sacred language their majority fails to comprehend—a bit like the DARK AGE Catholic experience of Latin;

- Obsessive-compulsive attendance to ritual servitude, perfected festival appointments and kibla timing along with judicious avoidance of justice;

- Endemic shaman training complete with spells, amulets, holy hands and water, evil eyes, pre-occupations with jinn filled terror-threats, and jealous spouses who purchase the services of jinn mongering sorcerers;

- Favor-oriented cliques of politically appointed sycophants obsessed with long public prayers and robes while counting beads, merit marks, booty and monotonous mantras, along with the placement of VIP seat names at sundry public venues of pompous circumstance where hands are kissed and the victories of their enemies over the wealth and health of their nations are studiously ignored;

---

[94] Proper child-rearing is thus not limited to teaching a young person to control the overly violent reactions of his instinctual emotionalism; it also ought to teach him to appreciate the wisdom of nature contained and speaking through his instinctive endowment [*fitrah*]. - *Political Ponerology*, op. cit. p. 60.

- Repressive accommodation of sexploitable women and children with FGM and incest filled shrines for homes that boast altars for Iblissian media (TV);
- Traditional honors for dope-peddling bearded pederasts who kidnap innocents for sale to Guantanamo patrons while forcing women to live in bags and crying 'Allah u'Akbar';
- RPG trigger happy jihadists for hire who protect drug laced economies along the ancient silk road and slice the throats of anyone who doesn't see things their way;
- The pretense of long robed sanctimony held in common with most other religious deviations as pin stripe suits apologize for riba laced ventures and Jew inspired banking facilities with fractional reserves, and the worthless paper they use to confiscate the real wealth of honest labor;
- After a hiatus of a few hundred years, some have finally placed hard science back on government agendas for intermittent consideration without sufficient funding for R&D. Understandably, they have trouble finding Muslims who comprehend the significance or qualified professionals willing to work for slave wages.
- Farmed out essential technology contracts to non-Muslim enemies who do comprehend the terms 'robust and 'rigorous' and who do not appreciate working for incompetents who act like they're God's gift to skilled utilitarian professionals.
- A majority of women who go shopping during Jummah.

Generically speaking, and as this much abbreviated litany sadly indicates, Muslims apologize for the traditional arts of divisive tyranny, chauvinist repression, routine murder, political corruption and protective sectarianism (cronyism) while dubiously qualified meta-physicians and scholars—as reported by Imam Hanbal—compete for influence, perks and IOK salaries rather than the cosmopolitan unity protected by *al'hisbah* as experienced by the first generation's *siasya dunya*. All of these are clear expressions of the sub-human nature that avoids the Law of Moral Imperative as discussed in Part One and furthermore, when considering Ibn Hanbal's testimony, this has been going on for quite some time. In addition, bear in mind that the 'group feeling' of the cosmopolitan oriented *siasya dunya* (inclusive governance referred to by Ibn Khaldun) is a phenomenon that singularly inhibits the exclusivity of tribalism. Furthermore, tribal favoritism was forbidden to Muslims by the Prophet himself (pbh). Of course these inconvenient truths are not politically correct, and, as a result, they are not consequentially addressed in IOK forums or conferences on Islamic Science, albeit, lip service is permitted and even funded.

Hence, we have robustly established that Muslims systemically failed to institutionalize an academy of metaphysician counselors, scientists and firm-fisted governors impressive enough to intimidate the warlords of crusading papists, Jesuits, Freemasons, B'nai B'rith Zionists, Sabataen Khazars, and Maltese Knights of the Templars et. alia., as well as Rosicrucians, UN & NATO New Age sympathizers, Neo-Con mass-murderers, Fabian Socialists (communists really, like Obama) and sundry Kabbalists—all of whom, by the way, are somehow united and governed occultly by adepts of the Ancient Mystery Religions. And since all of these latter ascend ponerogenic thrones that wield post-Colonial cum Occidental 'Nation State', fiscal and Sino-Japanese Hammers throughout the world, Muslims consequently, and haplessly stand and suffer within the many arcs and shadows of clear and present professionally prosecuted harm.[95]

If you, especially if Muslim, had trouble understanding the last paragraph, that alone confirms my position.

> ... Nation States are social formations characterized by a uniform bureaucratic governance and technological communication populated by largely anonymous, replaceable citizens and sustained and reproduced by a (relatively) uniform educational system that instills common civic values as well as the knowledge necessary for sustaining the bureaucratic and technological "expert systems" on which modern industrial societies are based.[96]

---

[95] The Triad & Yakuzza Systems have initiation rituals every bit analogous to those of Occidental Freemasons. These groups aided, abetted and survived the ongoing capitalization of opium and heroin, cocaine and designer drug wars in league with Western occult auspices.

[96] E. Gellner, *Nations and Nationalisms*. Ithaca: Cornell University Press, 2006, pp. 55–57.

This is hardly the definition of an Islamic polity but it is, in fact, both politically and socially 'scientific'. Indeed, somebody has to manage the backstreets, alleys and ports of these anonymous monstrosities and it is certainly not officers of *al'hisbah* who would faithfully and sincerely attend respectable *Jummah* but rather those who never apply sermon driven principles to their duties unless it serves to support the mere image of Islam.

As for "Islamic Science" and its relation to the charade: one is forced to remark, yet again, that after sixty odd years of concerted effort and untold millions in expenditures globally, we note that religiously oriented Islamized training increases while Muslim on Muslim murders rise and materialism waxes strong as autonomy ebbs in the wake of Muslim mimicry of the West. Do IOK and Islamic Science movements somehow directly correlate with these humiliations? I venture to posit 'yes' because too much religiously oriented education prevents professional accomplishment due to its diversion of precious resources as well as attention and time from the sciences that are socially productive; i.e. those that meet existential human needs while protecting resources and developing balanced halal systems of wealth distribution. I attempt to rigorously establish this as fact in the next essays.

The reader may find my assessment a bit harsh but there is far more to come in this morbidity and mortality report. It is my professional responsibility to record this ghastly reality in order to diagnose the malady and improve treatments for the tumors of pride, lassitude, denial, ignorance and pretense that plague the ummah of Mohammad (pbh).

Mysticism, Sufi-claimers & the Crisis of Knowledge

> ... the concept of knowledge enjoyed an importance unparalleled in other civilization . . . Its insistence upon "knowledge" has no doubt made medieval Muslim civilization one of great scholarly and scientific productivity, and through it, Muslim civilization made its most lasting contribution to mankind. "Knowledge", as its center, also hardened Muslim civilization and made it impervious to anything that did not fall within its view of what constituted acceptable knowledge.
>
> - Franz Rosenthal [97]

What Happened?

> Sermons were certainly preached for the masses, although it may be seriously doubted that the sermons which were set down in writing and constituted a productive branch of literature continued to serve as popular reading. If "knowledge" seems to play an insignificant role in the homiletic literature, it was the natural result of the general outlook of all Muslim preaching. It was orientated toward the *other world* and, to an even greater degree, away from the total evil of this world. Its recommendations were therefore all negative as far as this world was concerned. There was no good reason to recommend something like "knowledge" that had so many positive worldly aspects in addition to its religious value. - ibid

Sounds a bit 'Catholic', as if Muslim elitists kept knowledge for themselves? 'Why would they do that?' unless Prof. Rosenthal's assessment dovetails with Imam Hanbal's report that his colleagues sold their services, which then indicates that sub-human nature is truly universal and traditionally honored as long as palms are crossed and sycophantic beaks of ponerogenesis are wet.

---

[97] *Knowledge Triumphant; The Concept of Knowledge in Medieval Islam*, Brill, London, 2007.

> The ponerogenesis of macrosocial phenomena — large scale evil — appears to be subject to the same laws of nature that operate within human questions on an individual or small-group level . . . The atrophy of natural critical faculties with respect to pathological individuals becomes [essential] . . . If we take into consideration those historical examples which should be qualified in that regard, we will most frequently observe the figure of an autocratic ruler whose mental mediocrity and infantile personality finally opened the door to the ponerogenesis of the phenomenon . . . Whenever a nation experiences a "system crisis" or a hyperactivity of ponerogenic processes within, it becomes the object of a pathocratic penetration whose purpose is to serve up the country as booty.
>
> - Political Ponerology, op. cit. p. 213

In addition to self-serving sanctimony, other contributing factors helped stimulate ongoing intellectual stagnation in the Muslim pond.

A philosopher of the recent past, looking at knowledge in its Western habitat, divided the whole of it into Bildungswissen, Erlösungswissen, and Herrschaftswissen (or Leistungswissen). The last kind of knowledge, the effort of science to control nature and society, is assumed to have been undeveloped in Antiquity and in the Middle Ages. Strong as both *Bildungswissen* and *Erlösungswissen* were in the past, *Bildungswissen*, the effort to improve the individual personality, is believed to be little cultivated now, and *Erlösungswissen*, the desire to learn about the divine order of the world and to achieve salvation, is, we are told, no longer of any real significance.[98]

And:

> If we look at Islam in this way, we find that metaphysical, ethical, and scientific knowledge, and, in addition, knowledge as the power tool of society, *were not all present in equal strength*, but they were present and active.[99]

---

[98] Cf. M. Scheler, *Die Wissensformen und die Gesellschaft*, 64 ff., 250 (Leipzig 1926), cited by Stark, *Sociology of Knowledge*, 117.

[99] Rosenthal, op.cit. p. 337

Since sermons left Muslim hearers bereft of earthly ambitions, much the same as Christian medieval serfs, doors opened wide for metaphysical opportunists with charisma as the scales of public discernment tipped in their favor. Excepting for the exceptionally vibrant oral Islamic traditions that centered on the mainstream dialogue as carried forward by a faithful minority, *speculative metaphysics and not a few astral-tramp travelogues were accepted on faith in the proponent's veracity* rather than exacting discipline or scientific observation. We must further add that although present studies in paranormal phenomenon and neuro-physiology have markedly advanced, generally speaking, the "unseen" sphere of "human knowledge" is tentative and provisional and hence, is justifiably called mysticism.

I and others propose that this retreat from reason and the offices of al'*hisbah* is no small contributor to generic Muslim ignorance. It also seems that a glacial mass of subjective metaphysical speculations has aided and abetted the collapse of political and economic autonomy in favor of nationalized superstitions. This tsunami flow of ideation eventually morphed to sanctimonious hypocrisy under the astute guidance of ponerocrats who conventionally worship the booty of materialism; folks like Ibn Maymun, the Fatimid patriarch and crypto-Jew.

Here is an observation on the historicity of supposed 'divine provisions' mistaken as miracles and saintly *baraoka* by superstitious fools:

> How was the miracle of the endless river of religious bounty maintained? It was in large part funded by the very lord who represents all the principles of what the saint's life is the antithesis, or it was the lord who sent the sheikh sacks of wheat and grain and seed, even money when necessary, and who leased out land to other members of the family.[100]

---

[100] Gary S. Gregg, Foreword by David Matsumoto; *The Middle East, A Cultural Psychology*, 124.

Eloquent casuists might argue that this was merely 'God's Way' and perhaps have grounds. But the lords of largess that concern this writer are occidental villains who used Chinese expertise, gold and gunpowder while ignoring her excellence and accomplishments,[101] to then claim the Americas and colonize most of the earth while conducting grand cultural wars as tendered by Lord's Macaullay and Curzon. These fellows and Freemasonic brethren and dames induced mass hypnosis within their colonies in order to systematically exploit the earth by focusing on material sciences which Muslims had meticulously handed over and then abandoned for the mirage of religious ideations and ritual fetish. The immeasurable economic advantages gained by the West after the defeat of the Ottoman's at Lepanto [102] and the return of Marco Polo and others to Venice, allowed the enemies of mankind to duly master and advance the hard sciences in parallel with Machiavellian PSYOPS to their advantage. Meanwhile, Muslims, sighed 'insh'Allah', prayed, and abandoned science to maintain harems, booty, religion and slaves while waiting for Allah's blessings and unconsciously and superstitiously perfecting the socio-political art of the ponerogenic repression that has now become the neo-patriarchal abyss of chauvinism:

> Zay'our links repression in the family to the prevalence of "irrational and superstitious" attitudes in the mass of the population, which facilitates control by the status quo and makes people blindly opposed to social change. He sees this as a structural aspect of the existing society.
>
> The scientific mind, which explains phenomena by reference to causes that are subject to examination and verification, has not taken root in the collective personality. The magical, supernatural orientation is still dominant and is active in the psychic structure of the individual. Thus,

---

[101] The Chinese, under a Muslim Admiral, actually circumnavigated the world nearly one-hundred years before Europeans made the claim. The latter used Chinese maps of the globe in their reckonings. Their phenomenal accomplishment has been completely erased from Occidental history books. See: *1421, the year China Discovered the World*, by Gavin Menzies, Banatam Press, 2002.

[102] The Battle of Lepanto: 7 October 1571, a fleet of the Holy League, a coalition of southern European Catholic maritime states, decisively defeated the main fleet of the Ottoman Empire,

> rationality is not the governing principle of individual behavior or of social action in general. There are [in society] two sectors existing next to one another, one magical, the other scientific; traditional structures coexist alongside modern structures, a primitive, dependent economy alongside a rational modern economy. - Hisham Sharabi, op. cit.

A clear example of this is seen in Yemen where parents who fail to take preventative measures ascribe early childhood injuries to fate; a clear example of a collective moronic thought process.[103] There is more:

> Without acquiescing to the vagaries of postmodernism on political power, it is the crisis of knowledge that has thrown the Ummah into an abyss. No exotic claims about alien intervention can absolve Muslims of their intellectual docility … Muslims have nothing to offer from their cognitive repository. Even their material wealth has failed in putting a stop to the Serbian aggression. The two civilizations stand bankrupt but on different accounts. Thus resurfaces the question of knowledge and power. The way the Muslim intellect faces this predicament will shape its destiny.[104]

Had enough? I think not dear reader, this brief is still building. After reading the following paragraph you will better understand why even the most sympathetic of Orientalists gaze upon Islam with condescension while paying taxes for its rapine.

> In the early twentieth century, ulema forbade the learning of foreign languages and dissection of human bodies in the medical school in Iran. The ulama at the Islamic university of Al-Azhar in Cairo taught the Ptolemaic astronomical system (in which the sun circles the earth) until compelled to adopt the Copernican system by the Egyptian government in 1961.[105]

---

[103] Abed Alamid. *Non-Intentional Injuries in Yemini Children*, Ph.D. Thesis, Univ. Technology, KL, Malaysia, 2013.

[104] "The Soul of the World" by Dr. Munawar A. Anees, Editor-in-Chief, *Periodica Islamica*, 1995.

[105] Mackey, *The Iranians : Persia, Islam and the Soul of a Nation*, 1996, p.179; *In the Path of God : Islam and Political Power* by Daniel Pipes, c1983 p.113.

PART TWO: ESSAYS ON ISLAMIZATION & ISLAMIC SCIENCE
Chap. 2: Mysticism, Sufi-Claimers & the Crisis of Knowledge

Al-Azhar was created in the tenth century and is hailed as one of the oldest universities in the world. However, at the dawn of the twentieth century, the blind Egyptian author, Taha Husayn, complained about the repression I've cited as well as the total lack of critical thinking he encountered at the institution:

> The four years I spent [at al-Azhar, from 1902] seemed to me like forty, so utterly drawn out they were ... It was life of unrelieved repetition, with never a new thing, from the time the study began until it was over. After the dawn prayer came the study of Tawhid, the doctrine of [Allah's] unity; then fiqh, or jurisprudence, after sunrise; then the study of Arabic grammar during the forenoon, following a dull meal; then more grammar in the wake of the noon prayer. After this came a grudging bit of leisure and then, again, another snatch of wearisome food until the evening prayer was performed. I then proceeded to the logic class some shaikh or other conducted. Throughout these studies it was all merely a case of hearing reiterated words and traditional talk which aroused no chord in my heart, nor taste in my appetite. There was no food for one's intelligence, *no new knowledge adding to one's store.*" [106]
>
> ... Consequently, our situation changed from that of honor to becoming the lowest of nations compared to others . . . losing our habitations and dignity. All this took place in such a manner due to our own attitude thinking that . . . the advancement of learning and the development of skills are not related to religion and as a result we neglect them . . . What I can understand from the statements of the Sufis . . . is that those under 'Divine' attraction, who are "pulled by Allah" to experience a number of noble spiritual states and lofty stations . . . are not aware of their reason . . . *the person is unconscious of his reason and he is not conscious of himself.* [xxxvi]

Abandoning knowledge for the ancient Hindu amentia just cited doesn't sound very Islamic, scientific or rational to this writer. In other words, Sufi-claimers and their disciples became too 'heavenly' oriented to be of much earthly good. I should also mention satanic agents like Idris Shah who are purposely placed in their midst to promote the

---

[106] Fjordman; "The Truth About "Islamic Science" – *Global Politician,* 11/20/2007

futility. Holding a people back from progress is an ancient satanic ploy that has been purposely used by ponerocrats since the Sumerian Swindle. If you lack this historical perspective, you have been suitably swindled and subjected to a purposely misguided review of history by masters of the left Hand Path of Satanism.

One sees the same menace in Christendom, a group of sects known to have been infiltrated for this same purpose by Satanists, including Sabataen Jews in league with ancient Latins (*latin* means 'hidden'); especially the modern evangelical movement that blindly supports Zionism. This depressing estate is a far cry from whence Islam began its ascendance as the world-worthy vice-gerent of its Prophet.

Some scholars do apply principles drawn from the cognitive sciences to address the generic resistance to nomality as presented by magical thinking, religious fetishism, and the acquired systems that have adapted to social repression, but impediments are daunting. In addition, please note that what is termed 'secular' below is an attempt to validate models of forensic examination of the human psyche; specifically, the souls and minds that are repressed by well qualified Muslim reactionaries:

> Muhammad Arkoun's concern is similar to Jabiri's, but narrower and therefore more focused. His aim is to break the monopoly of traditional and neopatriarchal interpretation of the sacred and literary texts of Islamic culture. He seeks to do this by first establishing new ground for the (re)reading of the Quran, a reading that would put aside philological and Orientalist methods and rely instead on the modern disciplines of linguistics, semiology, anthropology, sociology, and history. Secularism involves taking an intellectual position with regard to two issues:
>
>> The first is linked to the problem of knowledge. How can the meaning of events be grasped? How can we understand reality in an accurate and precise way? Is it not impermissible to deny anyone, for no matter what reason, the right to understand?
>>
>> The second is, how can we communicate knowledge after its discovery and crystallization? When we discover new results in any field of knowledge our responsibility to communicate these results is as important as their discovery. . . . I have personally experienced a great

difficulty, and still do, with [communicating] my findings in the field of Islamic and Arab thought. It is a difficult problem.[107]

The questions posed by the gentleman are these:

- What of exoteric knowledge and scientific validity?

- How do we meld them to social advance in order to release people from superstition and obsessive-compulsive fetishism?

Despite the unimpeachable veracity of Al'Qur'an, men seem to excel at impeding the practical application of its extremely sound and clear directives. It appears that the forces that withstand Muhammad Arkoun's struggle are analogous to those that held Europeans in suspense by Catholic ecclesiarches for upwards of a thousand years. But what is the scientific basis for the phenomenon?

> Some theories, themselves products of arduous thought, ironically depreciate the activity in which the theorists are invested: they reduce thinking to cognition, or situate it in a wide band of transcendental regulations that curtail its inventiveness, or contract it into a bland intellectualism that neglects its affective sources, somatic entanglements, and effects. But the inventive and compositional dimensions of thinking ['Right Brained' activities] are essential to freedom of the self and to cultivation of generosity in ethics and politics. Thinking participates in that uncertain process by which new possibilities are ushered into being. One invention may be a new identity that jostles the roster of established constituencies as it struggles to find space. Another may be a thought-imbued disposition, incorporated into the sensibility of an individual or folded into the ethos of engagement between constituencies.
>
> William E. Connolly; *Neuropolitics: Thinking, Culture*, Speed Regents of the University of Minnesota & Press, 2000.

Group hysteria is contagious by means of psychological resonance, identification, and imitation. Each human being has a predisposition for this malformation of the personality, albeit to varying degrees . . . The

---

[107] Hisham Sharabi, op. cit. // Muhammad Arkoun, *Lectures du Goran* (Paris, 1982), pp. 1-26. & "Interview," al-Wihdah (Paris, December, 1984), p. 130.

hysterical patterns for experience and behavior grow and spread downwards from the privileged classes until crossing the boundary of the first criterion of ponerology: *the atrophy of natural critical faculties with respect to pathological individuals* . . . When the habits of subconscious selection and substitution of thought-data spread to the macrosocial level, a society tends to develop contempt for factual criticism and to humiliate anyone sounding an alarm. Contempt is also shown for other nations which have maintained normal thought-patterns and for their opinions. Egotistic thought-terrorization is accomplished by the society itself and its processes of conversive thinking. This obviates the need for censorship of the press, theater, or broadcasting, as a pathologically hypersensitive censor lives within the citizens themselves . . . additional circumstances and factors must participate in such a period of a society's general spiritual crisis and cause its reason and social structure to degenerate in such a way as to bring about the spontaneous generation of this worst disease of society. Let us call this societal disease phenomenon "pathocracy"; it has emerged numerous times during the history of our planet.

Political Ponerology, op. cit. pp. 177, 183

Koro

Sufferers of the culture-bound condition Koro believe that their genitals are disappearing into their bodies, often as a result of inappropriate sexual acts. This symptom, distressing enough in itself, causes further anxiety because it is believed that the organ's disappearance will result in death. An outbreak of Koro in Singapore in 1967 resulted in hundreds of Chinese men seeking help at hospitals, some going so far as to tie pieces of string to their penises in hope of preventing the precious appendage from receding into their abdomens.[108]

Sounding alarms am I? Into which of these referenced folds do you think the group hysteria of Catholic ecclesiarches once fell and still resides? Into which hysterical fold do you think many a Muslim neo-patriarch or mullah falls? But hold your thoughts for there is far more to come in this brief.

---

[108] "Mendelson S. Conversion disorder and mass hysteria." *Huffington Post*. Web. 1 Feb. 2012.

Mysticism vs. Sufism

As I examined the matter, it became clear that mysticism and Sufism are not synonymous. On the non-synonymous side it is evident that the monism of ancient Dravidia had slowly migrated to ascetic disciplines and dogma of not a few Sufi-claiming sects. For example:

> The *Murshid* is not separate from God, nor from the saints. All Sufis [taken together] are one soul [a single united entity = monism]. By virtue of and by the blessings of his spiritual linkage [*Nisbat*] through Divine love, the *Murshid* is (regarded as) the manifestation of [His, i.e. God's] Essence and Attributes.[109]

This is a perfect recipe for the elitist separatism that is so beloved by archons of sanctimony. However, since mystics cannot prove their observations in the accepted manner that satisfies science as defined previously—especially mindless nomads adsorbed to delusions of the unseen—in order to justify and responsibly utilize the proposed East-West marriage desired by Islamic Scientists and IOK pundits, we should, therefore, redefine 'science' in order to embrace a consensus on subjective cognitions, impressions, imaginations and/or interpretations of the unseen—not to mention Revelation's lofty concerns. This is not an unreasonable suggestion considering the numerous methodologies applied by Western approaches to psychology, psychiatry and cognitive manipulation for political purposes (Neuropolitics) as utilized by *PSYOPS* professionals and paranormal operatives.

Albeit, these and other fields remain in flux due to extensive modifications emanating from numerous advances in neuroscience, and this is in addition to forays made by para-psychological studies at Princeton, the Universities of Virginia and Arizona, the Stanford Research Institute, Duke University, and privately-funded units in the Universities of Edinburgh, Northampton, Liverpool, Hope and London.

---

[109] *The Path of Tasawwuf* by HAZRAT MOHAMMAD KHADIM HASAN SHAH, R.A. translated and edited by SYED MUMTAZ ALI

There are more such sinistrations offered by government programs such as the sophisticated mind-control programs originating with Nazis like Dr. J. Mengele at the Jesuit friendly McGill University after WWII, or the US Army's 'Operation Stargate'. One should have knowledge of these endeavors, especially people sitting in chairs of leadership who aspire towards the advance of Islamic Science with *ummatic* application. "Why?" you might ask. To be better enabled to defend the ummah from satanic attack because the science of war demands that you know your enemy. After all, Allah established both enemy and rules of war in order to test His slaves.

> I don't know about the religious perspective. I think any time we humans encounter things we don't understand and can't measure we tend to put them into religion instead of science. I am trying to look at this work from a scientific perspective and I think that eventually we will understand it from that viewpoint. I've actually become much more skeptical over the years as I see how people can easily be fooled by seeing what they want to see. On the other hand, I have also become much more convinced by the data that there is something unusual going on, that doesn't fit our current understanding of science. But I reserve judgment on what that is. I think those who put this into either a religious or New Age framework are making a leap into what they think the mechanism is. For instance, fundamentalists might think it's the "work of the devil" and New-Agers might think it's that we are all somehow interconnected. Either theory could be right but that's a matter of faith, not science."
>
> Prof. Jessica Utts, Stargate Scientist, University of California,

> "I've been approached by the South Koreans, the French and the British to come and work for their special intelligence gathering programs. So have the Russians and the Chinese. Since Stargate was shut down, I've had to work in the private sector and it's well paid. But I am a loyal and patriotic American. I'm an all-American girl and I just have this gut feeling that within a short time Uncle Sam is going to need remote viewers to once again carry out psychic missions vital to our national security interests."
>
> Michelle Heaton, Stargate Psychic

PART TWO: ESSAYS ON ISLAMIZATION & ISLAMIC SCIENCE
Chap. 2: Chap. 2: Mysticism vs. Sufism

> The Stargate project is an edge around mind control – about which the Russians and the Chinese are experts. Journalists should keep digging into this topic. - U.S. Army Gen. Albion Knight, Jr., Stargate Director

> There is no doubt that modern physics has encountered a new level of reality, namely, natural phenomena of a supra-logical and supra-rational order, which call for the application of another kind of methodology. [110]
>
> - Emeritus Prof. Dato Osman Bakar

As evidence of Dr. Bakar's assertion I present the following detailed excerpt:

> <u>Chapter 3</u> presents the current state-of-art of quantum teleportation physics, its theoretical basis, technological development, and its applications. Key theoretical, experimental, and applications breakthroughs were identified, and a series of theoretical and experimental research programs are proposed to solve technical problems and advance quantum teleportation physics.
>
> <u>Chapter 4</u> gives an overview of alternative teleportation concepts that challenge the present physics paradigm. These concepts are based on the existence of parallel universes/spaces and/or extra space dimensions. The theoretical and experimental work that has been done to develop these concepts is reviewed, and a recommendation for further research is made.
>
> <u>Chapter 5</u> gives an in-depth overview of unusual teleportation phenomena that occur naturally and under laboratory conditions. The teleportation phenomenon discussed in the chapter is based on psychokinesis (PK), which is a category of psychotronics. The U.S. military-intelligence literature is reviewed, which relates the historical scientific research performed on PK-teleportation in the U.S., China and the former Soviet Union. The material discussed in the chapter largely challenges the current physics paradigm; however, extensive controlled and repeatable laboratory data exists to suggest that PK-teleportation is quite real and that it is controllable.
>
> Teleportation Physics Study, Eric W. Davis, Air Force Research Laboratory (AFMC) Edwards AFB, CA., Report # AFRL-PR-ED-TR-2003-0034, CONTRACT # F04611-99-C-0025 (25 Nov 2003)

---

[110] *Tawhid and Science*, 2nd Edition, ARAH, 2008, p. 34

Robert Jahn, Dean Emeritus of the School of Engineering Anomalies Research Laboratory at Princeton University repeatedly demonstrated consistent results in mentally affecting material substances. Aerospace engineer and physicist Jack Houck, along with Army Colonel J.B. Alexander used psycho-kinesis parties in which more than eighty-five percent of attendees learned how to bend metal and plastic. This roster is readily expanded, including the teleportation of small objects in China (National Defense Science Commission of China. Hence, if any Islamized (IOK) metaphysical-physical scientific synthesis is to occur by means of *ta'wil*,[111] and for the sake of *tawhid*, I suggest we invite real scientists and authentically trained oral Traditional Scholars of *al'Nur* (*raqi'awliya*)—those who've lovingly, systematically, cogently and cognitively memorized authentic Hadith, Al'Qur'an and *fiqh*—to the dunya paddock of contemporary IOK challenges and revitalize the academic debate with purpose, facts, evidence and cogent signs as well as naturally bred, politically-incorrect veracity and intact fitrah, unpolluted by the ponerogenic taint that attends tenured salaries and post-colonial retirement packages.

In my opinion, and unless logic fails me, it was made evident by the prophet's recitation in Gibrial's presence that our *Qari"* Sheikhs carry the *sunnah* in its purest form and this by means of something called *isnad*.[112] This phenomena is not a light anthropological *cum* divinely graced achievement and deserves not only respect and honor but also scientific analysis. But for this to occur these redoubtable savants would need to exchange marabout campfires and un-globalized villages for the sake of advancing *tawhidic* perspective and urbanized cerebration. In addition, and now that it's possible, comparative observations should be made by neuroscientists in order to observe and contrast sub-cranial physiognomy and physiology with their academic counterparts of pensionable fame. We could then balance results by contrasting both cohorts with Capitalist sponsored

---

[111] "Hermeneutic interpretation... at a higher level..." – ibid.

[112] A list of authorities who have transmitted a report.

academics of Jesuit *cum* Ivy League dye or Cambridgian weave. Imagine isolating a part of the brain that prefers the abstractions of *philosophia perennis* to the remarkably factual *isnad* — now that would be scientific!

Today's academic "*Alim*" have abandoned *Qari"* ranks for less demanding but more fashionable tailoring *ala* Occidental frameworks that add the taint of Secular Humanist iconography to Worldviews that have marginalized the straightforward sagacity of *isnadis* and Al'Qur'an. On occasion, I have even heard *Qari"* Sheikhs referred to as 'backward Fundamentalists', which is certainly a Neo-Colonial aphorism indicating 'insignificance'. I can't help but wonder what Sheikh Omar Muhktar (pbh) might think of that sentiment.

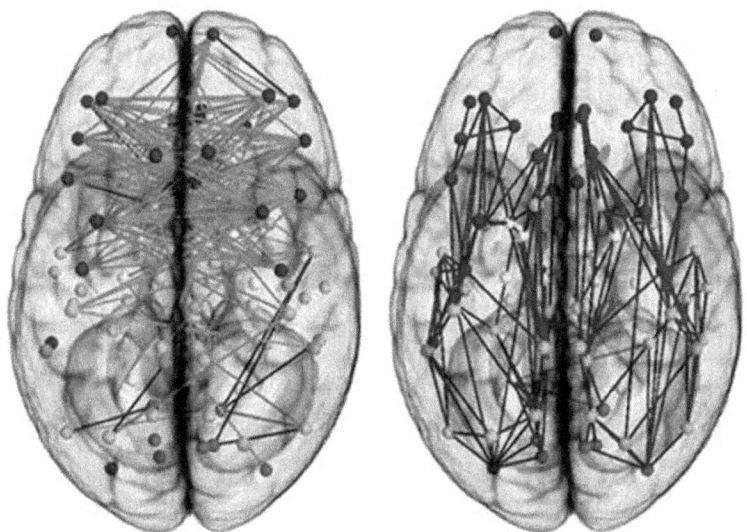

Scientists from Pennsylvania have found that the females are 'hard-wired' to be better at multi-tasking after scanning the brains of 949 men and women. Using hi-tech diffusion MRI imaging, they mapped the connections between the different parts of the brains. They found men's brains,right, in comparison, are better at concentrating on single complex tasks - whether it be reading a map or cooking a meal - and a woman's brain, left is better at multitasking.

Chapter Three

As I See It

Why Muslims Neglect the Sword of *al'Hisbah*

Beginning with the propaganda of Boy and Girl Scout iconography and moving right into the Holocaust scam,[113] the memes of the Western phase of the *New World Order* are actually culturally integrated as a continuum of Arcadian-Latin (Greco-Roman) hedonism. This ancient meme set permeates university fraternities and sororities and infuses the entire educational system for elitist oriented servants dressed in pinstripes, bow ties, stiletto heels and Ivy League sap. All of it is modeled on the Freemasonic system of privilege that attracts Jesuit intrigue[xxxvii] and serves Gnostic identity myths in the service of Hermetic magi of the Luciferian tradition. This tradition is the ancient cult of dragon royalty [114] (called 'Kings of the Earth' in both the Bible and Al'Qur'an), and was initially established by Cain & Sons, Inc. in Dravidia (the 'Land of Nod') long ago. It is the Serpent Society of Fertility Mystery Religions that included/includes Kurdish Yezid cousins, Benjamites, Danites and sundry Libertines who don capes of privilege. Most of these systems and others were taken up earnestly after the post-Babylonian oral accretion devolved to "Talmud", Halakah and "Kabbalah" by Pharisaic rabbis who later established precedents for the Eastern European Khazarian 'Jews who are not Jews'. Those pitiful creatures must not be misconstrued with the

---

[113] "The alleged Hitlerite gas chambers and the alleged genocide of the Jews constitute one and the same historical lie, which made possible a gigantic financial-political fraud, the principal beneficiaries of which are the State of Israel and international Zionism, and whose principal victims are the German people -- but not their leaders -- and the entire Palestinian people." - Prof. Robert Faurisson

[114] See the author's *Jerusalem, Sion & Zion*. A. S. Noordeen, KL, Malaysia, 2014; as well as *Cain's Creed, The Cult(s) of Rome*. ibid., 2013.

authentic cult of Bani-Israel, which, nevertheless, also abandoned its essentially Islamic origin.

The serpent cult's icons are transcendent imaginative symbols of intuition that deeply affect the human sub-conscious, such as the Statue of Liberty or the cisled stones of Mt. Rushmore. Essentially idols, they are traditionally linked to intuitive visions drawn from Fertility Cult Magicians who 'tie the knots' of cursing which the Prophet warned of when he wrote to the Shah of Persia. The Egyptian book of charms is similar and indirectly gave rise the term, Hermeneutics. Hermes, the Greek name for Thoth; the first Egyptian initiate-king whom interpolators audaciously and falsely claim was also the first Sufi Abbot, Prophet Idris (or Seth). King Thoth's blood-curdling oaths remain active in occult literature and fellowships to this day and many Hermeticists (Gnostics) still access and utilize them, thus, making claims—such as the British Monarchy's—to Adamic Prophethood patently false. The confrontation between Musa and Pharaoh also confirms this as fact as the Qur'an states it caused the repentance of Pharoah's chief magi who abandoned Gnosticism, symbolism and the practice of magick to consequently suffer tradition satanic crucifixion as per their indelible oaths. Neither repentance nor Musa saved them from the ordeal to which they were sworn.

I found the praise of metaphysical 'symbolism', therefore, as made by Muslim Perrenialists, disturbingly ascribed to the process of *ta'wil* as an "empirical direct experience of the spirit or 'unseen'. Prof. Osman Bakar goes so far as to call the highly subjective method 'Orthodox Islamic Illumination'.[115] As I recall it, 'Illumination' was one of Adam Weishoupt's—a Jesuit mole allied with Sabataens—favorite words of subversion. Professor Weishoupt also liked the word, 'dupe', a descriptive he reserved for academicians and clerics who adored symbols like the *Owl of Isis* and *Eye of Horus* or Pyramids that have since become popular trademarks in Muslim Urbania.

Before being visited by the "Virgin Mary", and prior to dedicating his army of black robes and hearts to the mother goddess in 'sworn-to-

---

[115] *Tawhid and Science*, ibid.

bleed-or-else' service to Rome's Papacy, 'Illumination' was also what Ignatius Loyola claimed as an initiate of the *Alumbrados* cult.[116] Illumination was also lauded by Baron Rudolf von Sebottendorf; the man who founded the *Thule Society* after being guided by Bektashi Sufis from the remote haunts of Marabout Turkey. [xxxviii] This particular deviant approach to non-Islamic *tasawwuf* aided Hitler's covey of occult metaphysicians (mostly Jews) as *der Fuehrer* kissed the hand of his master, the future Pope Pious XII who had secretly mentored Hitler from his young adulthood. Hitler dutifully modeled his Gestapo and SS Corps on the absolute blind-following (*taqlid*) of the Jesuit Army with Himmler's uncle (a Jesuit priest of the Fourth Vow) as its shadow director.[117] Jesuits also wrote *Mein Kamph* and one of their outstanding pupils at contemporary Georgetown University studiously penned the *Patriot Act* that launched the current pathological police state in America along with its atrocious crusade against reason—all without a single congressman having read it. I also discovered that Jesuits lent a generous hand to the *Protocols of Zion* after Medieval and Renaissance precedents. It is wise to remember that Jesuit agents don't always wear the dog collar and that the Pope has traditionally blessed both sides of dialectic militarism since Napoleon's sortie ushered the re-installation of Loyola's curs. If you don't know these particular facts of history you really should ask your Professors why? They will, most likely, not have an acceptable answer and will be tempted to dismiss you. Hence, I suggest you reserve special honors for those who don't.

> *Above all*, I have learned from the Jesuits. And so did Lenin too, as far as I recall. The world has never known anything quite so splendid as the hierarchical structure of the Catholic Church. There were quite a few things I simply appropriated from the Jesuits for the use of the Party.
>
> - Adolph Hitler

---

[116] A Gnostic cult traceable to Afghanistan; see *Cain's Creed*, op. cit.

[117] See: *The Hand of Iblis*, op.cit., for details.

PART TWO: ESSAYS ON ISLAMIZATION & ISLAMIC SCIENCE
Chap. 3: AS I SEE IT_The Sword of Al'Hisbah

This latter Illuminated phenomenon was so beloved in the Middle East that fascist fires were pathologically kindled wherever Freemasonic feet found a place to trod. These enlightened boots carried men such as Mohammad Rashid Rida, publisher of *The Lighthouse*[xxxix]—a mouthpiece of Salafiyya propaganda from 1897–1944—and a confidant of Mohammad Abduh, another colonized Freemason who just happened to "reform" Al Azhar and introduce Baring Bank riba to Cairo. These and other boy-scouts lent substantial literary hands to Lord Curzon's crew that brought down the Caliphate, which, in turn, gave Jerusalem to the British and German Kabbalist Zionists who financed Allenby's boot on Sala'u'din's grave. Lest we forget, we should also mention the Grand Mufti of Jerusalem's WWII who raised a 500,000 man army of Muslims that joined Hitler's SS corps under a satanic oath and *bayat* after which they fought and maimed and were maimed and killed for *der Fuehrer*'s cause, which they mistook for Allah's.

> SAY, `I do not say to you: I possess the treasures of ALLAH, nor do I know the unseen; nor do I say to you: I am an angel, I follow only that which is revealed to me.' Say, `Can a blind man and one who sees be alike?' Will you not then reflect... And with HIM are the keys of the unseen; none knows them but HE. (S. 6:50, 59)

Hence, I propose that illumination is dubious at best; especially now that it casts its shadow over the damnably-grand manipulation of the *ummah* to its irreparable harm. I personally suggest avoiding the term when referencing Islam's traditional dialogue.

On another front, several *surats* and *hadith* confirm that what is claimed by artisans of the improbable is actually impossible if not ridiculous unless the Illuminati "Light Bearer" Lucifer lends a hand to the divinely sanctioned miscarriage of the hierophant. Therefore, what many subjectively experience and claim or merely read about as the path of *haqiqah* (soul purification: which is an ancient Gnostic concept claiming union with the divine) leading to the illumination that permits "intellectual intuition" to perceive truth directly *vis-à-vis* symbolism as per Herrs Schuon, Nasr and Bakar, *et alia*. is, at the very best, dubious.[118]

Aside from the delusions of conceit that captured multifarious imaginations and led to Romanist sponsored genocides, we should note that none of the Muslim fellows just mentioned are traditionally trained *Alim* in the complete and time-honored Islamic sense and context. I have this on the authority of Dr. Arrifin Suhaimi (retired vice rector of IIUM, and Asst. Director of PERKIM in KL, Malaysia). He specifically related this to me personally during a conversation in 2010 and went further to mention that none of these professors of illumination can possibly measure up to the standards set by genuinely marginalized *Qari"*—a group of gentlemen they seem to have displaced from dais of honor in deference to Jesuit focused Islamic scholarship and High Tea. Bearing this in mind, therefore, the term 'academic' is a formidable scientific term that thoroughly applies in the matter.

Moving on, after fourteen hundred odd years I am compelled to ask why it is that Muslims did not continue their ascension based on Institutions of authentically guided *haqiqah* which would have granted evidence of the eminence and imminence of divine guidance and protection? To the contrary, we have the present ummah groveling at banks, oil soaked conglomerates, armies and universities funded or owned by pre-eminent *Bal Shems* of Iblis, or papist Illuminati such as the Jesuits John Esposito and John Voll, personages whom Perennialists admire sufficiently to repeatedly invite into Muslim academic and public forums.

A claim greater than Loyola's Illumination was made by the Catholic theosophist, Rudolph Steiner (discussed later). It's on rarely read public record that Dr. Steiner was once a member of a very private cult known as the Golden Dawn, a group of initiates favored by top British Royals of Lord Curzon's day and rumored to be the Rothschild's personal coven. The Golden Dawn also ushered Mr. Aleister Crowley into influential cliques and espionage circles. He was a

---

[118] *Tawhid and Science*, ibid, pp 36 - 38

disgusting sub-human and Catholic who restored the OTO (Order Templar Orientalis) as a fierce coven filled to the brim with globalists, Freemasons, crypto-Catholics, Illuminati and professional sexual predators of the highest order.

I wish to make it clear that I do not doubt the power of 'creative intuition' as divinely dispensed "wherever the wind listed" by Allah SWT to any pious *tassawuf* hierophant or freewheeling scientists like Nicholas Tesla. Nevertheless, as a prior Catholic, Anthroposophist, Theosophist, Freemason and well read student of the occult now returned to Islam's fold, I have known a number of well placed enemies of Islam intimately from within the camps of their worldview's adepts. As such, I am forced to question sources that gave birth to and nourished the Cause of *Religio Perennis* as well as the Muslim principals who promote it—folks who, to my knowledge, boast not a *Qari"*, *salihin*, recognized traditional *alim* or *awliya* in their midst.

The IOK group especially seems to initially hail from institutions founded, funded or directly affiliated with Occidental Hermeticists, Batinites, Jesuits, Freemasons, Rhodes Scholars, Illuminati filled UN Foundations, or Institutes inundated with Rockefeller, Fulbright, CFR and UN Theosophists, *et alia*; not to mention funds from our befouled and befuddled black gold-diggers of the Middle East who've made partners with the enemies of their protectorates. These groups are indelibly infiltrated by Euro-friendly intelligence agents documented to have had intimate relations with Nazis, Mossad, the CIA and MI6.[119] I am deeply disturbed by the proximity of Muslim scholars to institutions and personages of the greatest importance to societies that are professionally associated with dissecting and murdering the ummah and who wish to establish their future world capital in Jerusalem.

But neither am I calling for miracles or ghost-busting psychic phenomena. Nevertheless, rather than reams of academic brouhaha on the matter, I'd prefer to review hard evidence of Muslim superiority by means of the example of our prophet (bph) according to divine

---

[119] See: *The Hand of Iblis*, op.cit. for details

directives in keeping with his *sunnah* as promised by Allah. This should be an estate that would allow wisdom enough to prepare for war and prevail against the many incursions and insults Muslims generically suffer. This is also an estate that appears to deny Gnostic claims of direct perception of the unseen, unless Allah opens the heavens of His will rather than having the barrier breeched by human effort.

Hence again, I must ask: *Qua est is* ? Are such phenomena reserved for White Tower Shamans or for cloisters that have withstood centuries of mankind's foolishness? This is surely not an unreasonable query but I fear it is a tall if not laughable order for venerable lords of laudable Western scientific thoroughness, not to mention Muslim academics and sultans of consumption who'd rather not confront the su-peerage of marginalized Qari''. If it were otherwise, indeed, I believe Nuclear Magnetic Resonant brain mapping of authentic Imams would already have been done. Frankly, I doubt Muslim academia would dare approach such a study as it would demonstrate an incompetence they sub-consciously avoid discovering, an estate of mind which is professionally diagnosed as cognitive dissonance.

I have wasted many an hour listening to Ph.D. sophism on the Middle East from experts who are continually consulted. The only known Imam of merit in this realm who clearly understands what is taking place is Maulana Imran Hosein whom they wouldn't dare invite to London, Georgetown or Kuala Lumpur fetes for the numerous reasons I have cited above. Instead, Muslim academics roll out carpets for Madame Clinton and her Jesuit mentors while brother Imran publishes his own materials in order to more eruditely and plainly educate the *ummah* correctly because official *alim* have failed and wouldn't dare sully their politically-correct reputations by lending hand or imprint.

On another hand, non-scientists—a term that qualifies most Muslim writers on the subject of Islamic Science—are extremely slow to appreciate what I've just written due to in-bred deference to well-heeled political correctness and mind-warping abstractions that put bungalows and gold around and on their women. Unfortunately, and as experience is also knowledge, this trenchant college is permanently handicapped by the very privilege that prevents hands and gray matter from getting soiled in lab coats. Hence, their inexperience and ignorance of scientific rigor only adds to the generic disregard and disrespect for dons of authentic imagination.

Even the eminent S.H. Nasr left the study of hard science to pursue *Sophia Perennis*, a siren to whom he's been engaged for sixty odd years. Nevertheless, as encouraged by the occult lobbies of well synchronized Western counterparts, his clan of sophists continues to impress each other with inundations of comforting conjecture and easy-chair rhetoric, carefully avoiding the mirrors of authentic wisdom, hard science, and most especially the practical matters of politically incorrect action. They prefer book launches, jet lag and dining on the well connected doles of dubious sponsors. In true Jacobin style, they keep everyone's eye on Madame Sophia's abstracted wardrobe and Islam's lost Glory; which are calculated PSYOPS concerns that are analyzed below and which equate with the Emperor's new wardrobe for courts of the misguided — the result of strong delusion:

> ... in his attempt to solve the problems of an intellectual and religious nature faced by the Malay community during his time. 'Abd al-Samad perceived the basic problem faced by Malays was their confusion on the orthodoxy of the Sufi tradition as intellectually adhered to and religiously practiced by some of the Malay scholars and their followers in the Sufi orders (*turuq*). He connected this problem to two main factors: first, the lack of knowledge among the Malays on the essential teachings of *tasawwuf*; and second, scholars who suffered from self-delusion and who misled their students.[120]

> A pathocracy's ideology [e.g., Brave New World] changes its function, just as occurs with a mentally ill person's delusional system. It stops being a human conviction outlining methods of action and takes on other duties [religious?] which are not openly defined. It becomes a disguising story concealing the new reality from people's critical consciousness, both inside and outside one's nation . . . The deformed ideological systems which grew from historical conditions and a given civilization's

---

[120] *ABD AL-S{AMAD AL-PALIMBA'NI ON SCHOLARS, BOOKS AND SELF-DELUSION* DR. MEGAWATI MORIS, Pub. INTERNATIONAL ISLAMIC UNIV MALAYSIA, 2010

weaknesses should be understood insofar as they are a disguised operational instrument or Trojan horse for pathocratic infection [i.e. trans-generational propagation].

> - Political Ponerology, ibid. p. 296

The dialogues of the collective academic delusion qualify as a sport that catalyzes divorce from sounder reason and beneficial utilitarian knowledge. This always seems to initiate with persons who think they possess portions of especially reserved knowledge that empowers many pundits as Brahmin know-it-alls. Much like their Masonic counterparts, they are 'in the know' as was Rene' Gueron, a Jesuit educated, Freemason, Theosophist and freewheeling metaphysician who maintained intimate ties with papists throughout his most productive years.[121] He was, in fact, and perhaps remains, the occulted Perrenialist patriarch; a bit of an Ismai'ili analogue.

On the other hand, and as it was with the failed utopianites of the Harvard study (cited in Part One), authentic knowledge married to the reasonable activities that bring sustainable benefit appear to go wanting:

> Confucius further noted that knowledge is the innate ability to distinguish one's possession of knowledge from one's non-possession of knowledge. He also made a point which was considered similarly as important by Muslim authorities, namely, that a combination of reason and knowledge is a necessary requirement and that the absence of the one or the other results in creating situations that are either useless or dangerous.[122]

Considering also:

> The willingness of ordinary people to let themselves be guided by slogans becomes obvious at certain periods in history and is easily accounted for. However, the endurance and effectiveness of slogans over long stretches

---

[121] *The Essential Rene Guenon: Metaphysics, Tradition, and the Crisis of Modernity*, by René Guénon, John Herlihy, Martin Lings, World Wisdom Inc. 2009.

[122] Cf. Forke, *Geschichte der alten chinesischen Philosophie*, 129.

of time or the entire lifetime of civilizations are difficult, if not impossible, to calculate and to explain. [123]

"Not so," says this writer, as we are certainly capable of explaining this deleterious divorce of reason from knowledge:

> Large portions of German society ingested psychopathological material together with that unrealistic way of thinking wherein slogans take on the power of arguments and real data are subjected to subconscious selection . . . This occurred during a time when a wave of hysteria was growing throughout Europe, including a tendency for emotions to dominate and for human behavior to contain an element of histrionics . . . [the phenomenon] progressively took over three empires and other countries on the mainland . . . [We have witnessed this phenomenon with the domino effect of the so-called 'Arab Spring'. - oz]
>
> Pathocracy will always find a positive response if some independent country is infected with an advanced state of hysterization, or if a small privileged caste oppresses and exploits other citizens, keeping them backward and in the dark; anyone willing to [provide a remedy] can then be hounded and his moral right to act be [brought into] question.[124] *Evil in the world, in fact, constitutes a continuum: one kind opens the door to another, irrespective of its qualitative essence or the ideological slogans cloaking it. - Political Ponerology, op.cit. p. 280*

There is far more to the phenomenon, but let us return to the subject at hand, which is Sufi-Claimer 'know-it-alls'.

Spending one's time speculating on the unseen seems a bit useless to common pedestrians cogitators. Hence, it is most definitely 'unreasonable' and even 'dangerous' when officially sanctioned (by default) in constituencies under slogans like '1-Malaysia' as proffered by politicians who demand party loyalty rather than the justice of *al'hisbah* or the erudition demanded by *Islam Hadhari*.[125]

---

[123] Rosenthal, op.cit. 335.

[124] "The further a society drifts from truth, the more it will hate those that speak it." - George Orwell

[125] See: New Straits Times, p. 24, 2 Dec 2011.

If thus far I have offered too little to place in the coffers of taking issue, be mindful that the call of 'universalism' (i.e. Perennialism) is Catholic and that of 'democracy' is Jacobin.[126] Both sirens are traditionally used to call 'would-be' saints into temples that conform to a misguidance commonly called 'Peace on Earth' surrounded by 'love, liberty, equality and justice for all' sponsored by Ladies Sophia and Liberty. Both longed-for estates are impossible to attain and any logician worth their salt admits they cannot be had until the wicked are finally and forever corralled by the Hand of the Almighty. Peace is a call that can only be maintained as a treaty between the 'demonstrably strong' as long as their strength is restrained but maintained, nourished and handed on. And as all power rests with God Almighty, this truth and its implications were made abundantly clear when Muslims lost their strength and autonomy after nearly 800 years at the Battle of Leponto, and again after WWI. As it is, the quest for "peace" made by many respectable pundits is a call that avoids scientific clarity and real politics and clearly belies its tenders as either complicit with ponerogenic tyranny or foolish idealists.

Of course this demands a necessary confrontation with criticism and most especially calls for proofs of exalted concepts that promise unity, ethereal rewards, and daily chicken soup along with un-islamic retirement packages imported from the construct larders of Rothschild Pension Managers. Peace is a concept that suits sentimental pacifists who march, write, sing and perhaps pray or sleep asexually with young virgins [as did Ghandi] rather than courageous realists who know they must pay the price for their position and would never dream of sullying a woman's reputation and life with such nonsense. The latter are men and women who take to the field with sword in hand and/or fully expect the malefic knock on the door at three in the morning.

The *Universal Soul* of the peace seeking *Religio Perennis* cult cannot be proven in the least and thus it is fertile imaginative soil for many causes that divert our attention from the institutional evil of real politics. It keeps us wondering and talking into the wee hours as if that

---

[126] Consciously subversive Freemasonry offered by the Grand Orient Lodge of France. Some, like myself, would consider it murderously Bolshevik.

were life's purpose. The existence of this Hinduphilic imaginaire is mentioned on page seventy-five of Dr. Osman Bakar's otherwise unparalled book on *Tawhid and Science*. He claims it is a ginormous unseen entity bequeathed by Traditional Islam to Muslims as orthodox Islamic Science. — Is it? — I have read the Koran several times and seem to have missed the dissertation. It therefore must be in one of the Batinite passages my profane disposition occludes.

Distressingly, many authors by-pass Islam's classic logicians in favor of the esoteric transcendence beloved of Jesuits and their metaphysical kinfolk that subsumes Islam within folds of ecumenical fervor; which, for those of us who professionally recognize satanic agents and agencies, allows me to submit that this is the true purpose of *religio perennis* and its proponents, both witting and not. And, for the record, I fully believe Prof. Bakar, whom I love, is one of the latter.

Kali as derived from the original mother goddess, Shakti or Lilith, the consort of Iblis (Samael, from the Babylonian Talmud), dancing on her husband, the Universal Soul. Inset is 19th century Mauri War Mask, very similar to Japanese and Taiwanese war masks. Now you know where the tongue gesture comes from.

The Surrender of Faith & Reason

> In the Arab world, in the name of security, nationalism in the university has come to represent not freedom but accommodation, not brilliance and daring but caution and fear, not the advancement of knowledge but of self-preservation ... To make the practice of intellectual discourse dependent on conformity to a predetermined political ideology is to nullify intellect altogether.
>
> E. W. Said: "Identity, Authority and Freedom," in *Transition*, vol. 54, 1991, Duke Univ.

The late Dr. Said described Political Ponerology and its harmful effect on academia quite well. This approach to the advancement of 'self-preservation' and aggrandizement is far from the professed constitutions of many a Muslim business, state and institution. It is completely antithetical to IOK's "Islamic Science" platform. Indeed, such a system is Darwinian and the hominid sub-species that imposes and pursues it can hardly be described as Muslim.

In order to preserve Islamizing simulations along with the invented *isms* that pass for knowledge, many IOK confrères live in deference to High Teas funded by slogan mongers such as the 'One Malaysia' lot who've corralled 'pluralist' minions for the graft of incredibly corrupt sycophants and Anglo-centric adepts. Anyone who follows SE Asian politics knows this pretentious lot as the same folk who dropped *Islam Hadhari* like a hot durian. Need I say why? Ok, I will.

> 'One Malaysia' is a patriotic and globalist slogan while *Islam Hadhari* is, well, Islamic.

When you add patriotism to the nationalist pride of Arab or Malay Neo-Patriarchy (to be defined below) you get the following:

- narcissist sociopathy with
- a dollop of male chauvinism
- in addition to reductionism

- a distinct lack of *Bildungswissen*: the effort to improve individual personality; something relative value salesmen distinctively removed from traditional British and American models in favor of Fabian Socialism.

All of which confronts Muslims with the indelibly complex problems of repression *ala* neo-patriarchy, as labeled by psychologists and sociologists, respectively. These phenomena are usually fomented *en masse* by spellbinding ponerogenic narcissists, a condition that is infectious:

> Triumphant repression of self-critical or unpleasant concepts from the field of consciousness [cognitive dissonance] gradually gives rise to the phenomena of conversion thinking, or paralogistics, paramoralisms, and the use of reversion blockades. They stream so profusely from the mind and mouth of the spellbinder [charismatic sophists] that they flood the average person's mind. Everything becomes subordinated to the spellbinder's over compensatory conviction that they are exceptional, sometimes even messianic. An ideology emerges from this conviction, true in part, whose value is supposedly superior. However, if we analyze the exact functions of such an ideology in the spellbinder's personality, we perceive that it is a nothing other than a means of self-charming, useful for repressing those tormenting self-critical associations into the subconscious.
>
> - Political Ponerology, op. cit. p. 155

The Lebanese social psychologist, Ali Zay'our, in his analysis of the patriarchal family in Arab society, approaches the problem from the standpoint of the production of personality. His central thesis focuses on the "lostness" of the individual in the father-dominated family and neo-patriarchally organized society, as well as the denial by both of the possibility of "self-fulfillment."

> The family is relentless in its repression. [The child] is brought up to become an obedient youth, subservient to those above him—his father, older brother, clan chief, president.

The father, the prototypical neopatriarchal figure, is the central agent of repression. His power and influence are "grounded in punishment."

> The main concern is that the child be obedient, well-mannered, ignorant about sexual matters, "better" than his fellows. . . . By being compared to others to underscore his failure, he is driven to view himself negatively and to lose self-esteem (to the extent of self-punishment at times).[127]

There is no sense of the proverbial Oriental equanimity to be had in these scientific observations on the extant reality of Muslim 'lostness'.

One may focus on the *Religio Perennis* of Sufi-claimers or the Malay Scholar's confusion over orthodoxy, or the neo-patriarchal repression just described as you like, but I'm afraid it will make no difference to the *ummah's* prognosis. Judging from the un-discussed rise in Muslim divorce rates and endemic assaults on feminine dignity, which Muslim governments treat with non-to-minimal disclosure policies, I'd say there's little room for critical assessment and consequent remedy while time, resources and votes are devoted to "paralogistics, paramoralisms, and the use of reversion blockades" as personalities expire in the heated air of chauvinist induced 'lostness'. In terms of Real Politics, this translates as 'no possibility for the impeachment of un-scientific superiors' who have given lip service and useless paper to IOK for sixty-odd years.

The very least that can be done is an attempt to salvage our waning *alim* from the euphoria of utilitarian lethargy—a group whom Imran Hosein calls "pathetic". For this, the discipline of 'logic' (*al'burhân*)[128] should be reintroduced. Logic is readily entertained by hard scientists but less so by the many who enjoy paralogistic didactics based on *Ali Baba* reasoning as complimentary adjuncts to Nationalist

---

[127] Hisham Sharabi; *NEOPATRIARCHY, A Theory of Distorted Change in Arab Society*, Oxford University Press, Inc., 1988 // Ali Zay'our; *The Psychoanalysis of the Arab Self* (Beirut, 1977) (in Arabic). For a living portrayal of the father as absolute patriarch, see the novel by Naguib Mahfouz, *Bayn al-Qasrayn* (Between Two Palaces) (Cairo, [1956]), pp. 6, 14, 19-20, 58, 140-141.

[128] The science of reasoning, proof, thinking, or inference; a chain of reasoning; ability in reasoning, proof. Ox. Dict., ibid.

dialogues and the generic 'Stockholm Syndrome' that describes post-Colonial Islamia:

> The historian Hisham Sharabi uses the term neopatriarchy to describe the "absence equally of genuine traditionalism and of genuine modernity. He in fact argues that it is conditions of "neopatriarchy"—in which true tradition has been destroyed but modernity not achieved—that transform patriarchal forms of authority into authoritarian ones.[129] "Over the last one hundred years," he writes, "the patriarchal structures of Arab society, far from being displaced or truly modernized, have only been strengthened and deformed in 'modernized' forms." From families to regimes and all along the networks of fluid proto-familial patron-clientage that link them, neopatriarchal forms of relationship adapt to conditions of underdevelopment, yielding a society of *"forced consensus based on ritual and coercion from top to bottom*, one that is "incapable of performing as an integrated social or political system, as an economy, or as a military structure." - Sharbi, *Neopatriarchy*

This *"forced consensus based on ritual and coercion from top to bottom"* is a form of Nazi[130] spellbinding misdirection (magic) that throws logic into airs of suspense while magi dissect a country's ability to integrate its resources after which they focus attention on emptying its coffers while religiously obsessed madcap sectarians bicker over useless details and think they've done something for the Cause of Allah. I imagine Iblis salivates at the number of fascinated souls trapped in this trans-generational cycle. This should be simple enough to understand, but if not, the renowned Naguib Mahfouz puts it in plainer terms:

> In this new society he [the Muslim neo-patriarch] has been afflicted with a split personality: half of him believes, prays, fasts and makes the pilgrimage. The other half renders his values void in banks and courts and

---

[129] Gary S. Gregg, Foreword by David Matsumoto; *The Middle East, A Cultural Psychology*, 245.

[130] Nazi (nasi) is a term that originally refers to the President of the Jewish Sanhedrin, its Chief High Priest or Bal Shem of authoritarian Gnostic Kabbalism.

in the streets, even in the cinemas and theaters, perhaps even at home among his family before the television set.

This schizophrenic pan-dementia is the result of en-masse' hypocrisy and the self-sanctioned repression of cognitive dissonance.[131] I have been telling people to exile Jesuits and discard the television for twenty years for this very reason, for wich I've been marginalized according to principles and princi-*pals* of ponerogenesis. Alhamduillah.

Servants of Western magi among Muslim Political Parties have become expert at this con game, which describes the etiology of an essentially untreated mass psychosis or what Dr. Lobaczewski calls a 'hysteroidal society'. How then can Muslims represent Islamic Science, Islamization and their Creator under such ponerogenic influence and cunning? I propose it is time to stop the surrender of reason to *PSYOP* magicians because (i) it is clearly not the *sunnah*; (ii) it is clearly not working; and (iii) it clearly serves retainers of malevolence.

If my several positions remain insufficient thus far to stimulate reasonable doubt as to the stagnant direction Islamization policy makers have taken, I pose the following challenge. After sixty years of IOK lectures, literature, conferences, pamphlets education sorties and other miscellaneous flotsam and jetsam:

1. Where is the fruit of this purported Tree of the Sunnah?
2. Where are the new generations of *tassawuf alawyi* involved in hard science on behalf of thoroughly Islamized Institutions underwritten by independently authentic Muslim Imamates?
3. Where has action cum practicum been achieved by IOK initiatives that return dominion to the *ummah* of our prophet (pbh) minus corrupt governance?
4. Why, after all this time, are post-Colonial Muslim polities capitulating one-by-one to the planned chaos of Papist Blackwater Crusades?
5. Why do the capitalist icons of the unholy Judeo-Christian Alliance remain honored in capitals and shopping malls of Muslim nations?

---

[131] The excessive mental stress and discomfort experienced by an individual who holds two or more contradictory beliefs, ideas, or values at the same time

PART TWO: ESSAYS ON ISLAMIZATION & ISLAMIC SCIENCE
Chap. 3: AS I SEE IT_ The Surrender of Faith & Reason

This is an estate that was specifically predicted in Hadith and Al'Qur'an to the effect that those who turn to the Alliance and kiss the unholy hand for protection and provision have lost their Islam. Furthermore, this is not an opinion open for debate but much rather a statement of fact.

In order to explain this surrender of faith and reason along with the Rights of God's people, one must honestly compare present and past with the cosmopolitan verve that infuses genuine universalism. Thus we can avoid folds within the papist ecumenical garb. For this, I turn not to the lapsed glory of Islam but to a master from the Orient:

> However, Chinese and, in particular, Neo-Confucian thought, was thoroughly dominated by the idea of the inseparability of knowledge from action. In the Chinese view, action, and not knowledge, is the chief concern of the individual and of society. Action was regarded "as more important, more trustworthy, more easily grasped, or more difficult, and hence, of greater concern."[132]
>
> In contrast to the Greeks, the Chinese engage only in practical work. They are men of the active life and, therefore, do not inquire into the motive powers behind their activities. - al-Jâhiz[133]

For today's neo-patriarchal Muslims you may rephrase a passage from above as follows:

> In the ne-patriarchal Muslim view, ritual, and not knowledge or action, is the chief concern of the individual and of society. - oz

Do hard scientists of the *tassawuf alawyi* mold exist? Are Muslim scientists found only in deviant Iran or Western Institutions under

---

[132] D. S. Nivison, *The Problem of "Knowledge" and "Action" in Chinese Thought since Wang Yang-ming*, in A. F. Wright (ed.), *Studies in Chinese Thought*, 114 (Chicago 1953). Mencius had no theory of knowledge, and all his thinking was about action, cf. I. A. Richards, *Mencius on the Mind*, 61 (New York 1932). For the identity of knowledge and action or the superiority of action over knowledge in Confucian tradition, cf. Wing-tsit Chan, Instructions, XXXV ff.

[133] Rosenthal, *Technique and Approach*, 71

Illuminati governance or in someone else's spacecraft-cum 'Star Wars' weapon systems as a politically-correct tag-along in anticipation of execrable papist photo ops? Or perhaps Neo-Patriarchal Sunnis are intelligently practicing *taquiyah* while holding Muslim League Wahhabi Conferences that re-invent wheels for the 'jet-set' writing of more Islamization proposals reviewed by facilitators in Georgetown, George Washington,[134] McGill, Fordham, and Temple Universities bearing the Fabian expertise of University of London economists and other CFR friendly neo-Orientalist scholars?[135]

Let us leave this loathsome pretense behind and turn to hard Islamic science. Neurophysiology has finally evolved sufficiently to prove that both Confucius and Islam's Traditional *tassawuf alawyi* were correct. Observe:

> ... My experiments ... have taught me that the artificial intelligence model is not how the brain works. Its connections are extraordinarily labile and dynamic. Perceptions emerge as a result of reverberations of signals between different levels of the sensory hierarchy, indeed even across different senses. The fact that visual input can eliminate the spasm of a nonexistent arm and then erase the associated memory of pain vividly illustrates how extensive and profound these interactions are.
>
> - V. S. Ramachandran, *Phantoms in the Brain*, 130.

Although many readers will fail to grasp these implications, when adding neurophysiology as created by Allah (swt) to the Oxford Don who proved that children naturally believe in God, I venture to say that

---

[134] It is to be noted here that this institution is entirely Freemasonic from its foundation to present Governance.

[135] Somewhat jokingly, the prominence of the persons I have chosen to investigate, have made them a Muslim 'jet-set' travelling world-wide from conference to conference discussing the interpretation, function and future of the Islamic tradition ... they constitute a set of Muslim individuals who belong to a Muslim elite. That is to say that they are all well-to-do and they have extensive influence among other Muslim intellectuals. – "The Islamization of science or the marginalization of Islam: The positions of Seyyed Hossein Nasr and Ziauddin Sardar" - Leif Stenberg, University of Lund, *Social Epistemology*, x, 3/4, 1996, 273-87.

non-Muslims are making greater inroads towards Islamizing Science without IOK's befuddling interference. Dr. Ramachandran's findings also imply that habits have the effect of overriding percepts in order to assure that certain thoughts and actions, whether for harm or benefit, are brought about, depending, of course, on guidance and input. This indicates that Muslim neo-patriarchal fetishists have indeed been conditioned, confirming that Skinner's operant thesis wasn't far from the mark.

As I see it then, it is no small wonder that Muslims endemically avoid the following:

(a) Consequent Contemplation (*taffakur*, for which they are incapable), and hence also

(b) Righteous Action (*al'hisbah*), and

(c) Real Scientific effort, since they are habituated to injustice, fetishism and the consequent repressive thought processes that disallow logic and authentic scientific rigor.

I experienced the latter phenomenon when called on the carpet for presenting the hard science of anomalous brain sexualization and orientation at a conference that was ostensibly on Islamic Science. My paper was subsequently struck from the 'proceedings' publication without an acceptable scientific explanation and I was treated like an errant Catholic schoolboy. Even the renowned science editor who had praised and accepted the paper and later congratulated my presentation was silenced by the dean's disapproval of something this leader of a preeminent post-graduate Islamic Institution clearly failed to comprehend. I can only conclude that it is not considered Islamic for the ummah to learn that neo-patriarchal repression actually aids the increasing numbers of homosexual births. [136]

The most lamentable fact of this experience was that I was the only presenter of genuinely hard science at a two day conference on

---

[136] I refer the reader to my Book: *The Taqua of Marriage,* AS Noordeen, 2011. There you will find a complete dissertation on the matter.

'Islamic Science' attended by IOK globe trotters. Furthermore, with the help of Allah (swt), I had actually managed to Islamize the findings of modern science and relate them to *halal* treatment as recommended by the *sunnah* for women and children with regard to the immense responsibilities of husband and Muslim leaders. In retrospect, and especially after researching the material for this book, I conclude it was perhaps a bit too much *Islamization* for repressed minds to take all in one sitting. Nevertheless, and in deference to traditional fetishists who excel in ritual, a poorly crafted paper on the hygienic advantages of *wudu* was deemed perfectly suitable for *Proceedings* publication — "sad enough business", indeed.

The repression afforded the *ummah* globally by the present authoritarian neo-patriarchal order is clearly the result of mental conditioning (see: Dr. Connolly's *Neuropolitics*) as promoted by occult societies that govern the world. Meaning, of course, this is not accidental but consciously effected by Machiavellian mentors of fellows like Syria's Assad[137] or misters Blair and Clinton, which further implies that most dedicated disciples fail to perceive the misdirection. Indeed, this is far worse than the 'bad enough business' mentioned by Ibn Khaldun as it is a malady that assaults genuine scholarship daily, as per the late Dr. Said. This now validated method of ponerogenic political science distinctly follows default determinants of spiritual law as defined in Part One and can be further elaborated by modern science, most especially, cognitive neuroscience.

Quick references to historical figures that partook in the ongoing conditioning are easily identified by unaffected students of truth. An example is the wondering Jew, Al'Afghani,[138] founder of the Salafiyyah

---

[137] "On 21 Mar. 2004 at the Damascus al-Shaab Presidential palace, The Grand Magistry of the Sacred Military Constantinian Order of Saint George, which is one of the oldest internationally recognized Roman Catholic dynastic Orders of knighthood in existence, bestowed President Bashar al-Assad the Orders Highest honor of the " Knight Grand Cross of the Order of Francesco I and the " Benemerenti " Gold medal of the Constantinian order." __ a sub-Chapter of the Knights of Malta, sworn to serve the Pope. He has since been suspended. Shimon Peres belongs to the same club.

[138] 'Wondering Jew' is both aphorism and allegory identifying the *Bal Shem*: i.e., the Babylonian Sorcerer considered to hold the Seal of Solomon's power over jinn.

movement who was not only a Shi'ite (Ismaili) disguised as a Sunni, but also employed by the British. He became grand master of Egyptian Freemasonry and drew numerous Colonial sycophants to the occult lodges of Islam's enemies, including his disciple, Mohammad Abduh, who became grand master in his wake. Abduh was sheikh to Mohd Rida and both had significant influence on Hassan Al'Bana whose Muslim Brotherhood was baptized in the Freemasonic mold and financed by British subordinates of Lords Curzon and Rothschild.

The entire purpose of the Salafiyyah movement was to keep the Muslim populace *repressed* by promoting manufactured imaginations of sanctimony that allow the mirage of pride and false hope under the guise of reform. This ideology inhibited rational thought with vain imaginations, which, in turn, forbade scientific progress in addition to substantive resistance to colonial masters who readily exchanged political gowns—meaning that when the French were finished the Brits took over, followed by the Americans and now NATO—all of whom are under Knights of Malta (Gog) management crews while Oriental Dragons keep China and Russia (Magog) dangling on the periphery as plausibly dangerous. Ignorant Muslims aided and abetted this contest which destroyed Africa's Horn and handed Palestine over to everlasting infamy.

Once Arabic simpletons became accustomed to the conditioned worldview of the Salafiyyah 'reform movement', mass political manipulation and management readily followed, including raising flags of divisive sectarianism and fabricated nationalism whenever and wherever required. It really is that simple. People pre-occupied with the fetishism of sanctimony and patriotism — which are essentially neuro-political equivalents no matter the creed or state — are incapable of the truly unified resistance that threatens governing elites which doesn't include colonized pawns like Mubarak who was also a Freemason. This happens because the body politic are far too impassioned and will trip, as any mob does, over their own ignorance while trying to please the romance of God and Country as lower appetites are satiated wither-so-ever the winds of whisperers bloweth.[139] The significance of these last few statements is manifest by your reading this without having prior knowledge of these facts and methods.

The same is true of the Muslim and Whahabi Brotherhoods excepting that Hassan Al'Bana was a well intentioned unconscious pawn who was out of his depth and consequently out-finessed and out-classed in a dangerous game conducted by Occult Masters from whom he was not divinely protected, a matter for discussion by those wiser than I, but consider the following:

- His seniors (male mentors) were all Freemasons including his family and Rida's direct line to Al'Afghani's misguidance;
- The British Suez Canal Company [Rothschild Zionist Jews] gave Al'Bana the money to get started;
- When they finally drove him to desperation, he was justifiably murdered (sacrificed) and removed as head of what became 'their' society, thus becoming a useful martyr for the ongoing cause;
- After which, his divisive company was infiltrated by superior assets from the continent:
    - German spies under the Knight of Malta, Sir Reinhardt Ghelen, whose Nazis also raised the Boy Scouts of Nasser's fascist Green Shirts, and then
    - Turned their expertise towards the British and Americans as they perfected the arts of respective MI6, CIA and Mossad societies (Al'Sissi is a Jew who's uncle is a Mossad officer). If you thought these were separate organizations, you have some catching up to do. But don't feel bad because many of their operatives don't know it either. It's a secret.

Here, the proof of the indictment is twofold:

---

[139] References and elaboration are provided in my treatise: *The Hand of Iblis*.

- the present domino effect across the crescent of crises which demonstrates that the *ummah* has no protection from Allah SWT, despite any and all attempts at so-called, Islamization:
  - utilization of post WWII 'cell groups' to promote civil wars, the Godless Baath Party, revolutions and coups to exacerbate Sunni-Shia strife;
  - the helplessness of the *ummah* to withstand these insults;
  - the perplexity of the *alim* and the treachery of reoccurring and unforgiveable Muslim on Muslim murders under their auspices;
- neither the MB nor the Salafiyyah have raised their women to true Islamic status:
  - in addition to grievous insults such as honor killing at the hands of demented chauvinists, the majority of Egyptian women, for example, still undergo hideous female genital mutilation in the name of Allah.

Spare me any apology for this chaos and pietistic depravity of mind and practice that destroys womanhood, family, society, religion and nation. All of this and far more are the direct results of the magic and political science taught by Harut and Marut and the jinn of Babylon to Jewish magi and others as related in Al'Qur'an and specifically warned against in the Prophet's letter to the Persian Shah.

Reflection and activity that fixate on metaphysics, soft science, religious protocols and Shari'ah while at the same time ignore the strong arm of *al'hsbah* (Real Politics), amounts to the impotence of monkish religiosity with bizarre taboos that separate genders and denies the frank discussion of sexuality among other moral and ethical matters. The legatees of King Nimrud's Babylonian and Pharaoh's Egyptian magi depend on these instruments of repression, which is why they make certain that inconsequential OIC and IOK Conferences are lavishly funded and attended by agents who keep people talking about everything but empowerment. When one adds Universalist simulation without societal implementations that defend the veracity, strength and dominion of Mohammad's *ummah* as his vice-gerent, the sum is not only futility but worse, it becomes less than zero. This is specifically because the causes of failure are not forcibly removed or remediated due to imbalances that are readily and demonstrably manipulated. I am not alone in this opinion:

> To any that desires the tilth of the Hereafter, We give Increase in his tilth, and to any that desires the tilth of this world, We grant somewhat thereof. (42:20).

Western countries have abided by these rules: of perseverance, labor, persistent work and rational means. They employed the rules of the universe which are related to digging the earth. It is like what He — Glorious and exalted is He — has said:

> "They dug the earth and built upon it more than these (those before them). Messengers of their own came unto them with clear proofs." (30:9)

Digging the earth is fulfilled by construction and by searching for metals and water. The civilizations which preceded them drew out the treasures of the earth — and all of this is Allah's way and whoever establishes these methods will find success. Hence, the question is not about having in possession the Qur'an or not understanding it. It is about failing to follow its teachings. We are not abiding by the Qur'an which ordered us to act:

> "And say (Oh Mohammad) ... unto them: Act." (9:105)

It ordered us to renounce our idleness and to prepare our strength:

> "Against them make ready your strength to the utmost of your power." (8:60)

Yet we fail to obey the Qur'anic injunctions and put them into execution. This matter, which is obvious, is about failure and neglect.

- Shaykh 'Abdallah b. Bayyah;
Trans. by Y. Ahmed, www.marifah.net -1429 H

Hence, one readily appreciates the relationship of inaction with strong delusions as offered by the overly religious mindset, and I might add superstitious preoccupations such as the Hindu 'World Soul' and "unity with The One". Hence, I clearly state that the enemies of Islam know that as long as Muslims contemplate useless concepts such as *philosophia perennis* and preoccupations with *wudu* etc., they will neglect the prescribed sword of *al'hisbah* that is meant to destroy the activities of the Lord of Poneros (Iblis) and his followers among men. In addition, and in closing this section, my several years among Malay Muslims has only confirmed this surrender of faith and reason and the extremely clear and exquisitely sound logic of Shaykh Bayyah and other scientists cited above—as the good man wrote: "It is obvious.

Crimes Against Humanity:

Mimicry & the Humiliation of Women

> The result may not much resemble the Western ideal of secular humanism's Cultural Context of Development, but it is a modern, self-conscious reworking of tradition, and not tradition as spontaneously lived before colonization.
>
> Gary S. Gregg, Foreword by David Matsumoto;
> *The Middle East, A Cultural Psychology*, p. 36.

Muslims made more than significant contributions to the hard sciences during their years of glory. They established systematic references and exacting categorizations in most major fields of study which amount to nothing less than a concrete 'codification of science' for the first time in the history of civilization. But begging Prof. Nasr's pardon, I dare say this doesn't require science to fall under the term 'Islamic Science' any more than terms like 'Buddhist Science', 'Christian' or 'Taoist Science' would. Besides, none of the grand Islamic pens of bygone glory ever used the term.

What is more relevant is that nascent Islam's remarkably swift success was preeminently due to unity and the polity's obedience to most of the tenets of their faith, reflecting that the principles of Mohammad's Medina speech were taken to heart and practiced which is the only matchmaker for the marriage of hard and soft sciences in the bright reflection of *tawhidic* consciousness. It is this mirror into which the writer gazes. Sadly, this is not accorded consequent consideration as it is no longer the case and as such, is much too sensitive and shameful a confession for Muslim leaders to attend and correct because, as they say in the West, "MONEY TALKS!"

> With the Industrial Revolution ... the game of science became the game of the rich, in which whoever is wealthiest has the best chance of being right ... In other words, the goal of contemporary science is no longer truth but performability, that is, the best possible input/output equation. Scientists, technicians and instruments are bought not to find truth, but to expand power. This shift of attention, from truth to perfomability, has impact in

present-day educational policy ... with emphasis on skills rather than ideals. — Hussein Heriyanto [140]

Hence, in the West, morals and ethics were abandoned except for the Liberal Arts and sundry podium lip services in order to pursue utilitarianism which continues to enhance the growing global demise. Muslims, on the other hand, seem to have abandoned utilitarianism for the imagined bliss of pleasing Allah without it.

The pre-modern immoral exploitation of God's resources specifically dates to Sumer, then to Rome, and from there to the shylocks of Venice and the First Crusade in the wake of the Great Khan's Hammering of a rather impudent Muslim leadership who thought they'd achieved tenure as God's chosen. Venice was the post-decline-of-Rome capital for nascent capitalists representing the old "money engines" of Latin palatines. Its system was based on the Black Hand Mafia traditions of usury, murder, genocide, theft, cunning and the Mongolian pilferage of Eastern gold reserves with whom they had made a deal after Conti's and Marco Polo's sojourns.[141] The wickedness matured to Capitalism's monetization of mankind's worldview as Orientalists sedulously drove these interests deep into Islamia's pockets and hearts.

No doubt this is one reason 'Muslim Ministers of Religion' now qualify for the position at Cabinet level without having the credentials of a traditional *Alim* or *Qari*''. An example is the tyrant of Sarawak, CM Taib Mahmud: the gentlemen thief who headed Malaysia's chief missionary society (PERKIM) for decades. The backwaters of similar ignominious stupidity have managed to progressively marginalize traditional Sheikhs, especially since Freemasons like Mohammad Abduh and his mentor Afghani paved the way for Ikwanian ascensions. As it is now, and as prophesied by Mohammad (wslm), the worst scoundrels or mournfully ignorant mullahs and unqualified academics are at helms of state, mosque, madrassa, bureaucracy and university

---

[140] *Secularization of Science as the Problem of Humanity:* Proceedings, op.cit. p. 68

[141] See the author's book *Cain's Creed, the Cult(s) of Rome* for details

while the best of Mohammad's rather singular sect have little or no voice, power, prestige or celebrity in present-day Muslim affairs.

> The Saudi ruling family is a vast mafia of princely parasites ... the American political and media elites have purposely served them for the continuation of dishonesty and injustice in Arabia.
>
> Stephen Schwartz, *The Two Faces of Islam*

Hence, the modern marriage between hard and soft sciences implied by the terms Islamic Science and *Hadhari* can hardly progress as required under the auspice of a much discussed but poorly employed *tawhid* or gestalt synthesis. Furthermore, IOK has and will continue to follow a similar course of temporal glory as exemplified by the now failing Western Masters who surreptitiously mated modern science with Iblissian Hermeticism.[142] The reason for this is that mimicry is no substitute for obedience to Mohammad's Medina directives which contain the Principles of Spiritual Law. In addition, to gain true success, Muslims must restrain the powerful offensives of Magi who are sworn to contain the Muslim *ummah* and cause its neutralization via any means, including the already cited repression. This is specifically according to Eliphas Levi, a 19th Century Catholic Priest, Freemason, Jew and Kabalist sorcerer who also endorsed the doctrine of a 'Universal Soul'.[143]

Considering the Anglo-Eurocentric monopoly of the world's wealth by the West since the 15th Century, Muslims, Africans and sundry Asiatics became increasingly subject to "money machines" and occult fellowships by means or religious fetishism and those cited earlier by Shaykh Bayyah, which are straightforward and need no grandiloquent apology unless you're in denial. The obvious implication is that sophisticated scheming by Occidental Secret Societies aimed at the destruction of authentic Monotheism and genuine Patriarchy is not

---

[142] Many of those intimately associated with the Manhattan project were Satanists, kabbalists, Freemasons and ex-Nazi occultists.

[143] See: *The Hand of Iblis*, op.cit. for details

the main impediment to Muslim advance. To the contrary, the real reason is God's predetermined judgment according the principles of Spiritual Determinism as made evident by the Great Khan's hammer.

Disobedience and ignorance, along with collective inaction and apathy are the actual causes of Islamia's lack of competitive ambition, social demise and perennial humiliation. We may add to this litany the following: haram innovations, superstition, abundant deviations and the God forsaken murderous male chauvinism already mentioned.[144] The latter is a leverage point traditionally used by adepts of Satan to control the disobedient children of Prophet Adam because wherever you see poverty it is married to sorcery and the repression/oppression of women—something learned by Babylonian Jews long ago from the angels, *Harut* and *Marut*:

> Hijazi[145] described four main types of defense mechanisms that subjugated persons adopt to bear their shame, fear, and rage:
>
> 1. withdrawal into self (including dreaming of the glorious past and "dissolving" into family and kin-groups);
> 2. identification with authority [any authority, even gangs];

---

[144] Asghar and Mr Hussain had decided that Miss Wilson was 'a loose cannon and they had to get rid of her', Sheffield Crown Court was told. Asghar then lured her to a late-night meeting by the Sheffield and Keadby Canal near her home and stabbed her several times. One wound was seven inches deep. Rotherham Safeguarding Children Board, which co-ordinates agency work, undertook a serious case review after Miss Wilson's murder but its findings have not been published. Earlier this year, the issue of vulnerable white girls being targeted by Asian men for sex prompted Jack Straw, the former home secretary, to claim some British Pakistani men regard white girls as 'easy meat'. He spoke out after two Asian men who raped girls in Derby were given indefinite jail terms.

- 'We need to get the Pakistani community to think much more clearly about why this is going on and to be more open about the problems that are leading to a number of Pakistani heritage men thinking it is OK to target white girls in this way,' he said. Web. 21 Dec 2011

[145] Hijazi, "'Ilm al-nafs fi al-'alam al-'arabi" (*Psychology in the Arab World*)

3. mythic/superstitious control of fate (achieving an illusion of efficacy and security by protecting one's self from the jinn, Satan, and Evil Eye and by practicing sorcery and fortune telling);

4. violence (sometimes directed self-destructively inward but more often displaced outward, readily taking "paranoid" and "fascist" forms).

He argues that the whole symbolic complex by which men dominate women serves as the key equilibrium-restoring mechanism for men, as it creates an illusory dignity of exercising authority, no matter how strongly they themselves may be subjected to the authority of other men. Yet none of these defenses provide a satisfactory equilibrium, and so people typically shift among them according to temperaments and circumstance.

The Middle East, A CULTURAL PSYCHOLOGY
by Gary Gregg, Oxf. U Press, 2005, 348.

An Iranian woman, beaten every day by her husband, asked a court to tell him only to beat her once a week, a newspaper said on Wednesday. Maryam, the middle-age woman, said she did not want to divorce her husband because she loved him, the Aftab-eyazd daily said. "Just tell him to beat me once a week… Beating is part of his nature and he cannot stop it," Maryam told the court. The Tehran court found the man guilty and banned him from beating the wife, the paper said. "If I do not beat her, she will not be scared enough to obey me," the husband said.[xl]

Reuters News Agency – September 22, 2004.

You have asked what is essential for those walking on the Path of Allah … The second condition is that true and complete repentance (*Taubatun Nasuh*) should be done in such a way that [a seeker of Allah] will not return to this humiliation [of sins]. - Imam Abu'Hamid Muhd. Al-Ghazali[xli]

Humiliation is an estate we seek to escape at all costs and it is always connected with the public unveiling of some sort of failure; the greatest temporal fiasco being the disclosures of religious and sexual hypocrisy, and the greatest eternal fiasco is yet to come. To deny this is an exercise in the penchant for apologetics regarding Muslim peccadilloes, felonious traditions, pederasts, rapists, murderers and mendacious leaders as well as their standard avoidance of criticism like the true pathocrats they are.

In addition, the neo-patriarchy of assuagement, so necessary for threatened male egos as just cited, is oft joined to the vain-glorious recapitulation of a history that is punctuated by gross rapscallion predilections such as the crypto-Jewish Fatimid saga. Islam's history since the second generation is capped by the present classroom avoidance of insufferable tyranny such as the Moghul insult to India, the demonstrations from N. Africa to the 'Arc of Crisis', or Indonesia's genocide in Papua New Guinea, not to mention the Cultural Revolution that murdered more than a million Indon progressives on behalf of papal knights in Washington D.C. and local punks.

The saga of intrigues punctuated with traditional fratricides is a continuum of woe that chronicles cowardly decamps from personal and collective liabilities by throwing stones, shoes, fingers, Korans and AK-47's at others while avoiding the mirror(s) of self-criticism. This is not only juvenile but antithetical to the implementation of the moral imperatives required by Islam's venerable scientific traditions. In short, Muslims no longer qualify for the position of Mohammad's bequest. Where then is the national repentance that is required from God's people as per Imam Al-Ghazali and the Divine Sunnah such as that which King Josiah commanded of his near-reprobated kingdom in ancient Judea?

In the eyes of Neo-Colonial power-mongers and their masters who know these matters rather intimately, our envoys are little more than idiot-savants at a costume party celebrating mankind's generic pretense of dignity. Why on earth would rational, educated men-of-the-world take regents from the land of Ikwania seriously when more than 80% of their women suffer sexual mutilation as a religious rite of passage; or from lands where the threat of honor killing remains a rule of thumb?[146] It is no wonder then that Western Institutions support writers like the B'nai B'rith darling, Bernard Lewis, [147] a man who

---

[146] See: *The Society of Muslim Brothers* by Richard P. Mitchell, Oxf Univ Press, 1969;

[147] Lewis advocates following Ataturk's example, another Freemason and Crypto-Jew.

praises their dubious rationale, collateral damage sorties and imperial stealth. This is so because the occult purpose of Black Magic (i.e., the traditional *khassa* propaganda and dialogue) is to enslave any people by preventing their progress. What better method is there than to repress the status of women? Keep women uneducated and subject to repression and so go their children. In Egypt, after two solid generations of thoroughly infiltrated Ikwanian influence, women are either mutilated and repressed or liberated and set free of Islam; anything but truly Islamized.

> "There is nothing whatsoever in shari'a, ethics, or medicine to justify female circumcision." – al Ahzar, Shaykh M. Shaltut

A sizeable percentage of the *ummah* still practice this barbarism in the land of the Brotherhood — 66.2% of the educated class and 97.5% of uneducated women in Egypt suffer either complete clitoral amputation or radical amputation of the entire vulva.[148] One would think that after three plus generations of Brotherhood Reforms they'd have reversed the savage atrocity by means of the grace of Allah's guidance and upheld the fatwa.[149] So much then, for sixty odd years of IOK influence. Tell me, where is the *tassawuf alawyi* correction of the Ikwan on this matter? Ah — I see. They have a tradition to follow:

> Beginning within a few decades after the Prophet, and by the 11th Century, almost each and every principle established by the Qur'an and the Prophet—confirming the rights and status of women ... had been to a greater or lesser extent negated."—"By the early 20th Century, the ummah had been reconstituted as a series of nation-states based on the European models, not only in the political, but also in the legal, educational, economic and other spheres ... placed in the hands of secular oriented elements ... nurtured by the former colonial powers. ... A disjuncture exists between theory and practice that dominates the political process ... the overall condition of democracy and human rights in the Muslim world in general, and especially at the official and government levels of its Arab core is truly dismal.

---

[148] *The Hidden Face of Eve*, Nawal El Saadawi, M.D. St. Martin's Press, 2007, p. 50

[149] *The Hand of Iblis*; op.cit., 2009

PART TWO: ESSAYS ON ISLAMIZATION & ISLAMIC SCIENCE
Chap. 3: AS I SEE IT_ Crimes Against Humanity

- Muddhatir'Abd Al-Rahim [150]

As damning an assessment as this is, even the words 'democracy' and 'human rights' demonstrate the enemy's success:

> Prof. Muddathir speaks of "human rights and democracy". The use of such terms in their Western, liberal connotation is a common disease displayed by those who mimic secular Western frameworks. Most of them picked these terms up when they left homelands to study abroad in the lands of their colonialists. In addition and of great significance, it is no secret that such terms were coined by liberal spin masters in order to deceive and to promote their Freemasonic [Jacobin] ideas of 'liberty, fraternity and equality'. – Mustapha Karalli, op.cit.

In short and in the eyes of professional manipulators, the polity of more than 1.6 billion Muslimites is a convenient if not experimental punching bag and trough for exploitation, besides being an irritating pebble in the shoe of hegemonic capos.

Thanks to intrinsic failures and the amplification of propaganda, today's Muslims are generally viewed as anything but respectable contributors to human progress by the five billion-plus balance of earthlamites. The impunity exercised in the systematic and heartless destruction of Palestine and Iraq[xlii] and the World Bank's incessant plunder are unfathomable without acknowledging this as reality. An example of a shockingly open outrage is the mockery offered by architects such as W. S. Atkins who built the UAE's Burj Al Arab hotel with the world's largest cross facing the *ka'ba*.

If Islamia cannot defend its honor, banks, borders, built environments or women and children from internal and external ravages and public mockery under the nose of ostentatious imams,

---

[150] *The Human Rights Tradition in Islam*, Praeger, 2005, p.70, 104

what weight bears the cause of so-called "Islamic Science" in the balance of these self-evident indictments of failure and humiliation as a culture let alone religion? What world power steeped in "Real Politics" would/will entertain the diplomats of such wretchedness except for the cause of additional fleecing and the continuum of cunning mockery?

The problem is, therefore, that Muslim academics may exquisitely recite, bicker about or define any terms or phenomenon they care to trifle with under these deplorable conditions, but until they turn the tables and confront their own corruption and that of their leaders, whom they are commanded by God to keep honest, and until common Muslims wean themselves from mystic delusions and the stupidity of noncompliance with Divine Imperatives, there is God's hell to pay for these crimes against their own humanity.

Realities Confronting Islamization Policies and Pundits

In answer to awesome social problems facing Europe at the time, the Gnostic German Philosopher, Rudolph Steiner, used the term 'Spiritual Science' to describe his magnificent foray into metaphysics. [xliii] He firmly re-established Gnostic Christianity with its Cosmic Christ as a global panacea called Anthroposophy.

According to him, Christ returned to the earth's astral dimension in 1933 to oppose Hitler's mob. Dr. Steiner bequeathed initiatory exercises for his disciples to achieve an exalted state of spiritual cognition so they could meet "Jesus" (Cosmic Light Bearer or Lucifer) consciously in the astral realm. However, few of his devotees were able to enter his subjective 'higher world' milieu and repeat the same "astral" observations exactly and as scientifically as he—not unlike the many Jesuits who fail to achieve Loyola's ecstasy or Sufi-Claimers running after *fana*. In fact, it is not unlikely that Herr Steiner was schooled by Jesuits as an Austrian Catholic school boy, and this is in addition to the jinn he is known to have frolicked with as a child, like a good little hobbit.

Consequently, much of his teaching (observations of the unseen) has been dogmatized and followers voraciously devour his written word and tradition like the faithful of any cult. Dr. Steiner — an Illuminatus, Catholic and Freemason with numerous Jewish hierophants — claimed to enter and observe unseen realms rigorously and at will minus amnesic euphoria. His mystical forays resulted in knowledge that, when applied to the material world, brought great benefit and even repeatable scientific advances in the realms of bio-dynamic farming, architecture, bio-sciences and medicine and other disciplines. His work is well known among middle and upper class Europeans and others in the West, including the American *Khassa*, most of whom adhere to principles of collective socialism and the New Age cosmic Christology of Pharaoh's sun-god savior, *Horus*.

I submit that academicians and patrons of the Islamization of Knowledge School are seeking a similar marriage minus the painstaking rigor the term 'Islamic Science' implies. It is far easier to undergo jet lag in four and five star hotels while writing pabulum and signing books that have little or no effect on common taxi drivers except to allow the *khassa* to burden them further. I am bold enough to posit that the idioms, 'IOK' and 'Islamic Science', represent the evangelical banners described by T. Adorno as 'identitarian thought'. Indeed, in my view they developed spontaneously as repressive defense mechanisms for a polity on the verge of disaster in order to ease the pain of extremis. [xliv] This naturally attracted the cunning endorsement of Occidental dons of deception who are subtle tacticians of distraction (magi). These ponerogenic professionals offered ready funds to endorse the naturally and desperately befuddled 'paramoralized' [151] *alim*. Why would they do such a thing? —to keep the *alim* talking and writing rather than fighting and impeaching the extant reality of corrupt leadership and forbidden liaisons. It really is that simple. If you feel like the fool they made of you, I congratulate your chagrin because that's a great step towards repentance.

---

[151] Paramoralistic ... suggestions so often accompany various kinds of evil that they seem quite irreplaceable. Unfortunately, it has become a frequent phenomenon for individuals, oppressive groups, or patho-political systems to invent ever-new moral criteria for someone's convenience. Such suggestions often partially deprive people of their moral reasoning and deform its development in youngsters. Paramoralism factories have been founded worldwide, and a ponerologist finds it hard to believe that they are managed by psychologically normal people.

The conversive features in the genesis of paramoralisms seem to prove they are derived from mostly subconscious rejection (and repression from the field of consciousness) of something completely different, which we call the voice of conscience. Thanks to its specific psychological knowledge and its conviction that normal people are naive, a pathocracy is able to improve its "anti-psycho-therapeutic" techniques and, pathologically and egotistically as usual, to insinuate its deviant world of concepts to others in other countries, thus making them susceptible to conquest and domination. This is being very effectively used at the present time under the guise of "The War on Terror", a completely manufactured device that utilizes "false flag operations" to herd people into "support camps" for the U.S. imperialist agenda.

Political Ponerology, op cit. p. 211

Not that I doubt Muslim eschatology, but I lay these charges as a hard scientist and former metaphysician of the Anthroposophical and Freemasonic molds. I have experienced the rigor that accompanies both occult studies and laboratory science. I was a professional musician, Theosophist, sexual partner to a practicing witch, Anthroposophist, Freemason, Christian Preacher, Casualty Physician, US Army infantryman, farmer, and a biochemistry student prior to my medical degree and later reversion to Islam. These primary experiences and studies all taught me what most Muslim *alim* either do not know at all or have only read about. For example, I spoke with probably the most highly respected contemporary Malay Shaykh and Scholar (a neighbor and collegue) who had no idea of the actual practices that accompany Gnosticism's fertility cults. Now if this man did not know the ways of his enemy, what then about his peers, government superiors, and the minions who lean on his knowledge?

Another reason I foster the charge is because the term 'Islamic Science' was never used prior to 1948, which was a rather significant year of disaster for the *ummah*. Consider also that its genesis is from a Shi'ite Professor who now—like Al'Afghani—claims to be Sunni and was also a *cum laude* pupil of Frithjof Schuon, an acknowledged Catholic Areopagite and initiate of the sun-god Christology thesis so beloved by Dr. Steiner. Herr Schuon was a man whose Gnostic doctrine of *Religio Perennis* also included Egyptian Hermeticism with a tilt of the hat to Jesuit Mariolatry; a creed that subsumes all religions and demotes Islam in favor of papist ecumenicism. I can only conclude therefore, that the movement is highly suspect, especially since Prof. Nasr's seat of tenure is a Freemasonic stronghold: George Washington University, named after the 'theophanized demigod'.

It is extremely important for the uninitiated Mulsim to know without doubt that the occult Jesuit and Freemasonic histories contain the imposition and/or support of several ideologues such as Schuon to include crypto-Jewish villains like Ataturk (a Sabataen Jew), Freemasons like Abduh and his Sheikh, al'Afghani, as well as Stalin and even Rasputin,[xlv] a devotee of an ancient Dyonesian (Bacchante) cultus that spawned Sabataen hedonists. To support my reservations regarding Prof Nasr's spellbinding clan, I offer the following passage to critical thinkers from his own pen:

> On the *Survey of Metaphysics and Esoterism* by Frithjof Schuon: A Review by S. H. Nasr;
>
> This book is a veritable *summa* of traditional doctrines at the heart of which stands metaphysics. It is, in a sense, a synthesis of the works of the author written over the past half-century and casts a light of exceptional intensity upon complex metaphysical issues, various facets of man's inner life and the spiritual significance of existence itself in relation to the Supreme Principle. [152,153]

My concerns are shared by others who are gravely alarmed by the IOK movement's proximity to principals and institutions known for profound subterfuge and a continuum of post-Reformation genocides well into the twentieth century. We are also forced to ask what the author means by the subtle capitalization of "Supreme Principle" The allusion is typical of the purposely undefined, ideological-voodoo-abstractions for which Hermetic initiates and their cronies are infamous, and which Dr. Andrew M. Lobaczewski calls paramoralistic suggestions made by sophisticated spellbinders (professional sophists).

Luciferian Freemasons refer to their god as the "Supreme Architect of the Universe", and the Jesuit inner circle of the 'fourth vow' distinctly holds Luciferian Gnosticism with its 'Supreme Principle' (Illumination) at its root. Both are groups that accept the 'Universal Soul' or bisexual *Animus Mundi* of the ancient world in synchrony with the Freemasonic Baphomet and Sigil (see below). Unfortunately, their lesser members and sub-cults such as Rotarians, Knights of Columbus

---

[152] "… pure metaphysics, by which Guénon [a Freemason] means a supra-rational knowledge of the Divine, a gnosis, and not a rationalist system or theological dogma - its goal is the realization of the superior states of being and finally the union between the individual self and the Principle. Guénon calls this union "the Supreme Identity"… By "Supreme Identity", Guénon and Schuon do not refer to the personal God of exoteric theology but to a supra-personal Essence, the Beyond-Being, the Absolute both totally transcendent and immanent to the manifestation." Whatever that means? - oz

[153] *The Essential Writings of Frithjof Schuon* (S.H. Nasr, Ed.), 1986, Element, 1991

and other Boy-Scout[154] camps actually believe the phrase refers to 'God the Creator', when in fact, it is an occult designation for Satan as Lucifer the 'Light Bearer. Furthermore, the Freemasonic 'G' represents 'Gnosticism' and hence, end of discussion.

Pentagram (sigil) in the upright aspect represents the Right Hand Path of Satanism which is reserved for the marking of public institutions and their patrons who are governed by occult entities.

In the inverse position (left)it is reserved for the marking of institutions and persons governed by the Left Hand Path. Both are used for the casting of spells to bewitch the polity. Hence, I call the NWO the 'Cult of the Star'.

Marble statue of Washington sculpted by Horatio Greenough. Va. Statesman Henry Wise said "The man does not live, and never did live, that saw Washington without his shirt." So why portray him like that? Hmmmm...

Consider soberly that traditional Islamic scholars,[xlvi] whom many are wont to quote, never entertained the concepts of Islamic Science or IOK due to their consciousness of *tawhid*, which is the natural non-

---

[154] More than one-third of all recruits into Freemasonry come from the Boy Scouts.

pathologically deterred expression of *fitrah* mentioned by the Oxford Don. This inherent gift of grace inspired astounding scholarship of methodical thoroughness for both hard and soft sciences in a well balanced mix that forestalled the boredom, stagnation and deviance bred by tedious preoccupations with paramoral piety. These exalted hearts and minds neither had nor perceived need for either term and knew that the taxonomy was not only unnecessary but also unscientific. Furthermore, ordinary cogitators like myself see both idioms as implied incongruities or at least redundancies. Hence, it appears to some that the cause of IOK's Islamic Science is a patronizing undertaking of advocates in need of an identity boost who never undertook nor published hard scientific results or entertained al'Ghazali's *fana* as primary experiences. Frankly, I believe many naively succumbed to the delusion that IOK represents the real work of *jihad*. Subsequently, they have surrendered their potentials to hierophants of Iblissian finesse' who erode the fundamentals of Islam's Sword with dialogues and tomes on "Supreme Principles" and useless Islamization efforts that further advance the cause of the rather singular neo-patriarchy described previously.

I advisedly suspect, therefore, that IOK and Islamic Science initiatives are diversionary tactics employed so that Knights of Malta utilizing World Bank IFI's and NSA Economic Hit-men[xlvii] can administer customary rapine and plunder without any organized opposition from well educated Muslim *alim* with knowledgeable constituencies. The IOK and Islamic Science Institutions are so thoroughly integrated and stage-managed by occult Hermetic fellowships and worldview (think Georgetown, Rhodes and Fulbright), that while one arm plunders the other arm send's aide and re-educators to rebuild the pillaged polity's next generation in the beast's image — call it PSYOP academic evangelism.

Communism's consensus education with Learning Outcomes and Objectives is a dandy way of establishing authoritarian central committees that eliminate local autonomy. This is accomplished *via* Hegel's dialectic with Fabian cum Zionist protocols of the Yale Bonesman John Dewey, et. alia. Its reductionism entails so much preoccupation with extremely rational minutiae there is no time left for the Islamic synthesis demanded by Tawhid or to actually spend with students. This is the same condign methodology that was birthed out of Freudian madness courtesy of London's Tavistock Institute by Fabian Socialists and handed piecemeal to the Universities of Chicago and Columbia et alia[155] over the last century — methods which Muslims now follow everywhere and which obstruct the guided path of any prospective *alim* who raises his or her head in the cause of gestalt vision and local autonomy.

Nevertheless and despite of all these impediments, Emeritus Prof. Osman Bakar does offer the following defense for what he calls the 'Process of Islamization':

> When we look at literature in different languages, apart from English, Malay, Arabic, Persian, Turkish, etc., the word Islamization, as it is generally used, is applied to various things in a given context like a geo-cultural region, for example: Haribandar, the Dutch Orientalist, the specialist in Islam in South East Asia long before Prof. al-Attas, has already used the word Islamization, in this sense. He used it, for example, in his book, *The Rising of the Sun* (referring to the Japanese occupation in this part of the world). He talked about Islamization of the Malay Archipelago and that expression became the theme of Prof. al-Attas's Islamization. Certainly, he came before Prof. al-Attas, and he used the term Islamization of the Malay Archipelago. We can talk about Islamization of the Malay world, Islamization of Sub-Saharan Africa, Islamization of Central Asia, of the Balkans and so on. So people used that idiom. Of course, Islamization of a community, of a people, Islamization of the Malays, Islamization of the Turkish people, Islamization of the Sudanese, and so on: it is all valid and legitimate, meaning the term has been used for a people's or a community's application of Islamic principles. Moreover the word Islamization has been used in the context of 'worldview': Islamization of the worldview or Islamization of the Malay world-view. It has thus been used… [however], it is difficult to come up

---

[155] See *The Hand of Iblis* for details of this movement's relationship to the occult.

with a consensus on the term "Islamic." We can have a lot of agreements, commonalities, but to have one single definition, no. Thus, as for Islamicity, loosely we say conformity with Islam, etc., etc., and what do you mean by conformity with Islam, conformity to what? ...

And now, as for my own definition: Islamization is the process — of course it is a process (that's one thing we all agree on) — by which an entity (why do we use a general term entity? Because that entity could be a geographical region, could be people, could be a community, could be knowledge) — is transformed. The transformer could be the Holy Qur'an, could be the Sunnah, could be the whole teaching of Islam, it could be just some aspects of Islam...

My definition of Islamization of knowledge is that it is the process by which the whole body of human knowledge is particularized, classified, organized and systematized in conformity with Islamic epistemological principles.

— Lecture Series on the Islamization of Knowledge, ISTAC, 2007

His definition is what vexes non-Muslim scientists and Muslims like myself who've actually donned the white coat and entered modern labs and fields of scientific rigor; not that he errs philosophically, epistemologically or even historically, except for contentions that Islam has no universal definition and that knowledge is an "entity" — a disturbing concept when one reflects on its implications, especially since it managed to slip in at the end of a list of 'entities' all of which have well defined identities. It is the audacity of 'non-scientists' from a failed polity of fetishists to subsume robust men and women of science to this auspice that fosters both insult and irony.

Many lab-coated well researched and published scientists see scant justification to honor suggestions from non-scientists who hail from countries rife with parochial corruption that are completely dependent on their hard won advances and the goods and services of non-Muslim ethnicities such as Christians, Catholics, Hindus, Taoists, Confucians and Buddhists in addition to Occidentalized facilities for finance and developments owned by Kabbalists and members of secret societies of privilege that are mercilessly preying on polities they seek to Islamize in such a contorted image.

A credibility gap wells up viscerally here that is far too real to ignore if you are metaphysically awake. It is a void endorsed by "Muslim" leaders who've opened gates of despoliation while surrendering insufficient funds for the R & D required by indigenous scientists to independently compete with contemporary industries. In other words, supporters of Islamization are preaching to the choir when they should be tearing down the dais of pretense that supplies their inflated salaries.

In the words of both Mr. Harold Rosenthal (the reprobate Jew confessor) and the late Shaykh Ahmed Deedat, such spokesman have been metaphysically gelded by cunning partnerships-with and consequent impositions-of occult occidental perspectives in addition to ordinary cowardice and their addiction to the perquisites of a privileged 'White Tower' neo-patriarchy. Frankly, the mundane term, 'Brown Sahib', suits them perfectly.

In reference to Islamicity and the question posed by Professor Bakar regarding "conformity to what?", let me respond in terms that Muslims generically ignore in deference to the plasticity of soft science fetishism. This is to say, as a Medical cum Social scientist who addresses the answer in terms of neuroscience (Neuropolitics) in order to describe the human brain's natural design to thwart the hegemony of conformism.

The brain is inherently 'hard-wired' (*fitrah*) *not* to 'uncritically' adapt to the dubious interpolations of spellbinding speculation. As a matter of fact, this scientific verity is another example of the Islamization of knowledge carried out by non-Muslims:

> Again, it is not that rationalization never occurs without right hemisphere damage, but that *right hemisphere damage* both exacerbates it and gives the conformist left hemisphere hegemony in interpretation . . . the left hemisphere is conformist, largely indifferent to discrepancies, whereas the right hemisphere is the opposite: highly sensitive to perturbation.
>
> William E. Connolly; *Neuropolitics: Thinking, Culture, Speed*, Regents of the University of Minnesota & Press, 2000.

This then begs the question as to whether or not right hemispheric 'damage' or inhibition is induced by neo-patriarchal repression, propaganda, or more invasive forms of intervention such as environmental toxins and vaccines. Are there any un-gelded Muslims in white lab coats with right hemispheres sufficiently intact who remain bold enough to explore the answer as have Drs. Connolly and Lobaczewski? Of such is the need that goes begging in our *ummah*. Where are they, or have all succumbed to the left hemispheric dominance of this damnably repressive neo-patriarchy? As further hard evidence for the charge, I submit the following impressive and hard won Jesuit victory over Malaysian academia's IAIS, Prof. Dr. Bakar's think tank:

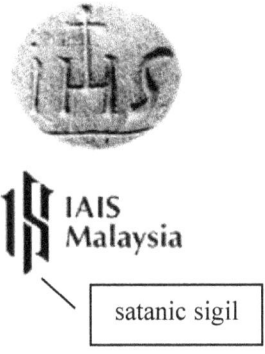

IAIS (an IOK Think-Tank for which Prof. Bakar is second in command), even sports a logo that mimics the Jesuit *IHS* with its traditional Gnostic anagram. I conclude therefore that just as the Malay ummah deserves their Sarawakian 'Pretender', so also Peninsular Malays deserve the delusion of the IAIS 'think tank' brigade and 'Twin Tower' worshippers of Lucifer who roll out red carpets for Jesuits on their behalf.

satanic sigil

Above taken from a Roman Catacomb

Anagram at left is taken from Dan Brown's *Angels & Demons*, a propaganda film that honors Templars and Rome's Curia as heroes. The Romanesque etchings specifically represent the actual nails used by Romans routinely for crucifixtions.

Essentially, the IAIS logo is a satanic sigil used to cast a spell over those who *unconsciously* honor it. How one derives IAIS from the proffered logo that abandons tradition Arabesque for the latinized Romanesque is indeed, a mystery.

The problem with Islamic Science and Islamization policy pundits is that very few of them understand the dilemma and many who think they do have abandoned the Traditional Islamic Dialogue to good but insufficiently educated men like Nick Aziz of Malaysia's opposition party. This lot favors liberal versions of the Prophet's religion (pbh) ala Prof. Nasr and IAIS-friendly Jesuit initiates like Fr. John Voll or Prof.

John Esperanza, who "think the entire globe is a Conference hall chaired by the West ..."[156] Well then, is this not the same antithetical-anti-Islamic hegemonic pluralism that attends globalist mania with Hermetic plans for a UN mandate and World Government with its headquarters in Jerusalem — 'chaired by the Zionist-Friendly West' of course? Isn't this ancient mystery religion the very reason Allah (swt) had our beloved Prophet change the *Kiblah*?

To briefly highlight the quintessential impasse just described, I remind us that Islam's traditional scholars of the Classical Age painstakingly indexed knowledge into two general categories under the heading of *ilm*:[157]

(1) the study of religion;
(2) the study of the human body and the world or cosmos in general;

This is to say: revealed knowledge, metaphysics and both the micro- and macro-cosmic hard-sciences.

They did this specifically according to the Prophet's instruction[158] and yet scholars such as *al-Razi*, *al-Biruni*, *al-Tusi* and *al-Farsietalia* had no need of the term, 'Islamic Science'. Today, however, in the midst of endemic ignorance of the true nature of the global political order and its history, as well as sectarianism and apathy towards the extremely hard work of scientific rigor, perhaps the need for the term has arisen in order to re-invigorate an errant polity and its woe-begone educational institutions. It could well be that a proper approach and perspective will counter-balance the last five hundred years of decline under extremism, Orientalist intrusions, interpolations by crypto-Jews and Jesuits, as well as the mystic impetus inspired by the endorphins of euphoric amentia, political rallies and the degenerate nihilism of the

---

[156] Bernard Lewis, John Esposito and Gilles Kepel, A Comparative Study: *Al-Shajarah*, ISTAC, 2010, v. 15, No 1.

[157] Arabic for knowledge and or science

[158] ISTAC Conference *Proceedings*, Ibid, p. 213

de-personalizing pop-occulture exported by the West and adopted by the East.

> For the decline of science, it is said that the tolerance towards science which was the orthodoxy of early Islam had been changed from the time of al-Ghazali (d. 1111 A.D.). This tolerance gave place to the persecution of the study of science because it [allegedly] led to the loss of belief in the origin of the world and in the Creator."
>
> 'Science and State in its Power and Weakness',
Muhammad D. Batayneh [159]

This is certainly not to blame the eminent al'Ghazali but rather the fans of the illusory *fana* cult who followed and misapplied his doctrines much as materialists did with Newton's work.

Hence, the question is: "What is the proper approach to the Islamization of Knowledge and dissemination of Islamic Science? I pray God to answer clearly, concisely and unfortunately, pessimistically in the next section.

---

[159] *Proceedings*, Islamic Science and the Contemporary World, Conference at ISTAC, KL, Jan. 2008. Pub. ISTAC, IIUM, 2008, p. 125

The Titanic Dilemma

Authentic Pedagogues, Reactionaries and Enemies

Prof. Batayneh's conclusion was fairly distasteful to those who refused to renew his contract at ISTAC-IIUM in KL, Malaysia. These are the same folks whose appointed representative called me on the carpet for presenting real science and later refused to renew mine as well. These predominantly Whahabi funded pundits claimed Dr. Batayneh was too old, despite the fact that he looked and acted ten years younger than many juniors and had just taken a second wife with great zest. The truth is that if I had had the choice, I would have chosen him as my father.

The cause of Islam's decline is similarly ironic because the same attitude had previously enveloped Christianity in the Darkness from which Muslims rescued it.

> Investigation of natural phenomena is superfluous and beyond the human mind, and the learning and study of these matters are impious and false.
>
> - Eusebius, c. 340 AD Church Historian

> Let us Christians prefer the simplicity of our faith which is stronger, to the demonstrations of human reason. - St. Basil

... etc, etc. *ad nauseum vobiscum*. The residue of this same deplorable sanctimony is now thickly varnished on the left cerebral hemispheres of Islamia's minions. Many deem religious ritual (God's Rites) and the practice of mouthing the 'remembrance' of God as sufficient exercise of their birthright; a moronic pedagogy of the Catholic specialists, which, no doubt, is reason enough for Salafis, Becktashis and Wahhabis to be welcomed within Romanist folds of the World Religious Parliament. This reminds me of the experimental innovation conducted by the Mogul Ali Akbar who ushered all creeds to his posthumously failed ecumenicist state — and sure it was that Jesuits resided there as well.

Prof. Muddathir Abdul-Rahim had this to say about the necessity for authentic Islamization:

> ... [Muslims] need the systematic development of a holistic understanding of the various branches of knowledge – including scientific enquiry and technical know-how – in which, consistently with the teachings of the Qur'an and the *tawhidic* world view of Islam, the material and spiritual aspects of nature and human experience will not be seen as dichotomous modes of existence but as a seamless continuum. [160]

Kudos, indeed. My second response, were I faculty recruiter, would be to offer top salaried positions to Muslims already trained in the desired disciplines and then insulate them from the monstrous brigade of pretenders. This would, of course, mean giving them incomes above that of bean counters who manage banks and the Datos, Datuks, Tan Sris, Tuns and Sultans of the let's-pretend-we're-producing-and-doing-something-of-worth mirage.

While I agree with Prof. Mudhathir, I see little need to develop another circus of pseudo-Islamified pedagogues lacking robust aptitudes for scientific rigor. Furthermore, the concept of *tawhid* cannot be assimilated without the work and actual street experience of obedience in relation to the principles of Mohammad's Medina Speech or the practice of *taqua* as exquisitely defined by the metaphysical sciences of Islam. This naturally implies that people who've done nothing but sit in White Towers are hardly qualified for the task. Besides, why re-invent the wheel rather than assure knowledge is taught in a balanced and scientific manner and correctly so by the 'knowledgeable' (meaning 'fully' rather than 'religiously' educated Muslim), and then adhered to as Al'Qur'an copiously instructs under officers dedicated to *al'hisbah*? If this were done, I am certain that countries such as Malaysia, Yemen and others would experience little Muslim brain drain, being mindful also that the Baghdad Academy was truly international and not a 'Muslim or Arab Only' club.

Such an approach would actually require dismissing and/or retraining the majority of teachers who presently think they're qualified because they have adopted British or American pedagogy. Mimics of the West create nifty boxes, cunning exam questions and

---

[160] *The Role of Governments*, ISTAC Conference Proceedings op.cit., p. 182

lovely flow charts with well defined goals and outcomes. Nevertheless, I assure you there is no *tawhid* found in such a non-synthesis reductionism as the persistent lowering of international standards annually reflects the reality. Quite to the contrary, one should scientifically conduct appropriate screening and streaming of student populations towards marks of excellence according to individual human capacities via assessing the several kinds of human intelligence given to each by God's grace. This cannot occur within folds of a centrally controlled and conditionally operative faculty conformed to curriculums that foolishly reward only one kind of intelligence. There were at least seven types of human intelligence the last time I counted. That was years ago when I was slogging the front-line trenches of American Emergency Rooms filled with the casualties of a failing nation and educational system. Contemporary research has increased their number:

> Gardner (1999) defines an intelligence as "biopsychological potential to process information that can be activated in a cultural setting to solve problems or create products that are of value in a culture" (pp. 33–34).

> According to Gardner, there are more ways to do this than just through logical and linguistic intelligence. Gardner believes that the purpose of schooling "should be to develop intelligences and to help people reach vocational and avocational goals that are appropriate to their particular spectrum of intelligences. People who are helped to do so, [he] believe[s], feel more engaged and competent and therefore more inclined to serve society in a constructive way."[161]

As stated previously, non-Muslims are indeed making greater Islamic contributions to knowledge than the entire IOK lot put together. Hence, they need to be accessed and engaged by a cosmopolitan *ummah*.

---

[161] An informal talk given on the 350th anniversary of Harvard University on 5 Sep 1986. *Harvard Education Review*, Harvard Publishing Group, 1987, 57, 187–93.

Our school systems presently educate and reward only two or three of these God-Given gifts of intelligence while the remaining majority is marginalized and hence, psychologically demeaned (i.e. repressed) which is neither Islamic nor scientific. It is, however, a *neo-patriarchal* norm that favors collectivist morons, the new post-modern, Muslim worldview standard.

The primary intent for developing MI (Multiple Intelligence) theory was to chart the evolution and topography of the human mind, not to prescribe educational practice. Nonetheless, MI theory has been discussed widely in the Educational field and has been particularly influential in elementary education, where it has provided a useful framework for improving school-based practice in the areas of curricula, instruction, and assessment... it offers an approach to intervention that focuses on strengths instead of deficits. By the same token, it extends the concept of the gifted child beyond those who excel in linguistic and logical pursuits to include children who achieve in a wide range of domains.[162]

Our Education System

"Everybody is a genius. But if you judge a fish by its ability to climb a tree, it will live its whole life believing that it is stupid."

- Albert Einstein

I venture to say some gifted Muslim scholar developed these same concepts to greater heights quite some time ago and that a present day student rediscovered them only to be ignored in the lemming run towards Western Cliffs of mimicry. I imagine also that Muslims have been far too preoccupied with ritual fetish and 'saving face' to either translate the treatise or take its content and student(s) seriously.

---

[162] Brill Encyclopedia of Education, 2004, p. 1200

Furthermore, in the present milieu of reductionist mimicry and politically correct brinksmanship, I imagine it would take another generation of IOK conferences to even broach the topic.

The retraining of teachers is what actually took place during the first two hundred years of Islam's infancy — minus IOK conferences and naturally so. It necessarily preceded the scientific explosion of the third century and beyond. Sadly, however, the present tolerance for professional inadequacies promotes repression rather than competence, especially so judging from what I've experienced in the academic domain of self-promotion, bribes, favoritism, plagiarism and outright intellectual property theft, etc. When we add these to the *ummah's* submission to Occidental governors whose ghastly gauchos of greed will never permit authenticity to inseminate, let alone flourish, I fear the prescriptions for authentic Islamic remedies will never be filled. The generic heedlessness and sectarianism of Muslim polities and policy-makers continually checkmates the process of *Islam Hadhari* so that the exercise remains little more than window dressing for cronyism, Ali Baba payoffs[163] and appointments, as well as politically-safe rhetoric — what I call propaganda mills for recycled humbug.

> And keep your soul content with those who call on their Lord morning and evening, seeking His Face; and let not your eyes pass beyond them, seeking the pomp and glitter of this Life; nor obey any whose heart We have *permitted to neglect* the remembrance of Us, one who follows his own desires, whose case has gone beyond all bounds. — Al-Kahf; 18:27

The ostentation of "Pomp and Glitter" both gelds and gilds the *ummah's* institutions and though many call on their Lord ritually they immediately join the ranks of *"permitted neglect"* by ignoring the corruption cited while inviting the counsel of enemies and imbibing the

---

[163] I have personally seen Muslims offer contracts based on >50% kickback payments to bureaucrats who grant the awards, which, after expenses and other such favors, in one proposed program would have left only 15-20% of the original award available for actual contractual servicing. I was once refused a contract because I would not agree to making a payment of 30% of the gross award to the granting institute's president.

forgetfulness of crossing bounds into globalism's Conference on Paradigm Drift with the West as Chair.

According to Prof. Wael Halliq, the communal worldview that once defined and characterized Muslim Society was one that palpably permeated the general public with a profoundly inherent awareness-of and submission-to implemented *Shari'ah* as opposed to the present swamps of accretion and neglect of justice. Professor Halliq claims that this communal perspective and attitude are what provided Muslims with the cohesive *elan'vitae* that allowed the sciences to robustly advance with vigor, morality and dignity. Everyone and everything was 'Islamic' without the designation and, hence—except for heresy mongers and crypto-magi like the *Ismai'ils*—there was little need for questions of split-hair Islamicity to arise. Alas, we may collectively lament the loss of implementation consequent to a consciousness that is soundly thrashed by today's dim lights of extremism, secular encroachment, material reductionism, moronic approaches to ritual, and artful dodgers of truth and obedience seated on dais of power and mammon. These circumstances are endemic, so much so, that Prof. Muddathir's recommendation and this quiescent diatribe must of necessity fall on a sequence of incompetent auditors, metaphysically gelded cowards, politically correct automatons, or marginalized truth seekers and doers. Under these conditions, the fact is that authentic Islamization can only occur as far from the urban urbane as possible: meaning amongst communities estranged 'from it all' exactly as the prophet (pbh) prophesied.

What significance does the term 'Islamic Science' have in such a corrupt milieu? I have read several articles on the hotly contested term and have yet to come across a serious characterization of the idiom that withstands criticism or confronts inhibiting corruptors head-on. Nevertheless, I will give it a go. Since Islam is a term that denotes peaceful submission to Allah SWT's absolute regency, and since science denotes the systematic study of the universe and all it holds—which does not include Allah SWT or His essence, (whatever that is) since He is indefinable and transcends creation and human cognition and comprehension—the term 'Islamic Science' may be succinctly defined in its gestalt sense of *Tawhidic* expression as:

> The 'systematic study of the universe according to divine command; including inherent, observed, and revealed knowledge.

This implies that non-Muslims may partake in the enterprise and that Imams attempting to describe Allah would be better off seeking improved living standards for their charges. In addition, the definition requires that leaders who support the cause need to shape up to Sala'u'din standards [xlviii] or resign before the grave cashes their reward checks and invites the boots of General Allenby's successors.

'Inherent' means those limited faculties and attributes with which things and creatures were/are created; observed means what we are capable of learning; and 'revealed' means knowledge as related by the Prophets. The given definition avoids speculation, redundancy and contradiction while at the same time admits the contemplative inspiration that is *taffakur's* attendance to authentic *tasawwuf* implied by the word 'study' rather than monotonous mantras leading to amentia or the dementia of jinn infestation, or the provisional imaginations that induce endogenous endorphins that are more powerful than morphine.

Nevertheless it will raise objections from non-believers in Allah's regency over mankind and creation, and create disquiet in the split-hair fogs that govern ruminations for Islamicity pundits who favor the Universalism of Romanist Patricians and sundry pantheist heart-throbs dressed in Ivy League comfort. In response to any doubt or unease, I can only say that, except for the Black Arts of Hermeticism and Lamaism behind which tree pagan kabbalists hide, all scientific queries man assumes are Islamic whether we admit it, like it, or even fail to describe the fact. The only qualifiers absent are human consciousness and the application of man's will: meaning the utilization of knowledge acquired, that being the conscious actualization of Islam's tenets by means of *adab*, which is the practice of justice that requires putting everything and everyone in its or their proper place according to traditional Islamic epistemology. Hence, I agree there with Prof Bakar but also reiterate that knowledge alone is insufficient for the task, which brings us full circle to honor the Confucian ethic of correct action.

The latter appears to be the authentic challenge and qualifier for man's benefit rather than loss. Furthermore, since half of the venue for accomplishing Islam's comprehensive practicum (*deen*) is marriage, and since Muslim marriages are increasingly at risk, this socially scientific indicator alone indicts Islam's Imams as dismal failures at true guidance or IOK, especially since the Islamization of Practice (IOP), rather than Knowledge, is what our societies truly need. In addition, and as if that's not enough to consider, of what use is any 'direct perception of the 'Supreme Principle' to the farmer or native who has lost land and income to speculators, or to women and children whom our leaders continually fail to protect from the unaccountable Muslims who abandon them without succor?

But let us not stop there in our discussion of neo-patriarchal futility and the grand psychological defense mechanism (projected conversion disorder) of IOK. To illustrate the empty-headed implications of the term 'Islamic Science' for extrinsic observers, consider the sub-science of Physiology, which is the study of the functions of living organisms and the interrelation of their parts. [xlix] This discipline is entirely Islamic in as much as it seeks to describe and comprehend the bio-dynamics of created organisms, all of which function according to the Word of Allah. Therefore, and despite the bias of religious belief imputed by the term 'Islamic', Physiology is inherently Islamic and needs no academic fetishist taut to remind us of the fact — reason enough for classical scholars never to have conceived the idiom to begin with.

There is indeed mammalian physiology, ichthyo-physiology, ornithyo-physiology, invertebrate-physiology, even jinni-physiology I imagine, but surely there is no Islamic, Christian, Buddhist, Hebrew or Taoist physiology excepting what proceeds from the anthropogenic perspective and teleological references defining what might be modified of an existential nature as a result of respective religious practices. Albeit, even these altered states of modified being are Islamic in as much as the guru's physiological state during trance or fasting, for example, is completely subject to Allah's preordained laws and limits.[l] The significant inference here is this:

> It is the individual human observer, the disciple, who needs Islamizing rather than any discipline or knowledge bank. After all, the Prophet (wslm) did not bring the Koran to birds, bees, fish, trees or rocks.

Of course this requires re-building the observer's worldview from the ground up which is the purpose of Islam's social venues. This consequently causes social scientific observers to bear in mind that marriage, family, market and community (including governance), in fact comprise 100% of the *deen*'s venue rather than madrassa, masjid or White Tower. Hence, and again, I and others perceive that the need for the term's advent since Prof. Nasr's 1948 thesis stems from the following reasons:

1. ideological manipulation on the part of Occult Sponsors [li] – as was the case with Darwin's *Origins* and Rousseau's '*Noble savage and Utopia*', both of which were used to promote anarchy and idealism;

2. Identitarian reactionism on behalf of those who feel obligated to defend a civilization that has lost its dignity and dominion because of moral, ethical, academic, religious, fiscal, scientific, social and political degeneration and decadence.

Both reasons give cause for grave concern and both have apologists. Furthermore, both give additional momentum to Western hegemony since reactionary responses are phlegmatic fronts that characteristically avoid real change in order to protect the status quo, which is the essence of neo-patriarchy. Magi know these matters well and hence created conservative parties with Luciferian values and Liberal oppositions with overly tolerant values that either independently and collectively cannot be balanced no matter how many 'laws' are passed, fists are pounded, or occupations mounted. There is no middle ground to be had in this approach to democracy which means that Muslims pursuing democratic solutions have been thoroughly hoodwinked.

With regards to the first charge, the reader must understand that the current practical use of Hegel's Dialectic proceeds from the Hermetic consortium that comprises a Satanic elite who preside over every significant institution of governance and education in the West, East, North and South. Is this a conspiracy? Of course it is. They do this in order to control consensus building on both sides of any issue or war and thereby assure management of the outcome either way. If the latter possibility appears lost, they induce chaos and start all over with whoever survives. A well known precedent is Lord Rothschild's manipulation of the London Stock Exchange via his machinations of both Nelson and Napoleon in the events leading to Waterloo. This standard Roman procedure, ala Julius Caesar, was adopted by Jesuits and other cults who've inherited ancient pagan crowns. It is the only explanation for why it is that Wall Street Jews funded both Hitler and Stalin or why Jesuits educated Karl Marx, Stalin and Clinton, not to mention Fidel Castro.

On the other hand, reactionism is not without apparent justification or idealist defenders:

> Probably, this Islamization would not be necessary if there were no secularization of science in the modern world. Again, the Islamization of Science would not be so urgent an agenda, if this secularization of science did not create dangerous threats or even destructive effects on the pillars of faith ... and we believers feel threatened theologically by these secular scientific theories ... therefore, the Islamization of Science as a form of naturalization should be done to minimize the negative impacts on the religious system and thus protect it from a complete ruin."
>
> Mulyadhi Kartanegara [164]

A key word used by Prof. Kartanegara is 'threatened'. The only reason the 'best of all *ummahs*' would feel this way is because they have

---

[164] Op. cit. p. 158

actually lost their faith by not realizing it through correct action. Hence, they are no longer the best and have adopted defensive posturing in order to aid the denial of sin; which means that the *ummah*, rather than knowledge, needs to be Islamized all over again. But since *Islam Hadhari* is no longer politically correct or better said, fashionable, this is an unlikely occurrence and defines the dilemma. People require Islamization, not knowledge! One could call this the RIOU Movement, or Re-Islamization of the *Ummah* in order to counteract the NPOU or Neo-Patriarchization of the *Ummah*. Both acronyms better reflect reality than does IOK.

Perhaps IOK contemporaries assume the role of reformers or agents of a much needed renaissance, and if so I applaud the intention but firmly criticize the focus and question their source of inspiration. Pursuant to the grand falling away from dominion via the demerits of heedlessness that were followed by an allowance of progressive Occidental infiltrations, I reluctantly agree that Muslim reactionaries may actually help forestall 'complete ruin' as a defense mechanism. Yet I insist, and will attempt to establish that there is a far greater priority than the religious tagging of any body of knowledge.

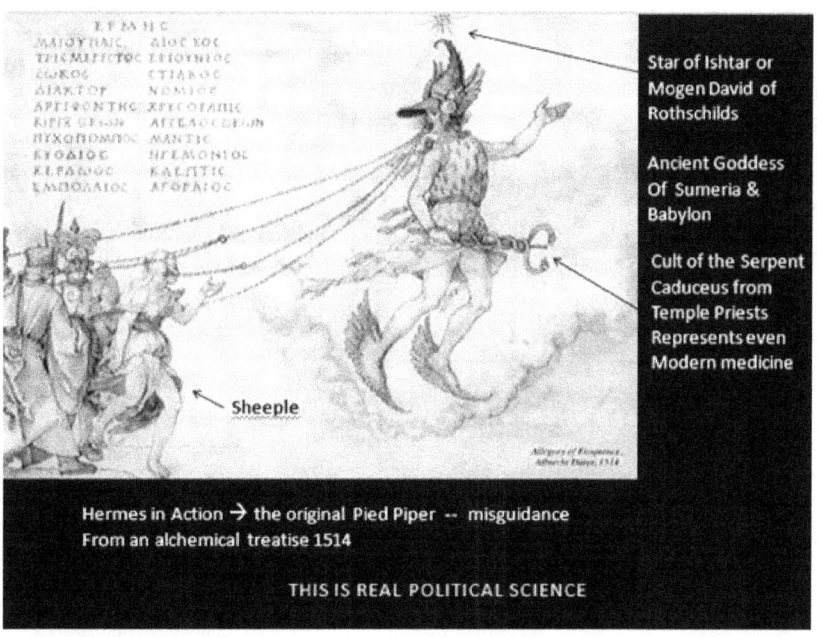

The Masquerade of Authenticity

As established above, physiology needs no Islamic adjective, neither do astronomy, physics, chemistry, mathematics, etc. etc. These fields are all inherently subject to *Al Musawwir* (SWT).

Nevertheless, there is indeed a colossal need for Prof. Muddhathir's 'holism' (Goethe's 'gestalt' worldview)[165] that requires progressive curricular adjustments towards the reflection of *tawhid* [166] in creation, though I dislike the term's 'New Age' implications. What holism implies is *akhira* or mindfulness of the continuum that exists between mind, body, spirit, cosmos, here and Hereafter. This is an approach that transcends and effaces the dichotomy of physical and metaphysical as manifest in the dependent unity and diversity of God's visible and purposeful Word of Creation and Command. Such an advance is reflected not by any delineation of a reduced curriculum, but rather by a teacher's heart to heart presentation of knowledge with regard for man's accountable post-mortem estate and the absolute inter-relatedness of all creation. In other words, it is, once again, man who needs the re-awakening of the childlike *tawhidic* consciousness he was born with rather than recycled treatises filled with rhetoric about bygone glory, dizzying categorizations and unreachable star-filled programs.

Specifically it implies that Islam need be actualized as the relevant and necessary solution for humanity's perplexity it is meant to be. As

---

[165] A configuration or pattern of elements so unified as a whole that it cannot be described merely as a sum of its parts.

[166] tawh'i^d (Arabic) The declaration that Allah is One. This constitutes one of the most fundamental beliefs in Islam, but the details of God's unity have been debated extensively by theologians. Many saw al-'asma^' al-h'usna^as attributes of God and indicating great complexity in His unity. The recitation of Q. 112 is held to be the starting point for understanding the unity of God.

discussed in Part One, this is best done in one's native tongue rather than the *lingua franca* of Muslim League Tartufferie. However, and despite the following observation, it also requires a corrective political surgery that dwarfs any concept of renaissance, which is why both Imam Mahdi and Prophet Isa (Jesus) are scheduled to end the present mask of authenticity:

> ... Islam is capable of providing a broader framework to eliminate the negative effects of secular science. It can establish sacred-religious science accommodating man's need for knowledge and science. Islam has a profound epistemology, which is appropriate for overcoming skepticism and relativism ... it has rich resources and great authority for the establishment of ethics and codes of conduct for scientific enterprises. — Hussein Heriyanto [lii]

A most excellent assessment, but for this to occur it is absolutely mandatory that Muslims repent of the moronic denial[167] of their neglect of Islam's personal and relational tenets of behavior regarding social welfare. This means that the extant "ethics and codes of conduct" Dr. Heriyanto so knowingly cites require activation rather than conferences and that, furthermore, for the effort's success, they must be applied first of all to leadership. This is a call that mandates the Imamate described by Imam Hanbal and obviously necessitates war since most contemporary leaders are far more than just reactionary: they are in league with Western Imperialists.

But since (i) war is an absurdity in a vacuum of authenticity as presently hedged in by awesome Iblissian encroachments and revolting Muslim ignorance; and since (ii) rebellion is forbidden as long as prayer

---

[167] <u>Denial</u> is refusal to acknowledge the existence or severity of unpleasant external realities or internal thoughts and feelings.

<u>The ponerogenic reality of human denial (repression of truth):</u> ". . . Invariably, when we analyze negative psychological attitudes, we always discern an affirmation which has been repressed from the field of consciousness. As a consequence, the constant subconscious effort of denying concepts about existing things engenders a zeal to eliminate them in other people." *Political Ponerology*, op. cit. p. 239. — Here lies the seat of persecution and even genocide.

is upheld; the only option is for *Alim* to have courage enough to stand at Friday prayer and ask Allah to impeach NATO-loving Kings, Presidents and Libyan traitors or aptly named Syrian *terrorists* among others. Imam Nik Aziz, a Malaysian Opposition leader, did this with regard to the country's mainstream political parties. Nevertheless, in the lack of such valor and oppositional unicity, it seems Allah SWT has seen fit to defer the triumph of truth until the iniquity of denial and pretense are fulfilled, whereupon traditional *Qari"* will announce the advent of Mahdi in Medina as prophesied; a moment that clearly delimits the futility of Islamization policies.

Meanwhile, those who stand above the corn should try to awaken the *ummah* as best they can to the clear and present dangers of Occidentalized enmity and enemies. They must be treated as such as commanded by the Prophet. Presently however, many *alim* are mesmerized by the requiem of "progress and its comforts". I used the term 'requiem' because the so called "progress" of modern (secular) science as accompanied by Romanist Universalism—the former being divorced from spiritual values and the latter being the Luciferian creed of ancient Babylon—only facilitates the acceleration of mankind's morbidity. The latter fact is patented by the multiplicity of modern illnesses, anti-social maladies and environmental havoc that have accompanied the most radioactive and barbaric century men have ever known. This wickedness is like the fuel rods in Japan that have dissolved into the earth, which implies that the post-Fukushima era holds little promise of improvement. And since "progress" is Islamically defined as 'success both here and hereafter', those who laud and submit-to the materialist dissolution without obedience to Allah only hasten their demise and that of their constituencies.

Such people develop cancer along with the modern infirmities of family dysfunction while heaping booty and conspicuously consuming the causes of environmental degradation and accelerated morbidity (decay) of all types causing dementias, neurotic dysfunctions, chronic immune disorders, anomalous sexual orientation and sociopathy. All of these are ponerogenic, being the direct consequences of inverse determinants of spiritual law that initiate default misguidance and judgment when mankind submits to the heedlessness of abject appetite satisfaction. Indeed, a 'bad enough business'.

Many are charmed by accolades for the pretentious achievements of deviant cultural norms that forgo clear thought as they contravene common sense, truth, and the genuine purposes of Islam under auspices of Hermetic icons such as the Star and Crescent or the red-white-and-blue banners of the Judeo-Christian Alliance. British Zionists chose Malaysia as a model Islamic State because malleable Malays are exquisitely amenable to such foolishness as their culture is habituated to denial, nepotism, religious fetishism and superstition — extremely fertile grounds for profitably civil ponerogenesis. This divorce of authentic Islam from both consciousness and practical implementation reflects the spiritual paralysis of ignorance joined to a malevolent psychic grip that causes premature entropic processes that mime the final separation of body and soul, and negate success in the Hereafter.

There is a titanic dilemma facing believers and non-believers in Allah's regency, both scientist and laymen. I will attempt to describe it because I disagree with Prof Heriyanto's implication that a sacred-religious science can be easily re-established because science does not need to be Islamized. To the contrary, it is scientists and those who fund and attend the results of their work (governance) that need Islamicity according to Sunnite principles of the Imamate. This should be the real focus of any effort to apply the term 'Islamic Science' to the contemporary insanity that's masquerades as authenticity. I believe that the most effective way to do this is by dropping IOK public campaigns in order to focus on management and leadership as do Jesuits who have successfully globalized their papist agenda in this manner. Banish them from your realms and dispense with rogue scholars and political appointees, and then re-educate or replace refractory teachers with well paid Islamized professionals and the polity will follow Islamicity guidelines as a natural matter of necessity. Why? Because Islam, like poneros, flows downhill; it is the sunnah.

If this were possible (which it is not), the sciences (knowledge) would automatically fall into place and pious step with little effort, just as they did previously in third century Islamia. This is an Islamization process that necessarily begins at the top of today's rather heedless pyramids of power. It is also a course of treatment that requires more time than it appears we have left, seeing it's 800 years since the Khan's Hammer destroyed the Abbasid edifice from which Islam and its sciences have never fully recovered and to which lands the Bush bunch and Blackwater Knights revisited for their own occult purposes. With regards to the latter, one must realize that Saddam Hussein was rebuilding Babylon after having thrown the Jesuits out in 1969.[168] Furthermore, Babylon is (a) a place where Talmudists took a thousand years to perfect their black arts, and (b) it is also a re-building project Allah said He would never again permit (see Isaiah 13:20).[169]

Frankly, I'm afraid it's too late for an Islamic renaissance but that doesn't mean we shouldn't make the attempt. Moreover, though the West could surely benefit from the sacred sciences of authentic Islam, there is little sense in trying to persuade them to do so when our leaders and polity fail to earnestly practice *al'hisbah* and the principles of Spiritual Law.

---

[168] Joseph MacDonnell. "The Jesuits of Baghdad: 1932-69." Web. 26 May 2003,

[169] Of note here is that conflicting OT prophecies suggest that Babylon must be rebuilt in order for its final destruction and utter desolation. Hence, the Magi of the NWO Consortium may wish to re-establish its ancient prominence after which Prophet Isa and Hadrat Mahdi will be sent to intervene. But it could also refer allegorically to the NWO's global control.

Real Political Science and the Resting of My Pen

> "The highest kind of jihad is to speak up for truth in the face of a government that deviates from the right path." [170]

> ... "If any of you sees something evil, he should set it right by his hand; if he is unable to do so, then by his tongue; and if he is unable to do even that, then within his heart-but this is the weakest form of faith." [171]

In concert with the Jesuit–friendly 'Occupy Movement' of the Guy Fawkes parody, Muslims claim that Zionist Bankers, Neo-colonialists and Uncle Sam's whiskers are the cause of their ongoing misery but this is the mere conversion disorder of psychological projection that invites ponerocrats to continue their reign. As an avoidance mechanism, it defers the pain of truth common to the self-delusion cited previously by utilizing neo-patriarchal constructs that cling to imaginations of Islam's 'Golden Age' which are so closely associated with the IOK movement. I am not alone in this opinion:

> "Genghis Khan awakened Islamia from its mirage of grandeur. The Mongol invasion came from the East, the Crusaders from the West. The two invasions exhausted the different abilities of the Islamic world. They impeded any plan for Muslims to recover from their declining situation. The Mongol invasion especially, had destroyed all the aspects of Islamic civilization, and brought an end to the Abbasid Caliphate of Baghdad."
>
> - Prof. Dr. Muhammad D. Batayneh, [172,173]

---

[170] Abu Da'ud, At-Tirmidhi & Ibn Majah, on auth. of Abu Sa'id al-Khudri

[171] Muslim, on auth. of Abu Sa'id al-Khudri

[172] "Science and State in its Power and Weakness." *Proceedings*, Islamic Science and the Contemporary World, ISTAC, KL. Malaysia. 2008. p. 128.

PART TWO: ESSAYS ON ISLAMIZATION & ISLAMIC SCIENCE
Chap. 3: AS I SEE IT_ Real Political Science

The words "declining" and "mirage" were used by Prof. Batayneh to describe the metaphysical reality. The fact that the Sultan murdered the last of three delegations sent by Ghengis Khan after dishonoring the first two is indicative of today's monitored educational system. I recently spoke to a group of Islamic graduate students from an ostensible IOK university of religious fetishism who were shocked to learn the truth of the matter and wondered why their professors never discussed the crime. Indeed, "why" is the pertinent question to which there are only two answers: denial and ignorance. Hence, we can admit that the 'decline' and 'mirage' of Islam continues.

To appreciate this as a statement of fact, please recall that the Keys to Jerusalem were handed to the unpretentious Hadrat Umar, a man who would abhor the ostentation that marks the bloated bellies and mentation of today's Imams. The horrific Mongol chastisement parallels but surely does not exceed the current permitted scourges on the continuum of Muslim dissembling, which further implies that contemporary sins exceed those of former generations. The lesson of this unpleasant historicity is that nations repeatedly suffer utter destruction,[liii] not because God gives His hammers to Khan's of chastisement, but because those who claim His favor arrogantly neglect His commands. Such disregard invites the intrusion and recurrence of nemesis because it autonomously attends the inverse determinants of Divine Imperatives as outlined in my opening chapters. Divine imperatives unquestionably embrace what I've called "The Rights of God" as a call to duty men cannot escape. When these rights are unattended in social practice, harm is the only possible result, both here and hereafter. This is authentic political science.

The Body Politic of Islam is a 'Living Organism' created and established by Allah SWT. Neither is it created or established by men.[liv] It cannot be imposed as a political institution any more than democracy can be foisted on a herd of elephants or monogamy on a

---

[173] NB: About 8% of Eurasian men, from the Pacific to the Caucasus, are the Great Khan's direct *paternal* descendents (approx 16 million men). This does not include those sired by his army. See *American Journal of Human Genetics*, March 2003.

lion. It simply is or it isn't by God's grace according to obedience and disobedience, respectively. This is to say that Islamic polities prosper in health or wither in malady according to the compliance of their constituencies to divine law. When the illness of neglect descends, the arrogance of pride ascends. Accordingly, this invites God's abhorrence and intervention by means of previously given Words of Divine Command. Furthermore, it cannot be treated artificially with programs, parliamentary decrees or self-styled reformers because there is no force in religion. The sooner Muslims realize this, the sooner they will exchange apology for repentance in pure fear of Allah SWT. The only remedy is that which is administered by Allah's grace in direct response to man's submission to critical truth.

Surely, we can study the polity's components and come to an understanding of its inherent qualities, institutions and mechanisms, and on occasion we may even apply the surgeon's knife or balms of admonishment; but Islam cannot be artificially inseminated, cloned, compromised with philosophical interpolations, boxed in curriculums, or restored to sentient potency by human effort. Its viability and authority as a Godly nation can only be divinely bestowed on obedient subjects who practice stern vigilance in the pursuit of all science. There can be no comprise of this necessity. No excuse or denial. With the help of God, Islamic governance may be inherited by the next generation by means of traditional Islamic education minus sanctimony and the cunning manipulation of Fabian pedantry. If you do not understand the last statement, it is another indication that you are ignorant of the wiles of Islam's enemies.

Alas, 'if the salt has lost its savor what good is it'? [iv] The potency needed for spiritually healthy reproduction depends upon salubrious leadership and the vigor of any Godly polity depends solely upon submission to His Will and not the traditions of half-educated imams who kow-tow and kiss the hands of sententious politicians and inscrutable sultans of dubious merit:

> A fourth major problem which obstructs the growth and development of research and advanced scholarship in Muslim countries today is the general lack of freedom and the all too frequent interference in academic

and scholarly institutions on the part of government and security forces. It is this, coupled with the paucity of financial, moral and technical support that has driven—and continues to drive—thousands upon thousands of scholars and scientists out of their homelands ... leading them to find both professional and personal fulfillment elsewhere.[lvi]

— Muddathir Abdel Rahim

How many times must 'Hammers of God' fall upon the Baghdads of Islamia before Muslims learn this lesson well enough to maintain genuine integrity rather than feign it? As far as this writer can see, its tainted polity needs gestalt soul laundering before collectively venturing abroad once more as mankind's "scientific" answer to perplexity.

The examples given of Divine Laws and their inverse determinants should suffice to open a metaphysical laundromat for Muslim chamberlains and chambermaids to entertain cleansing dialogues on the rapacious heedlessness and mind-boggling hypocrisy of their present leadership and selves. The talk of rising to World Class status in league with World Religious Parliaments of Maltese, Georgetown and Constantinian Knights of Occidental Academia and Governance is a whitewash over the pall of Muslim corruption and appeasement. I tremble at the thought should Allah permit this before granting the grace of collective repentance and authentic Renaissance.

In addition to the ancient occult conspiracy I've briefly introduced, what many socio-political Muslim "scientists" ignore is that they are lost in a maze of fabricated arguments on behalf of regimes that lie, lie, lie and then prevaricate while so-called "Royals" are shoved down the throats of beguiled worldview consumers. Authentic social unity, muliti-culturalism and pluralism are found only when the freely acknowledged leaders of a people come to agreement in cosmopolitan congruence minus vain imaginations. Where are they?

> On the Difference between Nation States & Empire: The Nation State is an *imagined* community to the extent that culturally and/or religiously salient symbols and narratives are manipulated in ways that lead often disparate peoples to accept the proposition that they have a unique

heritage that establishes them as a clearly defined and bounded community, the borders of which are co-terminus with those of the geographic space of the nation state. This is what distinguishes nations from empires, which define themselves as political and economic, but not cultural realties.

Java, Indonesia and Islam, Mark Woodward, Dept of Religious Studies Arizona State Univ., Springer Dordrecht, Heidelberg, London/NY, 2011.

Considering then:

(a) that 'just governance' as held by most balanced cogitators fails to countenance the bricolage of such fanciful imaginaires in

(b) partnership with untruths that veil iniquity;

(c) and that answers to my queries are only to be found in un-fabricated historcity alongside Divine Revelations as manifestly approved according to the highest faculties of logic;

to which Worldview is attributed the purest streams of untarnished truth or wisdom? In closing, and before answering this exquisitely divisive question, let us explore an analogy.

NATURAL MUSLIMS

Indigenous tribes may be described by some as peoples who lack science. Though they lack the technology that presently qualifies the term 'Modern Science', these peoples often practice the sciences of politics, ecology and sociology quite well with effective and efficient mechanisms that obviate modern bureaucracies. Few damage their environments as irreversibly as have progressive relatives under banners of 'modern science', and their intra- cum inter-tribal institutions of conflict resolution were generally of such a nature as to cause the least harm while bringing the most benefit, which is an Islamic principle of Shari'ah law. Many such groups demonstrated knowledge permeated with the gestalt consciousness reflecting eternal and imminent accountability, if not 'Islamic' specifics prior to the arrival of the "White Man's Burden'. In brief, they possessed wisdom ranging from elementary to profound levels of cognitive appreciation that streamlined executive function. Such peoples may be considered 'Natural Muslims' minus the more exquisite details and revelations that now identify the well defined way of life known as Islam.

Most of these cultures rationally believe in a singular Creator or Supreme Being (as opposed to Nasr's "Supreme Principle") and a God without partner who sent messengers to mankind. Native Americans were almost unanimously monotheist and prayed to 'The Great Spirit" and were conscientiously mindful of the 'Hereafter'. And from whence came this knowledge with its grace of wisdom? Indeed, they were born with the universal instinct Muslims call *fitrah* — a faculty my father called 'common sense' — meaning they were naturally born Muslims in keeping with the findings of Oxford's Dr. Justin Barrett cited previously. They also had prophets and exercised reasoning according to knowledge gained from revelations followed by intuitive contemplation, observation, and experience.

> Prophet Muhammad(s.a.a.w.) said, "No babe is born but upon Fitra (as a Muslim). It is his parents who make him a Jew or a Christian or a Polytheist." (Sahih Muslim, Book 033, Number 6426)

> In Soorah Al-A'raaf, Verses 172-173; Allah explained that when He created Adam, He caused all of Adam's descendants to come into existence and took a pledge from them saying, Am I not your Lord? To which they all replied, " Yes, we testify to It:'

The Divine order of Patriarchal governance was prevalent in most of these cultures, albeit some, like the Lakota, were balanced by matrilineal laws that avoided the unscrupulous amassing of wealth. Together, in well-balanced governance that avoided neo-patriarchal extremes by including the feminine perspective, these men and women administered their societies and environments while maintaining internal and external integrity. Thus, they preserved the *dignitas* of creation with the naturally ordered harmony inherently found in a *tawhidic* worldview, one that embraced creation's interrelatedness, inter-dependence and relevance regarding man's accountability and the afterlife. One might easily call this balance 'naturally Islamic'.

Indeed, the social structure and inter-tribal laws of the Iroquois Nation were so laudable that framers of the American Constitution incorporated many of their devices. This gives evidence of the more than adequate vicegerency of indigenous wisdom, despite some of the savage practices they employed such as scalping (which was actually imparted by French trappers, most of whom were Jesuit trained) that were—and still are—darkly eclipsed by Caucasians.

What ensued when the two cultures collided was a clash of world views in which materialist (Christian schizoid-god-men) perspectives dictated the terms of war according to calculated genocidal fury: the result of "spite and arrogance" as defined in Al'Qur'an. Despite their 'modern science' and predominantly 'Christian' Religion – which was anything but Monotheist when compared to the Ebionite polity of James the Just of first century Jerusalem – the mass murder and extinctions of native nations bears witness to a Catholic Euro-centric narcissism that frankly manifests fascist impunity and can be directly attributable to Deist doctrines, Jacobin Liberty Sirens, and male chauvinist governance despite its cloak of democratic equanimity.

This Aryan ethic may in turn be attributed to the Freemasonic superimpositions of its Babylonian/Egyptian cult on the Christian façade. An example of this invasive and subtle power is shown by the trans-generational occult gesture shared by men of ostensibly different creeds seen below:

The mass murderer Mr. Wilders (left) is not only a Talmudic Jew of the pretentious Aryan Ashkenazi cult, but also a Freemason.

Indeed, E.W. Said concluded that Orientalism was naught but Christian Evangelism, and evangelism has been esoterically governed by Freemasonry since the 18th Century as I've established in my book, The *Hand of Iblis*. All of these permutations have pagan roots in the ancient sun-god Mystery Religions under the auspice and worship of god-men heroes and goddesses rather than the Absolute Deity of professed Monotheism. In short, the Anglo-Amero-Eurocentric polity is governed by ignoramuses and hypocrites of the highest order who've rejected Allah's guidance in lieu of their own lusts, pride and arrogance as described in Al'Qur'an. While publicly professing secularism, their plutocrats secretly practice a well documented Luciferian cultus while darling apologists such as Mr. Silverstein, write as if what I've just related never happened:

> ... the majority of Islamic legal sources, and the earliest and most prestigious of them, advise Muslims to practice their faith with the assertiveness of a dominant religious culture. Therefore, what many Westerners might perceive amongst practicing Muslims to be an intransigence that hinders neighborly relations, or a general unwillingness to adapt their faith to the current cultures of non-Muslim countries, may be explained with reference to the course of Islamic history.
>
> *Adam J. Silverstein; Islamic History, A Very Short Introduction*, Oxford Univ. Press, 2010, p. 136.

Other writers are more realistic when discussing the West:

> The treatment of the hapless race of native Americans, which we are exterminating with such merciless and perfidious cruelty, [is] among the heinous sins of this nation, for which I believe God will one day bring [it] to judgment. — President John Quincy Adams

Indeed, this judgment has arrived. The Euro-centric imposition of this Hidden Hand of reprobate paganism adapted to pseudo-Christian morals has replaced any imminent sense of social accountability with an impious ethic best expressed as "the ends justify the means;" a theme hammered into Jesuit dogma by Ignatius Loyola that is accompanied by the real-politics of "might equals right" (ala Machiavelli) in Huntington's CFR sponsored call to another crusade.

> Pathocratic leadership believes that it can achieve a state wherein those "other" people's minds become dependent by means of the effects of their personality, perfidious pedagogical means, the means of mass-disinformation, and psychological terror; such faith has a basic meaning for them. In their conceptual world, pathocrats consider it virtually self-evident that the "others" should accept their obvious, realistic, and simple way of apprehending reality. - Political Ponerology, p. 231

These pathological doctrines are not found in genuine Monotheist scripture and we should bear in mind that Loyola was a Maranos-Jew who, along with Machiavelli, represent the traditional Roman mythos; an ideology that can hardly be described as either Christian or monotheist. Their sub-human ethos is held in common with all bullies as currently played-out by occult Bolsheviks who have actualized the 'Protocols of the Elders of Zion',[174] which comprise core principles for Nazism and as well as Adam Weishaupt's Illuminati and the Maltesean system of Freemasonic upper degree Initiation in their intimately related cults. Furthermore, let it be known that the groups just mentioned represent no more than an outer crust of the ancient demonism of the Serpent Cult (Sons of Cain) that lurks behind the

---

[174] The "Protocols of the Elders of Zion" is now well known to have been a hoaxed attribution to Jews.** However, the contents of the Protocols are clearly not "hoaxed ideas" since a reasonable assessment of the events in the United States over the past 50 years or so gives ample evidence of the application of these Protocols in order to bring about the current Neocon administration. Anyone who wishes to understand what has happened in the U.S. only needs to read the Protocols to understand that some group of deviant individuals took them to heart. The document, "Project For A New American Century", produced by the Neoconservatives reads as if it had been inspired by the Protocols. - Political Ponerology, op. cit. p 186

** They were, however, drawn out of Freemasonic French Lodges early in the 19th century and interpolated by a playwright. Furthermore, it is also well known that these Lodges were founded on Cabbalistic doctrine and frequented by Jews of the Frankist cult, which speaks for itself as to origin. In addition, Jesuits used similar tactics in the 17th and 18th centuries to attack others. See, *The Hand of Iblis* for further details.

residue of their mania as mentioned also by Jesus when he addressed the Scribes and Pharisees, calling them 'vipers'.

These elitist doctrines of Occidental political science as amended by neo-con wolves define the vices cited by Al'Qur'an as characteristic of the 'type three' humans I discussed in the Prologue. Despite rhetoric to the contrary, these attributes saturate the Western zeitgeist and surely have not stopped there as a result, thanks to Orientalist evangelicals, as per Dr. Said and PSYOP Cultural Warfare. They have permeated the halls and hearts of education, political, social and military sciences East of the Nile since Napoleon's Egyptian sortie, and have been accompanied by a generously exported sub-culture of moral chaos and dissipation, which describes a purposely prosecuted cultural war, as per Jesuit sponsored Rasputins, Sabataens, and Lords Curzon and Macaulay. This is not to say that their approach to modern-science, any more than classical-science, is dissolute etc., but it directly implies that the utilization of the knowledge gained under the auspice of such a benighted worldview can in no wise be justified as moral as defined by Islam or Goethe's ethically responsible gestalt perspective as practiced by Native Americans and other indigenes.

Nevertheless, it cannot be said that any science, excepting that of the divinely forbidden metaphysical black arts, is un-Islamic as science has no allegiance other than to whatever truth its methods and methodologists reveal. The law of gravity is not a conscious soul-imbued entity with a heart for understanding. It simply is. And so also are all scientific laws and/or facts of creation or inventions discovered or devised by men. A sword and gun have no cognizance. It can only be said that men and jinn are moral, amoral or immoral; ethical or an-/un-ethical, normally cognizant or pathologically inclined and thus impaired. Hence, whether people are Islamic subjects or un-Islamic outlaws of the Divine Imperatives is where we focus the crux of the matter under discussion.

If the majority of men and jinn are temporally unaccountable outlaws (i.e. un-Islamic, which, unfortunately, includes a majority of Muslims), and by virtue of pure reasoning quite incapable of discerning what is beneficial and harmful, then from Whom or What have such creatures outlawed themselves? The only answer is from Allah (SWT) according to the divine diktats of Holy Scripture and Prophetic examples, and the only unadulterated Holy Scripture is Al'Qur'an. And since, as a matter of confirmed bias I refuse to entertain polemics on the matter, I will simply move on with this as a given fact.

Conclusion

If (i), the truth of mankind's ultimate accountability is clearly delineated in Al'Qur'an; and (ii), the ancient Prophetic legacy was bequeathed to the *Qari"* by Mohammad (pbh) but rejected or not activated by the majority of mankind and Muslims; how can their collective knowledge be suffused with wisdom enough to acknowledge, seek and activate the purpose and pleasure of the Creator? More relevantly: how can such men consequently activate the cognition of rational and intuitive reasoning towards the utilization of knowledge that forbids evil action and enjoins good action as the result of scientific enquiry? In short, this empirically qualified estate cannot exist under conditions of endemic mental aberration which the Qur'an calls *insan* — i.e., the forgetfulness of Allah (being in loss) defined as the default status of Principle Three described in the opening chapters. Therefore, and in contradistinction to the commonly accepted and disarming definitions offered for the term 'Islamic Science', it is the *hearts* and *minds* of men that must be Islamized in order to presage a renaissance of Islamicity as it once was during Muslim infancy. The corollary here is that without the effective office of *al'hisbah* in the affairs of men who profess Islam, IOK is a useless construct.

In addition, since the traditional Islamic discourse has an ongoing history of some 1400 years plus, it is highly unlikely that such a knowledge bank needs re-Islamizing, which also makes IOK an irrational redundant collective for academics intent on re-inventing the wheel.

These conclusions demand that the habits of a sober and well defined 'Remembrance of Allah' (religion) must precede and permeate a society wherein the establishment of scientific disciplines are to occur in order to validate correct moral applications of the latter's fund of knowledge. This was also the conclusion determined by Ibn Khaldun who called the absence of Islam's *deen* "bad enough business." Unfortunately, the several processes of authentic Islamization are divorced from the current majority who consider themselves Muslim and unanimously neglect Principle Two, The Law of Obedience, in heinous ways. Activated obedience demands right actions as called for by Buddha and Confucius and eclipses the maintenance of ritual prayer, which, on its own, constitutes fetishism, a detestable substitute for submission to Allah SWT via righteous action. In addition, the current engagement of Islam's Academia and Imam's with ecumenical universalism belies a profound naiveté tainted with treason that represents surrender or partnership to/with Luciferian minions as clearly described in Al'Qur'an.

Hence, we surely do not need Islamic Science so much as we need Islamic Scientists and Leaders as defined by the three principles extracted from Mohammad's speech on his entry to Medina. As opposed to IOK, which is now a slogan worthy acronym of semiotic magic, a better way to accomplish Islamization is to place power, wealth and knowledgeable (*alim*) under the governance of authentic Muslims of the highest caliber. Therefore, if you're a sincere Muslim with your hand on the gauntlet rather than a dubiously conditioned patriotic heart, you now know what needs to be done. However, since such a feat is far from the hearts and minds of those who attend power, gauntlets and wealth, the entire exercise of writing and reading this book as an act of *jihad* is purely academic. Consequently, on this point, I rest my pen.

Appendix I

On Transcendence
Neuropolitics: Thinking, Culture, Speed

William E. Connolly
Pub., Regents of the University of Minnesota & Press, 2000

Apperception in explanation, recognition in morality, expression in aesthetic judgment—the Kantian models of explanation, morality, and aesthetics invoke in different ways an inscrutable supersensible field prior to consciousness that regulates its operations. The introduction of the transcendental field enabled Kant to devise a creative strategy to protect Christian freedom and morality from the corrosive effects of the Newtonian science of mechanics he also endorsed. The crucial move is "to ascribe the existence of a thing so far as it is determinable in time, and accordingly its causality under the law of natural necessity, merely to appearance, and to attribute freedom to the same being as a thing in itself." The Kantian supersensible field thus subsists below the level of consciousness and above the reach of modification through scientific knowledge, moral decision, or technical intervention. Such a philosophy enabled Kant to disparage naturalists such as Epicurus and Lucretius for sinking into a metaphysical dogmatism that pretends to know the "thing in itself" and for anchoring ethics in something as crude as the sensible realm.

But what happens if we set the half-second delay not in a supersensible domain but in the corporealization of culture and cultural inscriptions of corporeal processes? What if many messages flowing between multiple brain regions of differential capacities in the same person are too small and fast to be identified by consciousness but are, nonetheless, amenable to some degree to cultural inscription, experimental research, and technical intervention? Does this open a door not to disproof of the Kantian transcendental and proof of the alternative but to a contending interpretation of the transcendental field that moves closer to Lucretius? It may be that Kant's identification of an inscrutable transcendental field is profound, while his insistence that it must be eternal, supersensible, and authoritative in the last instance is open to modification. To contest the Kantian reading of the transcendental field, while appreciating that some such field is inscrutable to those implicated in it, is eventually to call into question both the Kantian images of thought and morality and the images of those neo-Kantians who often proceed as if they can avoid such a field altogether. Neo-Kantians tend to reduce arts of the self to "therapies" to deal with neuroses or blockages in the powers of normal rationality, recognition, deliberation, and decision, rather than ubiquitous exercises, tools, and techniques helping to shape thinking and sensibility in profound ways.

The key move is to translate the Kantian transcendental field into a layered, immanent field.

> If the unconscious dimension of thought is at once immanent in subsisting below the direct reach of consciousness, effective in influencing conduct on its own and also affecting conscious judgment, material in being embodied in neurological processes, and cultural in being given part of its shape by previous inscriptions of experience and new experimental interventions, then several theories of morality, ranging from the Kantian model of command through the Habermasian model of deliberative ethics and the Rawlsian model of justice, to the Taylorite model of attunement to a higher purpose in being, may deserve active contestation.

From the vantage point pursued here, some of the above theories systematically underplay the role of technique and artistry in thinking and ethics, while others overestimate the degree to which the cultivation of an ethical sensibility is linked to an intrinsic purpose susceptible to general attunement or recognition.

Appendix II

On The Universal Soul

Man's individual soul plays a crucial role in the perfection of Universal Soul. Because of Nasir-i Khusraw's premise that individual souls are actually a part of the Universal Soul (and not merely a trace, athar), each individual soul is instrumental in moving the Universal Soul closer to its perfection. This is achieved through individuals carrying out religious duties (the shari/'at) and through the souls using their individual intellects to gain knowledge. The doctrine of the soul is thereby shown to be at the center of Nasir-i Khusraw's cosmogony, ontology, epistemology, soteriology and eschatology.

> Title: "Nāṣir-i Khusraw's doctrine of the soul: from the universal intellect to the physical world in Isma'ili philosophy"; Physical Description: vi, 235 leaves, bound. Issue Date :1992 Description: Department: Middle East Languages and Cultures. Thesis (Ph. D.), Columbia University, 1992.

The Pythagoreans taught that the soul is a harmony, its essence consisting in those perfect mathematical ratios which are the law of the universe and the music of the heavenly spheres. With this doctrine was combined, according to Cicero, the belief in a universal world-spirit, from which all particular souls are derived.

> Maher, Michael, and Joseph Bolland."Soul."
> The Catholic Encyclopedia. Vol. 14. New York:
> Robert Appleton Company, 1912. 26 Feb. 2010

The Rosicrucian concept of the World Soul — the First Manifestation — corresponds to similar conceptions found, in various forms, in most of the ancient occult teachings of the several great esoteric schools of philosophy. In some philosophies it is known as the "Anima Mundi," or Life of the World, Soul of the World, or World Spirit. In others it is known as the Logos, or Word. In others, as the Demiurge. The spirit of the concept is this: that from the unconditioned essence of Infinite Unmanifestation there arose an Elemental and Universal Soul, clothed in the garments of the most tenuous, elemental form of Matter, which contained within itself the potency...

The symbol of the Cosmic Egg, of which the World Soul is the Animating Germ, is a very old one, and one widely spread in usage in the ancient world. As a prominent occultist has said: "Whence this universal symbol?

APPENDICES
II: Universal Soul

The first manifestation of the Kosmos in the form of an egg was the most widely diffused belief of antiquity. It was a symbol adopted among the Greeks, the Syrians, Persians, and Egyptians. In the Egyptian Ritual, Seb, the god of Time and of the Earth, is spoken of as having laid an egg, or the Universe. Ra is shown like Brahma gestating in the Egg of the Universe. With the Greeks the Orphic Egg was a part of the Dionysiac and other mysteries, during which the Mundane Egg was consecrated and its significance explained. The Christians – especially the Greek and Latin Churches – have fully adopted this symbol, and see in it a commemoration of life eternal, or salvation and resurrection. This is found in and corroborated by the custom of 'Easter Eggs.' From the 'Egg' of the pagan Druids, to the red Easter Egg of the Slav, a cycle has passed.

The concept of the World Soul, in some form of interpretation and under some one of many names, may be said to be practically universal. Among many of the ancient schools of philosophy it was taught that there was an Anima Mundi, or World Soul, of which all the individual souls were but apparently separated (though not actually separated) units. The conviction that Life was One is expressed through nearly all of the best of ancient philosophies; and, in fact, in subtly disguised forms, may be said to rest at the base of the best of modern philosophies.

In the philosophical concept of the Logos, we find another, and more advanced, form of this same fundamental concept. The term, Logos, first became prominent in the philosophy of Heraclitus of Ephesus, where it appears as the Law of Nature, objective in the world, giving order and regularity to the movement of things. The Logos formed an important part of the Stoic System of Philosophy. The Active Principle, abiding in the world, they called the Logos, the term being likewise applied to the Universal Productive Cause. An authority on the history of philosophy has said of the concept of the Logos: "The Logos, a being intermediate between God and the World, is diffused through the world of the senses. The Logos does not exist from Eternity like God, and yet its genesis is not like our own and that of all other created beings. It is the First-Begotten of God, and is for us imperfect beings almost as a God. Through the agency of the Logos, God created the World."

Other schools of philosophy, notably that founded by Schopenhauer, have postulated the presence of a Universal Spirit (whose chief attribute is Desire-Will) from whom the universe of creatures has proceeded. This Universal Spirit is held to be filled with a longing, craving, seeking, striving desire to express itself in phenomenal existence. Schopenhauer calls it "The Will to Live." It is described as instinctive rather than intellectual, and as creating intellect with which to better serve its purposes of self-expression. Other philosophers have proceeded along the main lines of the concept of Schopenhauer, with various modifications. The same idea is expressed by some of the old Buddhist philosophers, the very term "The Will-to-Live" being used to express the essential nature of the Universal Spirit. But, it must be noted, in such philosophies the Universal Spirit is considered rather as the Eternal Parent than as its First Manifestation.

> Secret Doctrine of the Rosicrucians, by Magus Incognito, [1918] pp 42–48, Cosmic Ideation, Mahat or Intelligence, Universal World-Soul; Cosmic Noumenon of Matter, the basis of the intelligent operations in and of Nature, also called Maha-Buddhi.

The Secret Doctrine by H. P. Blavatsky
Vol. 1 Theosophical University Press Online Edition Vol. 1

Finally, the Body of Bliss is an emanation of the Body of Essence (dharmakaya), which is the principle underlying the whole of the universe. This Body of Essence, the principle and rule of the universe, became synonymous with Nirvana. It was a kind of universal soul, and Nirvana became the transcendent joining with this universal soul.

One of the most important, perhaps the most important and central, of Ibn Arabi's ideas was that of the Logos, a term having the double meaning as "eternal wisdom" and "word" [Affifi, *Mystical Philosophy*, p. 91]. Originally, the term was coined by the Hellenistic Jewish philosopher Philo. Fluctuating between regarding the Logos as the first manifestation of the Godhead and a merely human or universal soul, Philo referred to it as the High Priest, the Intercessor or Paraclete, the Viceregent, the Glory of God, the Shadow of God, the Archetypal Idea, the principle of revelation, the first-born Son of God, the first of the Angels, and so on [A. E. Affifi, *The Mystical Philosophy of Muhyid Din-Ibnul Arabi*, pp. 91–2]. Here we have a confusion of mythological-religious, theological, and cosmological themes, many of which were taken up by Christianity.

Ibn Arabi shows the definite influence of Philo in his doctrine of the Logos; many of his descriptive terms are identical [Affifi, Mystical Philosophy, pp. 91–2]. But he also brings in Koranic, theological, Sufi, Neoplatonic, and other ideas as well [Ibid, p. 66]. He refers to the Logos (kalimah) as the Reality of Realities (Haqiqatu'l Haqa'iq - in contrast to this, the Sufi Hallaj used the similar term "Reality of Reality" (Haqiqatu'l Haqiqah) to refer to God Himself [p. 68 n.2]), the Reality of Mohammed, the Spirit of Mohammed, the First Intellect, the Most Mighty Spirit, the Most Exalted Pen (i.e. the Pen which God uses to inscribe the destiny of all things), the Throne (of God), the Perfect

APPENDICES
II: Universal Soul

Man, the Real Adam, the Origin of the Universe, the Real who is the Instrument of Creation, the Pole (Qutb, on which all Creation revolves), the Intermediary (between God and Creation), the Sphere of Life, the Servant of the All-embracing One, and so on [Affifi, *Mystical Philosophy*, p. 66, note].

Here, as with Philo, there is a confusion or hesitation between the emanationist idea of the first manifestation of the Godhead, and the dualistic monotheistic idea of the first created being who, whilst still extremely sublime, is nevertheless separated from God by an unbridgeable abyss. In other words, there is a confusion between the hypostases; in some appellations "the Logos" refers to the supernal Divine, in other appellations to a mere emanation, and not even a very high one (the Viceregent, the Servant, etc), of that Divine. This is the real weakness of any theistic metaphysics; the absoluteness and transcendence of the personal God acts as a distorting strait-jacket that most are unwilling or unable to break.

As A. E. Affifi explains [p. 77], Ibn Arabi's Logos has three aspects (or can be considered from three points of view):

1. the metaphysical aspect, as the Reality of Realities;
2. the mystical aspect, as the Reality of Mohammed;
3. the perfected human aspect, as the Perfect Ma

Considering the first of these aspects, the Reality of Realities (Haqiqatu'l Haqa'iq), Ibn Arabi says that this is the the First Intellect, the immanent Rational Principle in the universe (a Stoic idea), the "Idea of Ideas" (or Archetype of Archetypes - the great Alexandrian Christian theologian Origen likewise referred to the Logos as Idea Ideon [Affifi, *Mystical Philosophy*, p. 68 n.2]). It comprehends all archetypes and existing things absolutely, is neither a whole nor a part, neither does it increase or decrease. It contains the archetypes or realities (haqa'iq) of things, but is in itself homogonous. It is the consciousness of God, the content and substance of divine knowledge. It is the first manifestation or epiphany of God; God as the self-revealing Principle of the universe; God manifesting Himself as universal consciousness [A. E. Affifi, *The Mystical Philosophy of Muhyid Din-Ibnul Arabi*, p.68-70]

As for the second or mystical aspect, the Reality of Mohammed (al Haqiqatu'l Mohammadiyyah), the Logos is not the actual physical or human Mohammed, but the Reality (haqiqa) behind Mohammed, the active principle of all divine and esoteric Revelation. The Logos as the Reality of Mohammed has the characteristics of being the indwelling revealer of God, the transmitter of all divine knowledge, and the cosmological cause of all creation [pp. 74–5]. He is the active principle of divine knowledge [Parrinder, Avatar and Incarnation, p.204]

This distinction between the human and the transcendent Mohammed was a popular one in Sufi and esoteric Ismaili thought, by which the Sufis were able to reconcile the historical exoteric religious vehicle of Islam with the esoteric inward experience of the Divine. The same tendency occurred in the Mahayana Buddhist doctrine of the Trikaya or Three Bodies of the Buddha, according to which the historical Buddha was only the lowest member, the Nirmanakaya or "emanation body" of the Buddha principle; above the Nirmanakaya was the Sambhogakaya or divine Celestial body; and above that in turn the Dharmakaya or Truth Body, which was of the nature of Absolute Reality. In early Christianity too, especially Gnostic Christianity, this separation of the human from the Divine principle of Revelation occurred. Orthodox and fundamentalist Christian theologians called this understanding "docetism", and considered it a serious heresy. It reached its greatest development among the Christian Gnostics of the second and third centuries, with their distinction between the human Jesus and the true transcendent Christ, who only put on Jesus like a garment or a disguise. More recently, a similar idea has appeared among Christian theosophists such as Rudolph Steiner and Alice Bailey.

In Ibn Arabi's teaching, each prophet is called a logos but not the Logos, which latter term refers to the spiritual principle or Reality of Mohammed. Ibn Arabi calls everything a Logos – a "word" of God – inasmuch as it participates in the universal principle of reason and Life, but prophets and saints are distinguished because they manifest the activities and perfections of the universal Logos Mohammed to a perfect degree. The difference between the Spirit or Reality of Mohammed and the rest of the prophets and saints is like that between the whole and its parts; he unites in himself what exists in them separately [Affifi, *Mystical Philosophy*, p. 72]

Finally, regarding the third or individual aspect, the possibility of becoming the Logos exists potentially for all Muslims. The difference between one who is asleep and one who is spiritually awakened, and the different levels attained by the latter, depend on the degree of preparedness. Each Sufi seeks to became the Logos [Affifi, *Mystical Philosophy*, p. 11]. Here there is a certain parallel with Tibetan Buddhist Tantra, where the emphasis on the Trikaya at times shifts from the theological or "mystical" to the individual yogic (the Trikaya as the yogically transformed and perfected individual self).

APPENDICES
II: Universal Soul

In the mystical hierarchy, the Qutb or Pole is the Spiritual Head of the hierarchy of Prophets and Saints, the intermediary stage between the Godhead and the phenomenal world, the eternal and the temporal [Affifi, *Mystical Philosophy*, p. 74]. The Qutb is the "Pole" on which all Creation turns. According to Sufism, the Pole is realized in the Perfect Man, the individual human expression of the Logos.

As the Pole of Creation, the Qutb is comparable to the world-axis of Shamanism (which survives in Scandinavian mythology as the world-tree Ymir, and in Hindu and Buddhist cosmography as Mount Meru), the Tai Ch'i or "Great Pivot" or "Great Ridgepole" of Chinese (Neo-Taoist and Neo-Confucian) cosmology, the "Central Sun" of Blavatsky, that maintains the Cosmos. Just as the Sun is the central pivot and source of life and energy for the solar system, so the Qutb is like a "Sun" in the centre of the planes of being. But in saying this, one must be careful not to assume, as some theosophists and neo-theosophists actually do, that there is an actual physical central sun. This is just a metaphor, like "pole" or "world mountain".

The Divine Logos thus manifests as countless Avatars, Perfect Masters, Divine Presences, and so on; whether in human form as an actual physical Avatar, or in subtle non-incarnate form as a Presence that moves subtly in the spiritual Heart (Qalb) of each individual being. This is a process that is always continuing, for there is always the Divine Presence in the world, although in some periods it may be more accessible than others - thus the Ismailis speak of Cycles of Epiphany and Cycles of Occultation [Corbin, *Cyclical Time and Ismaili Gnosis*, pp. 80–81], and the Kabbalists of God revealing his Face and turning his Face away [Luzzatto, *General Principles of the Kabbalah,* p.47] - but even in the periods of concealing of the Light, there would still be avatars and masters for those who are sincere. At no time are souls stumbling in the world of darkness ever left without guidance or grace.

And it could even be said that every spiritual aspirant, through his or her sincere striving for and mystical devotion and surrender to the Divine, becomes a minor Qutb, helping to maintain the worlds through total surrender and selflessness; the sacrifice of the lower self on the altar of the higher self and the Divine above.

M. Allan Khazlav, *Ibn Arabi's Logos Doctrine*,
Web. 15 Mar. 2010

Appendix III

The Serpent Cult

Ye who say you are Jews, *but are not Jews*, the serpent is your father. Ye are of your father the Devil, and the lusts of your father ye will do. He was a murderer from the beginning, and abode not in the truth, because there is no truth in him. When he speaketh a lie, he speaketh of his own: for he is a liar, and the father of it. - John 8:44

I know your afflictions and your poverty—yet you are rich! I know the slander of those who say they are Jews*and are not*, but are a synagogue of Satan… I will make those who are of the synagogue of Satan, who claim to be Jews though they are not, but are liars—I will make them come and fall down at your feet and acknowledge that I have loved you. - Revelation 2:9

It showed that he (Cain) was as the firstborn of the serpent's seed." In John 8:44, Jesus was speaking to the Pharisees and proclaimed, 'Ye are of your father the devil. - *Matthew Henry's Commentary* (vol. 6 p. 1077)

For Complete Dissertation, see my book, *Jerusalem, Sion & Zion: Truth, Lies and Historicity*, A. S. Noordeen, K.L. Malaysia, 2014.

Appendix IV

http://www.parliamentofreligions.org/index.cfm

1893 – The Theosophical Society (a Group of Freemasons and Rosicrucian Magi) sponsors a Parliament of World Religions held in Chicago. The purpose of the convention is to introduce Hindu and Buddhist concepts, such as belief in reincarnation, to the West. The World Parliament of Religions includes shamans and witches of the world's pagan religions

At times it was hard to take the 1993 Parliament of the World's Religions seriously. On several occasions during the eight-day convocation (August 28-September 4), the wacky New Age undercurrent that moved through the event became evident. For example, in a plenary session entitled "Voices of Spirit and Tradition," it was laughable to find — alongside representatives of

APPENDICES
III & IV; The Serpent Cult & Council on World Religions

Native American, Chinese, and Indian traditions — an American woman from a pantheistic neopagan cult representing "the tradition of Egypt." Invoking not only the Egyptian goddess Isis but also the Greek goddess Diana, she (mis)informed us that in Egyptian tradition, everything is One and all is divine.

Robert Müller [former assistant UN Secretary, Freemason & Theosophist] offered the following advice: "Let all the religions work on what they have in common. And what divides them, put aside for the very end. If you want to have an agreement whether to believe in God, in several gods, or in no god you will never get an agreement because there's no commonality. So leave these aside, and take the subjects which we have in common," which he proceeded to describe as ethical concerns.

Archive for the '2014 Parliament' Category

CPWR Chair Named One of the World's Most Influential Muslims

Re: Imam Abdul Malik

Imam Abdul Malik Mujahid, chairman of the Council for a Parliament of the World's Religions, was cited in the latest issue of *"The Muslim 500: The World's Most Influential Muslims"* for his efforts to raise awareness and understanding about faith and social issues.

The widely viewed publication from the Royal Islamic Strategic Studies Centre, an independent research entity based in Amman, is a comprehensive study of global Muslim leadership in 14 categories including politics, religion, business, science, arts, media, sports, philanthropy and social issues. Imam Mujahid was included on the list for the first time. He is one of eight Americans identified as leaders in the category of Social Issues.

The report credited Imam Mujahid with a range of contributions including his work with broadcast media and his organizing efforts as the former chairman of the Council of Islamic Organizations of Greater Chicago and his current role as chairman of the Council for a Parliament of the World's Religions. Imam Mujahid, an award-winning author, is the president of Sound Vision in Chicago, which offers multimedia Islamic teaching materials. He is also the executive producer of Chicago's Radioislam.com and the host of a daily one hour talk program on WCEV 1450 AM.

"His development of the Radio Islam nightly talk show in Chicago is not only a source of support for Muslims, but an important educational link to non-

Muslims in the greater Chicago area," according to *"The Muslim 500"* publication. "Mujahid speaks with eloquence not only about the destructiveness of Islamophobia but also of the need for all people to come together in a spirit of justice and peace."

The Council for a Parliament of the World's Religions, based in Chicago, is an international, non-sectarian, non-profit organization, established in 1988 to host the 1993 Parliament of the World's Religions. Since the historic 1893 Parliament in Chicago, modern Parliaments have been held in Chicago (1993), Cape Town (1999), Barcelona (2004) and Melbourne (2009). These periodic Parliament events are the world's oldest and largest interreligious gatherings. The next Parliament is expected to draw more than 10,000 religious leaders, scholars, theologians, worshippers, observers and journalists to the city of Brussels in 2014.

INDEX

A

Abbasid, 231, 232
Abduh, 21, 190, 196, 206
Abduh, Mohammad, 172, 190
Abduh, Mohd., xxii, 45, 190
Abdul-Rahim, Prof. Muddahthir, 216
Abraham
   See also
      Ibrahim, 48, 56, 272
Abu 'Sa'id, 130
Abu Bakr, 46, 59
academia, xiii, xvi, 175
academics, xiii, 54, 84, 168, 175, 196, 203
Accountability, 93
Active Intellects, 129
adab, xix, 27, 55, 222
Adam, xi, 31, 40, 66, 78, 93, 170, 198, 237, 239, 240, 249
Adams, Pres. John Quincy, 239
admonition, xi, 25
Adorno, T., 205
agape, 105
Agapeo, 106, 107, 142
Ahab, King, 60
Ahmad, Mirza Ghulam, 109
Ahmad, Mirzam Ghulam, 109
akhira, 22, 147, 227
Al Musawwir, 227
Al'Afghani, xxii, 189, 191, 206
Al'Bana, Hassan, 49, 190, 191
al'burhân, 183
al'Nur, 167
al-Assad, Pres. Bashar, 189
Al-Attas, Prof. S.N., 132, 135
Al-Azhar, 159, 160
Alchemists, 141
Aleister Crowley, 173
Alexandrian schools of mysticism, 140
Al-Ghazali, 200
al'hisbah, 8
Ali, Hadrat, 87
   defeat by Mu'awiyah, 87
alim, 5, 140, 174, 175, 183, 205, 206, 229, 243

Alim, xvi, 18, 168, 173, 196, 209, 229
Allenby, 172, 222
Alliance, xx, 147, 185, 186, 230, 272
allopathic, 70, 71
Al-Misri, Dhun-Nun, 140
Al-Rahim, Muddhatir'Abd, 202
Alumbrados, 171
amana, 103
American Constitution, 238
Amish, 94, 96, 97
amma, 24
amulets, 151
anarchy, 224
anchorites, 92
Animus Mundi
   Universal Soul, 207
Anthroposophy, 130, 204
apartheid, 109, 115
Apotheosis
   of George Washington, 127
Arab League, 131
Arabic, 27, 48, 53, 54, 55, 136, 149, 160, 183, 190, 210, 214, 227
   classical, 53
Architect of the Universe, 207
Arkoun, Muhammad, 161, 162
Armageddon, 71
artificial intelligence, 187
Aryan, 238
ascetics, 93, 97
Ashkenazi, 238
Ashstarte, 60
assabiyah, 23
as-Sakkinah, 14
astral dimension, 204
astral travel, 135
Ataturk, 200, 206
Ataturk, Gemal, 49
Atheism, 43, 124
Atkins, W.S., 202
Attaturk, Gemal, xxii
authenticity, 25, 26, 220, 228, 230
authoritarianism, 184
authority, 14, 15, 57, 58, 59, 61, 64, 65, 66, 71, 119, 173, 184, 198, 199, 228, 234, 247

INDEX

Authority
    divinely authentic, 15
awliya, 174
azan, 55
Aziz, Nick, 62
Aziz, Nik, 229

B

B'nai B'rith, xxi, 200
Baal, 60, 88
Babel, 88
Babylon, 102, 132, 192, 231
Babylonian cult, 238
Baden-Powell, Lord
    Boy Scout Founder, 138
Baghdad, 16, 49, 116, 217, 232
Bakar, Prof Osman, 131, 134, 173, 180, 212
Bakar, Prof. Osman, 130, 131, 134, 166, 170, 180, 210
Bal Shems, 173
Baphomet, 99, 207
baraoka, 157
Baring Bank, 172
Batayneh, Muhammad D., 215, 232
Batinite, 138, 180
Batinites, 174
Bayyah, Shaykh 'Abdallah b., 193
BBC, xxi, 122
Becktashis, 216
Bektashi, 171
Benjamintes, 169
Bethel, 132
bid'ah, 136
Bilderburger, xxi
bilingual language, 51
biopsychological potential, 218
Black Arts, 222
Black Magic, 201
Blackwater, 147, 185, 231
blasphemy, xx, 126, 134
Blavatsky, H.P., 248
blind lead the blind, 73
Board of Censors, 68
Body Politic of Islam, 119, 233
bomohs, 134, 136
Book of Deeds, 33
booty, 97, 117, 229
Born-Again', 75
Boy Scouts, 138, 191, 208

brain drain, 217
British pedagogy, 217
British Royals, 173
British Zionists, 230
Bucaille, Dr. Maurice, xix
Buddha, 106, 243, 250
Buddhist, 74, 195, 223, 250, 251
bureaucratic governance, 153
Burj Al Arab hotel
    insult to Islam, 202

C

cabalist, 140
Cain, xxii, 11, 40, 96, 124, 130, 138, 144, 149, 169, 171, 240, 252
Caliphate, 61, 65, 66, 70, 172, 232
cancer, xx, 58, 229
Castro, Fidel, 225
casuistry, xx, 43
Catholic, 7, 26, 27, 54, 83, 93, 94, 129, 130, 149, 155, 158, 162, 163, 170, 171, 173, 174, 179, 188, 197, 204, 206, 216, 238, 246, 272
Catholicism, 124
Catholics, 10, 27, 151, 174, 211
Cause of Allah, xiv, 25
Cause of God, 109
celibacy, 93
Censorship, 68
cerebral left hemisphere
    hard wired to conform, 212
certitude, 35, 36
CFR, xxi, 174, 187, 240
charity, 25, 62, 81
chastisement
    divine, 233
chauvinism, 56, 158, 181, 198
chauvinist, 23, 119, 238
Cheney, Dick, 89, 126
children, 15, 17, 51, 76, 83, 91, 93, 96, 97, 113, 116, 117, 121, 122, 123, 187, 198, 202, 219
Christendom, 161
Christian Evangelists
    as examples of schzoidia, 90
Christians, 3, 21, 37, 56, 129, 211, 216, 247
Christology, 204
Church, 85, 171, 216, 272
CIA, xxi, 174, 191

INDEX

circumcision, female, 201
civic values, 153
Classical Arabic, 53, 54, 55, 56
clergy, 93
Clinton, 175, 225
clitoral amputation, 201
cognitive acquisition, 27
cognitive dissonance, 185
cognitive manipulation, 164
collectivism, 125, 150
colonial masters, 190
Comintern, 9, 128
commandment
    First Mosaic Law regarding
        idolatry, 83
commerce, 5, 95, 97, 114, 118, 130
communal pretense, 5
communalism, 150
Communism, 85
community, xi, xviii, 51, 59, 71, 78, 92, 93, 95, 96, 97, 176, 198, 210, 211, 224, 235
conformism, 212
Confucian tradition, 186
Confucius, 109, 177, 187, 223
conscience, 80
Consensus Education, 209
consensus, forced
    Muslim neo-patriarchy, 184
conservative, 224
conspiracy, xiii, xxi, 225, 235
Constantinian Order of Saint George
    Bashar al-Assad, 189
consumerism, 117
Cosmic Christ, 204
cosmopolitan, 150, 152, 186, 235
cost of living, 118
Council on Foreign Relations, 128
cowardice, 74
creation, xi, 8, 11, 30, 41, 77, 121, 122, 123, 221, 222, 237, 241, 250
creationist, xviii
credibility gap, 212
Crescent Moon, 88
crime, ix, xvii, 5, 98, 101
Criminal activity, 17
crusade, 40, 62
crusades, 58, 147
crypto-Jews, xxii, 49, 214
Cult of Cain, 130
cultural mores', 24

cultural pluralism, xiv
cultural war, 241
cunning, 12, 25, 26, 43, 61, 87, 91, 149, 151, 185, 196, 203, 205, 212, 217, 234
curses, 115
Curzon, Lord, 158, 172, 173, 190, 241

D

Da'ud, Prophet
    King David, 43, 59, 232
Dajjal, 71
Dajjal's, 71
dakwah, 7
Dakwah, 7
damnation, 24, 32
Danites, 169
Darwin, 224
David Copperfield, 131
Day of Judgment, 2, 15, 84, 114
Deedat, Ahmed, 212
deen, 132, 224
default determinants of spiritual laws, 4, 125
deification, 126
Deism, 123, 124, 126
dementia, 134
democracy, 66, 119, 125, 127, 179, 201, 202, 233
denial, xiii, xiv, 10, 24, 25, 32, 72, 73, 93, 123, 135, 154, 182, 197, 226, 228, 229, 230, 233, 234
denial-syndrome, xiii
depravity, 6, 93, 192
desertification, 116
destiny, 80, 105, 159, 249
deviation, 25, 44
deviations, 198
Dewey, John, 210
Dewy, John, 146
Dick Cheney, 145
Dionysius, 11
disobedience, 23, 24, 31, 32, 43, 47, 49, 60, 61, 64, 72, 107, 234
Disobedience to Allah
    discussion, 23
dissolution, 11
divine design, xviii
Divine Grace, 31

INDEX

divine guidance, 20, 81, 87, 92, 122, 123, 129, 150
divine laws, 1
divine sanction, 45
divorce rates, 183
Dragon Cult, xxii
Dravidia, 164, 169
Dreams and visions, 79
dualism, xi, 104
dunya, 133, 167

E

Ebionite, 238
Economic Hit Man, 7
Economic Hit-men, 209
ecumenicism, 206
Ecumenicism, 180
educational policy, 196
Egypt, 83, 138, 201
Einstein, Albert, 174
Eisenhower, President Dwight, 21
elan' vitae
   of early Islam, 221
Elijah, Prophet, 60
elitism, 22
emotionalism, 151
Empire, 12, 138, 235
empowerment
   IOK avoidance, 192
Enlightenment, xiii, 12
Enlightenment', xiii
entropy
   spiritual, 4, 16
environmental degradation, 229
equality, 12, 202
eschatology, xii, xv, 206, 246
Esoterism, 207
Esperanza, Prof. John
   Jesuit, 214
Esposito, John, 173, 214
ethics, 127, 162, 196, 201, 228, 244, 245
Evangelism, 239
Eve, 92, 93, 201
evil, x, xi, xiv, 1, 3, 4, 5, 8, 9, 11, 16, 17, 23, 27, 28, 30, 31, 32, 33, 34, 37, 50, 65, 74, 78, 80, 95, 102, 104, 105, 111, 113, 115, 120, 129, 133, 149, 151, 155, 156, 179, 205, 232, 242
   made easy, 104
Evil Eye, 199
Evolution, xviii
extremism, 23, 143, 214, 221

F

Fabian Socialism, 182
Fabian Socialists, 153, 210
faith, vi, 19, 31, 32, 33, 34, 37, 38, 39, 40, 42, 45, 56, 58, 77, 78, 79, 80, 81, 93, 98, 103, 116, 118, 121, 131, 140, 157, 165, 181, 186, 195, 216, 225, 232, 239
Faith, 32, 34, 64
Faithfulness, 74, 75
Fallen Angels, 99
families, 61, 66, 92, 94, 149, 184
family dysfunction, 229
fana, 209, 215
fascism, 11, 124
Fascist, xx
father, the Arab
   as agent of repression, 182
Fatimid, 49, 157, 200
fatwa
   female circumcision, 201
fear, 2, 5, 8, 10, 14, 22, 34, 64, 87, 106, 116, 141, 175, 181, 198, 220
fear of God, 10, 141
Fear of God
   Principle of Spiritual Determinism, 2
fear or *reverence* for God, 106
Fertility Cult, 170
fertility cults, 206
fetish, 46
fetishism, 46, 60, 70, 87, 97, 112, 144, 148, 161, 188, 190, 197, 212, 243
fiqh, 160, 167
First Crusade, 196
fitna, 62
Fitra, 237
fitrah, 14, 23, 91, 122, 147, 237
fools, 62
Fordham, 187
fortune telling, 199
free will, 32, 33
Free Will, 115
Freemason, xxii, 21, 45, 174, 187, 197, 200, 206, 207, 238

INDEX

Freemasonry
  Egyptian, 190
Freemasons, 26, 110, 141, 153, 174, 196, 197, 206, 207
free-will, 114, 115
Fukushima, 12, 229
Fulbright Scholars, xxi, 174, 209

G

gangs, 198
Gemal Attaturk, xxii
Genesis
  Book of, 82
Genghis Khan, 58, 232
genocide, 196, 200, 207
George Washington, 126
George Washington U, xix
Georgetown, xix, 175, 187, 209, 235
Germany, 28
gestalt, 20, 48, 90, 91, 145, 197, 210, 222, 227, 235, 236, 241
Gestapo, 171
Ghazali, Imam, 129, 134, 199, 209, 215
Ghelen, Sir Reinhardt, 191
Gibrial, 167
globalist conspiracy, xx, xxi
gnosis, 133, 139, 207
Gnostic, 172, 175, 204, 206, 250
Gnostic Christianity, 204
Gnosticism, 140, 141, 206, 207
Gnostics, 130, 170, 250
goats
  and desertification, 116
God's Cause, 110, 112
God's counsel, 81
God's protection, 27, 50
God's Word, 116
Goethe, xv, xvi, 42, 43, 143, 144, 145, 146, 227, 241, 272
Gog, 190
Golden Age, 144
  of Islam, 10, 232
Golden Dawn, 173
grace, 4, 8, 14, 15, 30, 33, 34, 35, 36, 37, 38, 39, 40, 42, 43, 44, 50, 60, 61, 65, 66, 72, 73, 74, 76, 77, 104, 107, 109, 111, 112, 119, 123, 126, 151, 233, 235, 237, 251
Grand Mufti of Jerusalem, 172
grave, 20, 68, 91, 104, 118, 172, 222, 224
Green Shirts, 191
Guenon, Rene, 137, 177
Gueron, Rene', 177
guidance, viii, xvii, 2, 10, 15, 20, 34, 36, 42, 61, 65, 66, 73, 74, 77, 78, 80, 81, 82, 87, 90, 101, 102, 105, 109, 112, 126, 127, 136, 151, 173, 188, 201, 223, 239, 251
Guidance
  divine, 23, 94
Guy Fawkes, 232

H

habit, 6, 27, 79, 119, 188, 242
Hallaj, 134, 248
Halliq, Prof. Wael, 221

I

'Hammer of God, 116

H

Hanbal, Imam, xii, 61, 152, 155
hanif, 48, 49, 132
haqiqah, 172, 173
haqqiah, 133
hard science, 188
harm, 3, 4, 22, 27, 31, 32, 71, 113, 115, 233, 236
Harry Potter, 130
Harut and Marut, 192
Harvard, xxi, 94, 96, 97, 177, 218
heavens, 132, 175
hedonism, 169
Hedonism, 116
heedlessness, 22, 220, 226, 230, 235
Hegel's Dialectic, 225
hereafter, 14, 31, 32, 77, 112, 229
Hereafter, 3, 99, 131, 193, 227, 230, 237
heresy, 221, 250
Heriyanto, Hussein, 196, 228
Hermes, 138, 140, 170
Hermeticism, 197, 206, 222
Hermeticists, 132, 138, 170, 174
hero worship, 23, 82
high culture, 9

INDEX

High Priest
   Nazi, Bal Shem, Sanhedrin, 184
hikmah, 147
Hindu, xvii, 160, 193, 251, 252
hisbah, xiii, 8, 17, 61, 127, 149, 154, 157, 178, 188, 192, 194, 217, 231, 242
Hisbah, vi, xii, 9, 17, 169
histrionics, 12, 24, 178
Hitler, 171, 204, 225
holiday, 81
holiness, 112
Holiness, 93
holism, 146, 227
homiletic literature, 155
honor, xiii, 12, 47, 63, 84, 88, 105, 107, 114, 160, 167, 173, 192, 200, 202, 211
Horus, 21, 170
Hosein, Imran, xxi, 99, 175, 183
human dignity, 20
human intelligence
   types of, 218
human rights, 114, 115, 201, 202
Humanism, 12, 20, 21, 23, 43, 85, 102, 124
humanists, 26, 81
Humiliation, vi, 143, 195, 199
Husayn, Taha, 160
Husbandry, 17
Hutterite, 94
Hykal, Mohd. H., 41
hypocrisy, 5, 6, 9, 77, 97, 157, 185, 199, 235
hypocrites, xiii, xix, 25, 39, 239

I

IAIS, 8, 213
IAIS logo, 213
Iblis, x, xiii, xxii, 39, 47, 65, 68, 144, 146, 171, 173, 174, 180, 184, 191, 194, 197, 201, 210, 239, 240, 271
Ibn 'Abbas, 73
Ibn Arabi, 248, 249, 250, 251
Ibn Khaldun, ix, xi, 1, 2, 89, 116, 124, 152, 189, 243
Ibn Maymun, 49, 157
Ibn Sina, 129, 131, 134
Ibrahim, 48, 62, 76, 81, 88
Icarius, 148

iconography, 84, 168, 169
icons, 20, 25, 62, 66, 82, 83, 88, 98, 102, 170, 185, 224, 230
idealism, 224
identitarian thought, 205
idolatry, 20, 25, 34, 44, 84, 87, 98, 110, 124, 126
   subliminal, 84
Idolatry, 60, 84
   defined, 84
Idris. *See* Seth
ignorance, viii, 10, 20, 21, 22, 27, 28, 50, 55, 77, 90, 123, 136, 154, 157, 176, 190, 198, 214, 228, 230, 233
IIUM, 173, 215, 216, 270
ijtihad, 7, 8
Illuminati, 172, 173, 174, 187, 240
illumination, 172
Illumination, 170, 171, 173, 207
illusory dignity, 199
ilm, 214
Imaan
   60 branches of, 130
Imamate, xiii, 228, 230
immortality, 133
impurity, 40, 47, 61
incest, 10, 152
Indonesia, 56, 128, 148, 200, 236
Industrial Revolution, 195
initiates, 48, 124, 173, 207, 213
initiation, 14, 153
Initiation, 240
innovation, 136, 137, 141, 216
insan, 242
insight, xvi, 3, 25, 42, 122
inspiration, 10, 20, 23, 25, 126, 147, 222, 226
integrity, 5, 15, 63, 71, 94, 95, 98, 235, 237
inverse determinants
   of spiritual law, 29, 122, 229, 233, 235
IOK, vi, xv, xvii, xxi, 6, 9, 54, 164, 167, 174, 181, 183, 185, 188, 189, 192, 197, 201, 205, 207, 208, 209, 220, 232, 242
Iraq, 10, 97, 99, 202
Iroquois, 238
Isa, 59, 70, 72, 98, 106, 107, 109, 110, 112, 228, 231
   Prophet (Jesus), 26, 33, 58, 66

INDEX

Isaiah
   prophet, 66
   Prophet (65 15), 56
Isaiah, Prophet, 56, 57, 66, 70, 231
Ishmai'ili, 49, 126
Ishtar, 88
Isis, 88, 170
Islam
   purpose of, 57
Islam Hadhari, 8, 9, 178, 181, 220, 226
Islamic Bank, 7
Islamic Science, vi, xii, xvii, xviii, xix, 2, 6, 9, 10, 56, 121, 132, 134, 143, 144, 148, 149, 153, 154, 160, 165, 175, 180, 181, 185, 188, 189, 195, 197, 203, 205, 206, 208, 209, 213, 214, 215, 221, 223, 230, 232, 242, 243
   defined by author, 222
Islamic State, 58, 59, 62, 230
Islamicity, 211, 212, 221
Islamists, xxi, 54, 129
ISLAMIZATION, vi, xv, xix, 8, 9, 120, 121, 128, 144, 151, 185, 187, 204, 205, 209, 210, 211, 212, 213, 215, 216, 221, 222, 225, 226, 229, 230, 243
Islamization of Knowledge, xvii, xix, 128, 205, 211, 215
Islamization of Practice, 223
Islamization of Science, 144, 225
Islamization-of-Knowledge, xv
Ismai'ili, 23
Ismai'ils, 221
Ismaili, 190, 250, 251
Ismailis, 251
isnad, 167
Israel, 49, 57, 60, 95, 170

J

jabarut, 133
Jacob
   Prophet, 57
Jacob, Prophet, 57, 132
Jacob's ladder, 132
Jacobin, xiii, 12, 59, 62, 106, 176, 179, 202, 238
James the Just
   Brother of Jesus, 238

Jerusalem, 169, 172, 174, 214, 233, 238, 252
Jesuit, 8, 43, 59, 129, 132, 138, 149, 165, 168, 169, 170, 171, 175, 177, 206, 207, 213, 232, 238, 239
Jesuits, xx, 128, 130, 141, 153, 171, 173, 174, 180, 185, 204, 214, 216, 225, 230, 231
Jesus, xvii, 3, 41, 57, 68, 72, 75, 93, 98, 109, 110, 133, 204, 228, 241, 250, 252
Jew, xxii, 74, 82, 87, 91, 152, 189, 197, 200, 212, 237, 238
Jews, 21, 31, 70, 109, 116, 129, 140, 171, 198, 225, 252
Jezebel, Queen, 60
jihad, 71, 74, 209, 232
jihadists, 152
jinn, x, 15, 92, 93, 113, 122, 129, 134, 151, 189, 199, 222, 241
Joseph, Prophet, 62
Josiah, King, 200
Judaism, 41
Judeo-Christian Alliance, 230
Judeo-Christian misguidance, 56
Judgment Day, 31, 134, 135
Julius Caesar, x, 225
Jummah, 152, 154
justice, 5, 12, 17, 32, 38, 59, 62, 74, 108, 113, 116, 117, 178, 221, 222, 245

K

Kabalism, 130
kabalists, 197, 222
Kabalists, 58, 102, 211
Kabbalah, 169, 251
Kafir, 33
Kali, 180
kalimah, 248
Karalli, Mustapha, 131, 136, 140, 202
Karamah, 131
Kartanegara, Prof. Mulyadhi, 144, 225
Keller, Shaykh Nuh Ha mim, 137
Kennedy, ix, x, xi, 146
   murders, 146
Khabil, 11
Khadafy, Colonel, xiv
Khadafy,Colonel, 63
Khalid, 22

INDEX

khassa, 23, 24, 29, 201, 205
Khassa, xxii, 204
Kiblah, 214
King James translation, 57
Kingdom of God, xi, 34, 66, 109
Kingdom of Heaven, 75, 109, 111
Knight of Malta, 191
Knights of Columbus, 207
Knights of Malta, xiv, xxii, 125, 190, 209
knowledge, iii, viii, xvi, xviii, xix, 1, 3, 4, 8, 16, 19, 21, 22, 25, 27, 28, 29, 34, 38, 40, 41, 42, 47, 48, 50, 55, 63, 67, 72, 88, 89, 90, 91, 94, 100, 103, 104, 106, 112, 122, 124, 126, 130, 132, 133, 136, 139, 145, 146, 147, 148, 153, 155, 156, 157, 159, 160, 161, 162, 165, 174, 175, 176, 177, 178, 181, 186, 204, 205, 206, 207, 211, 212, 214, 217, 218, 222, 224, 226, 227, 228, 230, 236, 237, 241, 242, 243, 244, 246, 249, 250
    forbidden, 130
knowledge and power, 159
knowledge of God, 90
Koro, 163
Kufr, 33

L

Lakota, 237
Lamaism, 222
language and culture, 52
languages
    learning, 53
Lao Tse, 109
Latin, 51, 54, 151, 196, 247, 272
Law of Communion, 78
Law of Community, 92
Law of Decay, 16
Law of Grace, 30
Law of Guidance, 103
Law of Humility, 99
Law of Knowledge, 88
Law of Love, 105
Law of Mercy, 75, 77
Law of Obedience, 14
Law of Submission, 15
Law of Truth, 72
Law of Unity, 45
Law of Worship, 83

Learning Outcomes and Objectives, 209
Lenin, 171
Leninist slogans, 125
Lepanto, 158
Leponto, Battle of, 179
Levi, Eliphas, 197
Lewis, Bernard, 200, 214
Liberal, xviii, 224
liberalism, 58, 69
Libertines, 169
liberty, xii, 12, 25, 62, 101, 179, 202
Light Bearer
    Lucifer, 172, 208
Lilith, 180
Lincoln, Abraham, x, 272
linguistic science, 54
logic, 7, 12, 144, 160, 167, 183, 184, 194, 236
logos, 62, 250
Logos, 246, 247, 248, 249, 250, 251
London School of Economics, xxi
London Stock Exchange, 225
love, 45, 75, 83, 84, 88, 105, 106, 107, 108, 111, 136, 139, 141, 142, 143, 145, 164
Love
    Agape, *Fileo*, and *Eros*, 106
love of God, 106, 141
Loyola, Ignatius, 171, 239
Lucifer, 110, 172, 208
Luciferian, xxii, 128, 169, 207, 224, 229, 239, 243
Luciferianism, x, xx

M

Machiavelli, xii, 240
Madina, 44
Mafia, xxii, 196
Magi, 9, 113, 170, 197, 224, 231
magic, 62, 99, 123, 129, 134, 148
magical
    thinking, 159
magical thinking, 133
Magog, 190, 238
Mahdi, 70, 228, 229, 231
Mahfouz, Naguib, 184
Mahmud, Taib, 196
Malay Neo-Patriarchy, 181
Malay scholars, 140, 176

INDEX

Malays, xiii, 50, 109, 132, 176, 210, 230
Malaysia, xiii, 8, 9, 28, 55, 62, 74, 118, 120, 131, 146, 148, 169, 173, 178, 181, 196, 213, 216, 217, 229, 230, 252
Malcolm X, xiii, 146
male chauvinism, 198
Maranos-Jew, 240
marifah, 133, 193
Mariolatry, 206
marriage, 17, 36, 47, 73, 74, 78, 112, 164, 195, 197, 205, 223, 224
Marriage, 11, 188
  as analogy for Communion with God, 78
Marx, Karl, 90, 225
materialism, 20, 26, 76, 157
Materialism, 94, 124, 126
mathematics, 99, 143, 227
matrilineal laws, 237
Mauri War Mask, 180
McGill
  university, 165, 187
McGill University, 165
Medina, xii, 25, 116, 117, 195, 197, 229, 243
Medina Speech, reference to
  of Mohammad, 217
Mein Kamph, 171
Melchizedek, 56
memes, 25, 169
men of understanding, 25
Mencius, 186
Mengele, Dr. J., 165
Mennonite, 94, 95, 97
mercantilism, 23
Mercy, 34, 75, 76, 77, 79
metaphysical laws, 104
metaphysics, xx, 91, 129, 147, 157, 192, 204, 207, 214, 249
Metaphysics, 177, 207
MI6, 174, 191
micropolitics, xii, xiii
Middle East, xxii, 10, 74, 147, 150, 157, 172, 175, 184, 195, 199, 246
might equals right, 240
Ministers of Religion, 196
minorities, 52
mischief, 48, 76, 132

misguidance, xvii, xxii, 11, 15, 26, 29, 56, 89, 126, 128, 129, 179, 191, 229
modern illnesses, 229
modernity, 121, 184
Modernity, xxi, 177
Moghul, 200
Mohammad's entry to Madinah, 2
Mongol, 50, 232, 233
monism, 124, 164
Monotheism, 132, 239
monotheist, 8, 48, 57, 237, 240
moral force, xi, 10
moral governance, 115
moral idiocy, 4
Moral Imperative, 109
moral Imperatives, 6
Moral Imperatives
  Discussion, 4
Moral Law, 113
morality, 20, 73, 109, 110, 111, 127, 221, 244, 245
morals, 196
Moses, 14, 59, 82, 100, 133
Mossad, xxi, 174, 191
Mother Theresa, 93
Mu'awiyah, 86, 87, 91
Mubarak, Hosni
  Freemasonic Pawn, 190
Mujahid, Imam Abdul Malik, 253
mujtahids, 7
Mukhtar, Omar, 63, 131
mullahs, 88, 119, 125, 196
Multiple Intelligence theory, 219
murder, 37, 40, 49, 91, 113, 114, 125, 196, 198, 238
Murshid, 164
Musa, Prophet
  Moses, 170
Muslim Academics, xiv
Muslim Brotherhood, 190, 191
Muslim domestic violence, 199
Muslim marriages, 223
Mystery Religion, 54
Mystery Religions, 43, 239
mysticism, 157, 164
Mythras, 20, 88

N

nano-thermite, xxi

INDEX

9/11, xxi
Napoleon, 128, 171, 225, 241
narcissism, 23, 238
Nasr, Seyyed Hossein, xvii, xviii, 10, 131, 137, 173, 176, 187, 195, 206, 207, 213, 224, 237
Nation State, 153, 235
Nation States, 12, 153, 235
national repentance, 200
national security, 165
nationalism, 65, 181, 190
Nationalism, 12, 69, 90, 138
nationalist pride, 181
nation-states, 136, 201
Native Americans, 237, 241
NATO, xix, 126, 131, 229
Nazi, 23, 184, 197
Nazis, 165, 174
Nazism, 240
neo-patriarchal chauvinism, 158
neo-patriarchal constructs, 232
neo-patriarchal fetishists, 188
neopatriarchy, 184
neo-patriarchy, 6, 91, 99, 149, 182
neo-patriarchy, 184
neo-patriarchy, 200
neo-patriarchy, 209
neo-patriarchy, 213
neo-Pythagorean philosophy, 99
nepotism, 21
neuro-physiology, 157
Neurophysiology, 187
Neuropolitics, vii, xii, 162, 212, 244
Neuro-Sociology, xiv
neutralization
   as psyop war strategy, 9
New Age, 81, 146, 165, 227
New Imperialism, 124
New Imperialist, xiv
New World Order, iii, xxi, 58, 169
NGO, 62
nihilism, 23, 215
Nimrud, 24, 88
   King, 102, 192
Noah, Prophet, 56, 88
Nod, land of, 169
noumena
   of Ibn Sina, 129
NSA, 209
nuclear waste, 12

O

Obedience to God
   Principle of Spritual Determinism, 2
occult societies, 189
Occupy Movement, 232
OIC, xxii, 131, 192
One Malaysia, 8
Operation Stargate
   US Army Parapsychology Program, 165
opium economies, 152
oppressors, 6
opulence, 22, 26
Order Templar Orientalis, 174
Orientalism, 140, 239
Orientalist, 140, 141, 187, 210, 214
Orientalists, xix, 140, 159, 196, 241
Origen, 249
orthodoxy
   Islamic, 135, 138, 176, 215
Osama bin Laden, xxi
ostentation, 220, 233
OTO, 174
Ottoman, 11, 88, 158
Ottoman Turks, 88

P

pagan, 43, 60, 124, 206, 222, 225, 239, 247
paganism, 239
pagans, 132
pageantry, 22, 82
Paine, Thomas, xvii
Pakistan, 88
Palestine, 202
pantheism, 124
Papists, xxi
Papua New Guinea, 200
Paradigm Drift, 221
Paradise, 38, 44, 107, 118
parallel universes, 166
Paramoralism, 205
paranormal, 110, 157
parapsychology, 164
Parliament of World Religions, 252
pathocracy, xiv, 46, 48, 101, 111, 125, 176, 205
patriotic loyalty, 25

INDEX

patriotism, 181, 190
Peace, 30, 56, 109, 111, 112, 120, 179
peace and security, 14
Peace of God, 30, 111
Peace on Earth, 179
peace with God, 110
pederasts, 152, 199
pederasty, 10
Perennialism, 137, 179
Perennialist, 132, 134
Perfect Man, 23, 249, 251
PERKIM, 173, 196
Persia, 99, 159
Pharaoh, 170, 204
Pharisees, 169, 241, 252
Philo of Alexandria, 248, 249
philosophia perennis, 168, 193
philosophy, 45, 99, 106, 124, 145, 147, 244, 246, 247
physics, xviii, 121, 166, 227
Physics, 20, 143
Physiology, 223
piety, 2, 19, 20, 28, 41, 60, 79
Pike, Albert, 113
Pilate, Pontious, 72
Pilate, Pontius, 72
Pious XII, Pope, 171
PK-teleportation, 166
plagiarism, 21, 220
pluralism, xiv, 12, 125, 214, 235
pluralistic societies, 62
Pol Pot, 9, 145
political manipulation, 190
political parties, 61, 64, 66, 149
Political Ponerology,, xi, xiii, 24, 46, 63, 76, 88, 89, 90, 94, 100, 101, 102, 103, 109, 111, 125, 130, 151, 156, 163, 177, 178, 182, 205, 228
political science, 189
politics, 65, 66, 162, 236, 240
poltergeist, 130, 134
polygamists, 93
Polytheist, 237
Pomp and Glitter, 220
poneros, 5, 50, 230
Positivists, 144
power, 1, 3, 7, 23, 30, 33, 36, 42, 43, 45, 47, 57, 60, 61, 62, 64, 65, 66, 67, 68, 71, 82, 84, 87, 110, 131, 133, 156, 159, 174, 179, 182, 189, 193, 195, 197, 200, 203, 221, 231, 238, 243
inherent, 67
Power, v, 3, 47, 58, 63, 64, 65, 66, 67, 159, 215, 232
pragmatics, 87
in semiotics, 87
prayer and patience, 79
preaching, 155, 212
predestination, 1, 2, 13, 32
pride, 22, 47, 49, 78, 102, 123, 154, 234, 239
Priest, 197, 248
Princeton, xxi, 164
Prodigal Son, 11, 76, 105
propaganda, 15, 26, 61, 82, 147, 172, 201, 202, 213, 220
Prophets, 14, 26, 44, 66, 72, 80, 93, 132, 222, 251
Protocols of the Elders of Zion, 240
psychiatry, 164
Psychic, 165
psychic missions, 165
psychic phenomena, 174
psychokinesis, 166
psychological gelding, 10
psychological projection, 232
psychology, 164
psychotronics, 166
psyop, 164, 185
Ptolemaic astronomical system taught in Al-Azhar, 159
public trust, 17, 18
Purity, 46, 48
Pyramids, 21, 170

Q

Qari, xxi, 126, 168, 173, 174, 175, 196, 229, 242
qari', 7
Qari'', 126, 167, 168, 173, 174, 175, 196, 229, 242
Qiblah, 22
quiddity, 129
Quietists, 139
Qutb, 249, 251

R

R&D

INDEX

Malaysia, 28
rage, 14, 198
Rahman, Fazlur, 144
Ramachandran, Dr. V.S. Neurophysiologist, 187
Ramadan, 74
raqi'awliya, 167
rationalism, 12, 24
rationality, 159, 245
reactionary, 5, 224
reactionism, 69, 224, 225
Real Politics, xix, xx, xxi, 129, 183, 192, 203
reason, 7, 9, 20, 22, 32, 33, 38, 41, 42, 43, 61, 62, 70, 72, 76, 77, 79, 81, 82, 89, 108, 111, 115, 131, 155, 157, 160, 161, 171, 175, 177, 178, 185, 186, 196, 197, 198, 206, 214, 216, 223, 225, 250
reductionism, xv, 19, 29, 143, 147, 181, 210, 218, 221
Reformation, 26, 207
Religio Perennialism, 130
Religio Perennis, xx, 19, 174, 179, 183, 206
religious conflict, 47
religious conviction, 35, 36
religious instruction, 56
religious mania, 158
religious training, 89
remembrance of God, 4, 79, 137, 216
Remembrance of God, v, 20, 25, 27
    Principle of Spiritual Determinism, 3
remorse, 76, 77
remote viewers
    astral travel, parapsychology, 165
repentance, 20, 37, 39, 69, 76, 77, 170, 199, 200, 205, 234, 235
repression, 149, 152, 158, 160, 161, 182, 183, 185, 188, 189, 192, 197, 198, 205
    in the family, 158
reprobate, 37, 40, 123, 147, 169, 239
reprobation, 5, 11, 100, 123
Reprobation, 6
Revelation, 10, 19, 43, 73, 164, 250, 252
Reverence of God, 4
Rhodes Scholars, 174
Rhodes Scolars, 174, 209
riba, xiv, 10, 23, 152
Rida, Mohd, 190, 191
Rida, Mohd. Rashid, xxii
Rida. Mohd. Rashid, 172
Righteous Caliphs, 49
Righteous dominion, 6
Rightly Guided Caliphs, 117
rightly guided Caliphs, 70
Rights of God, v, xi, xiii, 1, 5, 8, 186, 233
ritual, 9, 74, 78, 79, 81, 82, 101, 110, 123, 184, 216, 219, 221, 243
Rockefeller, 174
Rockefeller, David, 9
Romance, 106
Romanists, 26, 132
Rome, xii, xiv, 11, 169, 171, 196, 271, 272
Rosicrucian, 141, 169, 246
Rosicrucians, 153, 248
Rotarians, 207
Rothschild, xxii, 128, 173, 179, 191, 225
Rousseau, 224
Royal Islamic Strategic Studies Centre, 253
ruling class, 24
Rumsfeld, Donald, 89, 126

S

Sabaeans, 99
Sabataen, xxii
Sabean, 74, 102
Sabeans, 99
Said, E.W., xiv, 239
saints, 44, 164, 179, 250
Sala'u'din, 111, 172, 222
Salafiyyah, 189, 190, 192
Salam, Muhammad Salam, xix
Saliba, Professor, xviii, xix
salihin, 174
Salt of the Earth, 15
Samael, 180
sanctimony, 20, 152, 190, 192, 216, 234
Sanhedrin, 184
Sarawak, 196
Sardar, Ziaruddin, xvii, 187

INDEX

Satan, 1, 15, 16, 26, 31, 32, 33, 40, 46, 47, 82, 103, 198, 199, 208, 252
satanic agents, 160
Satanic elite, 225
satanic governance, 90
Satanism, 23
    Left Hand Path, 124
    Right Hand Path, 124
Saudi family, 197
<u>Schizoid characters</u>, 90
SCHIZOIDIA, 89
scholars
    tradition Islamic, 208
Schuon, Frithjof, xx, 126, 137, 173, 206, 207
science, xviii, xix, 10, 25, 41, 42, 43, 44, 51, 90, 91, 92, 132, 135, 143, 144, 147, 148, 152, 156, 164, 165, 176, 183, 185, 187, 192, 195, 197, 214, 215, 221, 223, 225, 228, 229, 230, 234, 236, 238, 241, 244
scientific progress
    reasons for ummah's lack of, 190
SCOPUS, xix
scoundrels, 196
Scribes and Pharisees, 241
Sebottendorf, Baron Rudolf von, 171
second death, 12, 37
<u>Secret Societies</u>, 78, 103, 197
sectarianism, 127, 149, 152, 190, 214, 220
secular, xvi, 6, 7, 20, 26, 58, 62, 63, 65, 95, 96, 161, 195, 201, 202, 221, 225, 228, 229
secular government, 63
secular pluralism, 20, 62
secularism, 4, 239
Seerah, 59, 64
self-delusion
    of Malay Scholars, 176
self-sufficiency, 104
semantics, 87
semiosis, 87
semiotics, xii, 84, 113
Semite, 50, 57
Semites, 116
Sermons
    effects on ummah, 155
Serpent Cult, vii, 130, 240, 252
Serpent Society, 169
Seth, Prophet, 170
sexual delight, 112
sexual intimacy, 107
sexual matters
    Muslim ignorance, 183
sexual orientation, 229
Shakti, 180
shamans, 81, 134, 136
shame, 14, 198
Shamil al-Daghestani, 131
Shari'ah, 1, 58, 114, 133, 192, 221, 236
Shaw, G.B., 146
Shi'ite, 82, 190, 206
shirk, 20, 40, 44, 136
shura, 54
Shura, 70
Siddiqui, Dr. Kalim, 64
sigil, 207, 213
sin, 26, 31, 34, 39, 59, 77, 103, 114, 115
    the right to sin, 114
Sinai, Mt., 81
sincere of heart, 74
Skinner, B.F., 188
skirtoid
    pathologic personality type, 84
slogans, 25, 62, 66, 102, 177, 178
sloth, 14, 49, 113, 116
social disorder, 18
sociopathy, xiv, xv, 181, 229
Sodom, 11
Solomon, Prophet, 134
Solzhenitsyn, Alexander, xvii
Sophia Perennis, 176
sophism, 175
sophists, 8, 71, 100, 126, 176
sorcerers, xiii, 151
sorcery, 3, 46, 132, 135, 198, 199
special interests, 21, 64
Spirit
    Divine Word of Command, 76
spiritual cognition, 204
Spiritual Determinism, v, 2, 198
spiritual law, 5, 27, 105, 107, 111, 122, 229
Spiritual Law, v, xx, 2, 31, 32, 54, 72, 101, 104, 113, 121, 197, 231
Spiritual Science, 204
spiritualist, 136
SS, 171, 172
SS Corps, 171

INDEX

Stalin, 225
Stanford Research Institute, 164
Star and Crescent, 62, 84, 230
Star of Isis
   re
      Star & Crescent, 88
status quo, 158, 224
Steiner, Rudolph, 173, 204, 250
Stockholm Syndrome, 184
Strauss, Leo, 89, 91
Suez Canal Company
   & Al'Bana, 191
Sufi tradition
   Malay confusion, 176
Sufi-claimer, 44, 129
Sufi-claimers, 41, 133, 137, 141, 155, 160, 183
Sufis, 131, 136, 137, 139, 160, 164, 250
Sufism, 132, 135, 139, 164, 251
Suhaimi, Dr. Arrifin, 173
Suhaimi, Prof. Dato Arrifin, 173
Sumer, 196
supernatural, 110, 111, 112, 131, 158
superstition, 50, 88, 126, 162, 198
Supreme Principle, 207, 223
sustainability, 95
sychophants, 151
Symbolism
   idolatry and the first
      commandment, 84
symbols, 82, 83, 84, 170, 235
synthesis, 91, 145, 167, 197, 207

T

taffakur, 81, 188, 222
Talmud, 41, 126, 169, 180
talmudist Jews, 140
Tantra, 250
taqua, 60, 65, 73, 82, 89, 93, 113, 217
   loss of, 89
tareeqahs, 137
tasawwuf, 129, 136, 137, 139, 140, 148, 171, 176, 222
   definition, 136
tauba, 69
Taubatun Nasuh, 199
Tavistock, 210
Tavistock Institute, 210

tawhid, xi, 123, 146, 167, 197, 217, 218, 227
Tawhid, 131, 134, 140, 160, 166, 170, 173, 180, 210
tawhidic, 19, 147, 167, 195, 208, 217, 227, 237
teachers, 9, 217, 220
teleportation phenomena, 166
television, 185
Temple
   university, 187
Tesla, Nicholas, 174
The Great Spirit, 237
The Left Hand Path of Satanism, 124
The Right Path of Satanism, 124
theft, 196
Theology, 41, 43, 44, 99
Theomania, 141
Theosophical Society, 252
Theosophists, 174
theosophy, 126, 139
thieves, xix
thinking
   impotance of in reference to
      intellectual freedom, 162
Thoth, 170
Thoth, King, 138, 140, 170
traditionalism, genuine
   absence, 184
Triad, 153
tribal bias, 109
tribalism, 22, 23, 24, 47, 152
Turkey, xviii, 171
TV - television, 96
tyranny, 15, 65, 152, 200

U

ullama, 26
Umar, Hadrat, 22, 233
UN, 128, 174, 214
unbelief, 34
underdevelopment, 184
unity, 12, 36, 41, 43, 44, 45, 50, 51, 56, 63, 68, 78, 87, 90, 122, 131, 152, 160, 227, 235
Unity, v, 43, 45, 46, 47, 48, 49, 58, 60, 66, 70, 71, 73, 112, 130, 138, 148
Unity & Power, 48
Unity and Power, 48, 71
Unity with God, 112, 130

INDEX

Universal Soul, vii, 179, 197, 207, 246
Universalism, xx, 126, 130, 222, 229
University of California, 165
University of London, 187
unseen worlds, 129
unseen, the, 2, 129, 130, 131, 132, 136, 139, 157, 164, 170, 172, 175, 178, 180, 204
usury, 26, 74, 96, 196
utilitarianism, 196

V

Venice, 196
violence, 199
virtue, 2, 5, 30, 33, 35, 37, 50, 60, 107, 108, 109, 112, 122, 123, 147, 164, 241
Voll, Fr. John
    Jesuit Priest, 173, 213
Voll, John, 173
von Sebottendorf, Baron Rudolf, 171
vulva
    radical amputation, 201

W

Wahhabi, 23, 137
Wahhabis, 136, 137, 216
waliy, 131
Wall Street, 12, 225
walliyah, 15
war, 9, 32, 107, 114, 116, 118, 165, 175, 225, 228, 238, 240
Washington DC, 126, 200
Washington, Pres. George, xix, 23, 127, 187, 206
whisperers, 191

White Tower Neo-Patriarchy, 212
White Towers, 217
wickedness, x, xiv, 31, 32, 47, 63, 179, 196, 229
Will of God, 38, 64
wisdom, viii, xiv, 4, 5, 8, 12, 25, 36, 41, 73, 81, 91, 101, 106, 117, 141, 145, 151, 175, 176, 236, 237, 238, 242, 248
Wisdom, 4, 38, 72, 73, 112, 177
women
    status eroded, 201
Word of God, 115
World Bank, 202, 209
World Government
    Jerusalem, 214
World Parliaments of Churches, 128
World Religious Parliament, 216
World Soul, 193, 246, 247
worship, 25, 40, 60, 64, 79, 81, 83, 98, 110, 239
Worship, v, 83, 84, 88
WTC towers, xxi
wudu, 189, 193

Y

Yakuzza, 153
Yale, xxi, 146, 210

Z

zakat
    in Malaysia, 118
Zay'our, Ali, 182, 183
Zionist, 57, 210, 232
Zionist Jew, 89
Zionists, x, xxii, 71, 75, 153, 172, 232

About the Author

A globally known author and researcher on the New World Order, Freemasonry and Secret Societies as well as Human Development and Sexuality.

He is married to Malee Zaida Manowang of Phayao, Thailand.

Senior Lecturer (1 Aug 2011 – April 2014) Homeopathic Medicine, Medical Ethics & Islamic Revealed Knowledge – Allianze University Medical School, secunded to Insaniah Medical College

April 2014: Invited by UNITAR University, Shah, Alam to help develop a new Liberal Arts Program in Comparative Cultural Studies

Senior Research Fellow (Jul 2008 – Jul 2011)
International Institute of Islamic Thought & Civilization (ISTAC) IIUM, KL, Malaysia; English ed., books, Journal, Articles, Conference & Administrative Proceedings; Coordinator for Research & Publications; Contributing Editor, Al-Sajarah (Journal)

Dr. Zaid was raised a Catholic along the river front industrial towns south of Philadelphia. A professional musician for over 20 years from the age of 13, he served in the US Army in Europe during the Vietnam War. He has 13 years of formal post-secondary education: 3 yrs Liberal Arts as a Music Major; 3 yrs Pre-Med science, and 7 yrs post-graduate training in Medicine (M.D. from U. of S. Dakota, 1987, with Family Practice Residency Training at Pontiac General Hospital, Mi. USA, 1990). He practiced medicine for more than twenty years; including ten years as an inner-city E.R. Doctor in the U.S. and Caribbean, as well as in Australia amongst Queensland's Aborigines and on the Gold Coast. He is also a trained Homeopath.

While living in Europe Dr. Zaid became intimate with the doctrines of Dr. Rudolph Steiner to the point of 'Initiation' and later lectured on Anthroposophy for three years in Ann Arbor, Michigan. He became a Freemason, recanted and became a 'Born-Again' Christian Missionary.

From 1999 to 2005, he lived and farmed in Borneo with his third wife (a Native Dyak) and their two sons but divorced after his conversion to Islam in 2004, at which time he lost everything at age 55.

After his conversion—being unable to practice Medicine in Malaysia—to earn a living Dr Zaid edited texts for the International Institute of Islamic Thought and Civilization (ISTAC) and Islamic Books Trust in Kuala Lumpur, as well as thesis papers for students of the U. of Malaya. He also taught 'English' to international students at two other Malaysian universities, and for a year in Bangkok. During this time he authored his first Book, *Trinity*. Emeritus Prof. Dr. Osman Bakar—formerly of Georgetown University—reviewed this title

About The Author

and invited Dr. Zaid to return to ISTAC as full time Editor and Research Fellow in July of 2007.

- Published Books:

1) *The Hand of Iblis: an Anatomy of Evil* Summary Observations on the New World Order (780 pp) Analysis & History, AS Noordeen, 2009 ISBN 978-983-065-295-5 translated to Bahasa Indonesian and Spanish

2) *Trinity, The Metamorphosis of Myth* Comparative Religion & Christology, (160 pp) Penpress, England 2008 ISBN 978-1-906206-43-7; 2nd ed. June, 2013, AS Noordeen, KL.

3) *Forgotten Saints: The Gospel of Barnabas:* Survey and Commentary (Monograph) (90 pp) AS Noordeen, 2010 SBN 978-983-065-312-9

4) *The Taqua of Marriage* Sociology, Psychology & Human Development; (189 pp), AS Noordeen (Aug 2011) ISBN 978-973-065-321-1

5) *Cain's Creed, The Cult of Rome,* A Deconstruction of the Monotheist Saga AS Noordeen, KL, 2012 ISBN: 978-983-065-339-6

6) *Jerusalem, Zion & Sion: Truth Lies and Historicity* (160 pp) AS Noordeen, 2014. Currently being translated to Spanish.

Endnotes

[i] *FORWARD to. The Introduction and Book One of the World History.* Kitab al-Ibar, and *Erroneous Figures, Israelites* p. 8.

[ii] *Rome's Responsibility for the Assassination of Abraham Lincoln* by Thomas Mealey Harris, 1817-1906, Brigadier General; Subject: Lincoln, Abraham, 1809-1865; Catholic Church; Publisher: Pittsburgh, Pa., Williams Pub. Co.; Call number: 9135328

Also See: Avro Manhattan's works, ordered chronologically:
- *The Rumbling of the Apocalypse (1934)*
- *Towards the new Italy (Preface by H.G. Wells) (1943)*
- *Latin America and the Vatican (1946)*
- *The Catholic Church Against the Twentieth Century (1947; 2nd edition 1950)*
- *The Vatican in Asia (1948)*
- *Religion in Russia (1949)*
- *Vatican in World Politics (1949)*
- *Catholic Imperialism and World Freedom (1952; 2nd edition 1959)*
- *Terror Over Yugoslavia, the Threat to Europe (1953)*
- *The Dollar and the Vatican (1956)*
- *Vatican Imperialism in the Twentieth Century (1965)*
- *Vatican Moscow Alliance (1982)*
- *The Vatican Billions (1983)*
- *Catholic Terror in Ireland (1988)*
- *Vietnam ... why did we go? (1984)*
- *Murder in the Vatican, American Russian and Papal Plots (1985)*
- *The Vatican's Holocaust (1986)*

[iii] *How the Media and the Experts Determine How We See the Rest of the World*: Softcover, Taylor & Francis Group, ISBN 0710205414

[iv] *Proceedings*, Southern Illinois Goethe Celebration, 1950, p. 37.

ENDNOTES

[v] The Islamization of science or the marginalization of Islam: "The positions of Seyyed Hossein Nasr and Ziauddin Sardar"; Leif Stenberg, University of Lund; *Social Epistemology*, x, 3/4, 1996, 273-87

[vi] "A False Quest for a True Islam" by *Taner Edis, Council for Secular Humanism,* 24 Feb 2010; Dr. Edis is an associate professor of physics at Truman State University. His latest book is *An Illusion of Harmony: Science and Religion in Islam* (Prometheus Books, 2007).

[vii] *Re-writing the History of Science in the Islamic Civilization*: Report of George Saliba's visit to Lahore, November 2007, by Dr Muhammad Sabieh Anwar, Khwarzimic Science Society Centre of Excellence in Solid State Physics, Punjab University, Quaid-e-Azam Campus, Lahore 54590, Pakistan, http://www.khwarzimic.org/

[viii] *The Soul of the World* By Dr. Munawar A. Anees, Editor-in-Chief, *Periodica Islamica,* 1995

[ix] *Rewriting the History of Science*, op.cit.

[x] *THE MUQADDIMAH, The Introduction and Book One of the World History, Kitab al-Ibar*, p. 132; Vol. 2. P. 212, Ibn Khadun, Translated from the Arabic by FRANZ ROSENTHAL.

[xi] According to Riane Eisler, in her seminal work, *The Chalice and The Blade*, the notion of dominance as a 'natural social order' has philosophical roots in the 'might makes right' ideology originated by the **Sophists**, a group of men who, with regard to morals and ethics, exemplified the thinking of political rulers throughout history from its beginnings in Ancient Greece.

Theirs was the first official lie-by-design-for-political-gain school of thought.

- Unlike other philosophers who contemplated the big ethical questions of life, the Sophists were primarily interested in the mechanics of *how language can be used to control human behavior.*

- Sophists were paid well to help rulers write speeches and win court cases through the use of *twisted arguments and paradox* (not unlike what is known in modern times as *Orwellian doublethink*).

- A 'might makes right' ideology posits that the right to rule over others is just, and earned, on the basis of proving one's strength, wealth and, or armed might.

- Members of the ruling class competed with one another to attain what was considered the top prize (to do wrong and not get caught), and to avoid what was the worst humiliation (to be wronged and not get revenge).

- Fabricated lies of the doublethink variety were necessary for one very good reason, well understood by political rulers and sociology researchers alike — *physical strength or violencealone do not work to oppress* or dominate human beings.

> Athena Staik *Eroticized Dominance: Predatory Behaviors as Cultural Norms and Political* Tools,Web. 26 Nov. 2011

[xii] "It [the Abbasid Caliphate in Baghdad] recruited them to fulfill the objectives of its scientific plan that they had to undertake to develop the knowledge in order to achieve a life of prosperity, urbanization and strength, regardless of color, race, nationality and religion. By the end of the phase of translation, physicians and scientists in the Islamic world stood on a firm foundation." — *Science and State in its Power and Weakness*, Proceedings, Islamic Science and the Contemporary World, Conference at ISTAC, KL, Jan. 2008. Pub. ISTAC, IIUM, 2008, p. 121

[xiii] Muslim, *Mukhtasar Sahih Muslim*, p.329, # 1226 — *The Dignity of Man*, Mohd. Hashim Kamali, Ilmiah Pub. 2002, p. 58.

[xiv] *Decline and Fall of Islamic Scientific Tradition*, Alparslan Acikgenc. Proceedings, ISTAC Conference on Islamic Science in Contemporary Education, Jan. 2008, Kuala Lumpur, Malaysia.

[xv] Every Occidental Board of Governance—Religious, Political, and Institutional— is directly or indirectly governed by Freemasons whose occult fellowship is the result of esoteric metaphysics directly influenced and guided by the Kabbala, the Talmud, and occult doctrines of the sun-god mystery religions of antiquity. See my Books: *Trinity, The Metamorphosis of Myth, Cain's Creed, The Genesis of Terror*, and *The Hand of Iblis, Summary Observations on the New World Order*, for dissertations and history of this Occidental cum Orientalist malady.

[xvi] Vol 7, Book 72, Hadith 693, Bukhari

[xvii] For example: In 2009, along with Umno cronies and several Government Linked Companies, Malaysians shifted billions out of the country – about 50 percent of its GDP, which in 2008 was some RM739 billion. In its latest report,

UBS Securities Asia wrote: "Question: which Asian country had the biggest FX reserve losses in 2009? The answer is Malaysia, and by a very wide margin; we estimate that official reserves fell by well more than one-quarter on a valuation-adjusted basis. Why is this bizarre? Well, in the first place because Malaysia runs a current account surplus – and not just a mild surplus but rather the largest in Asia, around 17% of GDP. Other structural surplus neighbors like China, Hong Kong, Singapore, Taiwan and Thailand have all seen sizeable increases in FX reserves over the past 12 months and yet Malaysian reserves nearly collapsed. How did this happen? In short, Malaysia must have seen massive foreign capital outflows – and sure enough, when we measure implied net flows, the numbers are simply stunning: peak outflows of nearly 50% of GDP, i.e., more than twice as large … Malaysians need to be brave if the current tailspin into backwardness and poverty is to be arrested and reversed. Otherwise, from becoming a developed country by 2020, we may well slip further in the ranks of the third world, economically overtaken by Vietnam and politically comparable to Myanmar."

- Wong, Choon Mei, *Pendapat dan Analysis,* 12 Feb, 2010

[xviii] Vol 6. Book 60, Hadith 070, Bukhari.

[xix] Vol 9, Book 092, Hadith 421, 422, Bukhari;

[xx] *Instruction of the Student: The Method of Learning (Ta'lim al-Muta'allim Tariq al-Ta'allum)*, Imam Al-Zarnuji, Trns. G.E. von Grunebaum and Theodur M. Abel, Starlatch Press, Chicago, 1947 & 2008.

[xxi] Economic Report, 2001, Ministry of Finance, Malaysia and as cited in *Abdulai* (2001).

[xxii] GENERAL GUIDELINES FOR AN ISLAMIC POLITY:

NB: evidence for many of the follwing assertions can be seen in Note XXV on *Tassawuf*, where the Islamic leadership by authentic Sufi Sheikhs is itemized.

A. All pagans should be forbidden to practice their faith within the borders of an Islamic residential community. This essentially means the formation a limited apartheid state. If pagans choose to remain and ask for asylum, they should pay the Tax of subjugation as per the Sunnah and Al'Qur'an. Otherwise it is clear that the State is indeed "Plural", i.e., secular and hence not Islamic. The destruction of Pagan shrines and temples within a Muslim precinct is mandatory. If they fight, fight them until they either submit or leave because their chief goal is defiance of Allah's Law and the worshipof demons and jinn.

Muhammad said: 'slaughter is better than such mischief' and went further to state that such people only instill perversity among believers.

B. Islamic *administrations* (executives, military and police) should purge themselves of hypocrites whenever possible; i.e. of all Freemasons, including the destruction of their Lodges; of Sufi-claimers, shamans who commune with jinn, and all sectarians including Muslim extremists, Christians, Jews and Pagans. On this, there can be no compromise.

C. Christians and Jews should be permitted to practice their faith but forbidden to proselytize or ally with each other because this may put them on an equal footing with Islamic power. Idols and crosses bearing an idol (crucifix) should be removed from all public exhibits. These people must also pay the tax of submission or leave the state. Church properties should be limited to sites of worship and schools. Church organizations should be forbidden to engage in commerce, manufacture, agriculture, or government (except as consultants); and absolutely no provision should be made for overseas representation, especially from the Papal State; all Missionaries should be expelled from the country, and all church employees should be salaried according to standards established by the Muslim State, including provision for retirement contributions.

D. Jews should be examined by knowledgeable doctors of the Mosaic Law. Those not in compliance with the hanif of Abraham (Kabbalists and Talmudists, and especially Frankist Sabataens, for example), or those practicing usury and/or business monopoly, should be given time to repent after which they must be expelled from the state should they fail. Those who remain in peace must pay the tax of submission and remain carefully scrutinized even when integrated.

E. All Banks must be prohibited from lending with interest or charging exorbitant fees. Further, limitations apply to investment banking and loans subject to fierce Islamic scruples, thus making them liable to profit or loss along with their underwritten enterprises. Usury, in any form, must be completely annihilated. All interest due on any loan must be forgiven and principal-only payments made.

F. All vestiges of sexually immoral TV, advertisement or exhibitionism such as mimicry of the 'American Idol' programs should be forbidden. If this means curtailment by means of censorship, including the limitation of Satellite TV to wholesome channels, then so be it. And none but a qualified and

ENDNOTES

knowledgeable Muslim may own and operate the Media to which the State's citizens are subject. If no capable entity (company) exists, then the media should be completely withdrawn.

G. Profit levels, especially for essentials, should be monitored and strictly limited by the Ulama, and any practitioner of opulence immediately curtailed as an oppressor of the poor. Speculation, including futures and derivatives in the stock market must be forbidden, as it is gambling or usurious manipulation; and salaries of Public Corporate Executives should be curtailed to modest rofessional levels on par with the alim.

H. State lands, utilities, natural resources, public transport, communications, fuel supply, and distribution of goods should be under the direct scrutiny of government aegis. Experts in each field must manage these systems subcontracted to private capable entrepreneurs without monopoly or the slightest hint of nepotism or tribal favoritism. There must be no privatization of essential goods and services without severe governmental oversight.

I. Marriage: women and children must be emphatically protected without recourse to the chauvinist bias that elevates most men to dictator rather than husband. Any rapist or paedophile must be put to death and abusers of women severely punished. Furthermore, all Homosexuals, bi-sexuals, transvestites, and hardened criminals not deserving capital punishment, etc., should be relegated to places of refuge according to the Prophet's directive. Such places (cities) of criminal refuge may be within the Islamic Province and yet be isolated such that any resident leaving without warrant (internal passport) is subject to immediate execution.

J. Anyone found practicing the occult arts must be put to death. This means bomohs and shamans, etc., even within cities of refuge.

K. Teacher salaries should be comparable to those of corporate executives. Education in comparative religion, ethics, morality, social and physical sciences, and any skill incumbent to man's success must become mandatory and streamed according to the various intelligences as gifted by Allah.

L. Al'Qur'an should be taught in the native tongue and Arabic reserved for prayer, recitation, scholars and individuals gifted and motivated to learn it fluently. Under no means should it be forced upon any individual.

M. Women should be encouraged to participate in Friday jummah as in the days of Sirah, and when qualified, be elevated to positions of sub-cabinet authority under the protection and guidance of their husbands. Unmarried women, and those not subject to the protection of a competent husband, father, brother or male relative should be proscribed from senior public offices unless especially approved by the Senior Council of Shura.

N. Manslaughter should be weighed far more carefully; blood whit rather than imprisonment should return to its proper place; repeat offenders put to death (e.g. drunken drivers). Prisons should be transformed into well balanced work camps with restitution, remedial goals and education as well as profit in mind. Those refractory, i.e., hardened criminals and their women, should be exiled to *Cities of Refuge* where any escape attempt prompts immediate execution. All hardened thieves must lose the hand and repay what they have stolen (unless forgiven) if they wish to remain part of the community, and even if it means life-long servitude, especially white collar criminals and politicians. Better shame now than in the hereafter.

O. A all out and merciless military war (jihad) must be waged against organized crime.

P. All police should exhibit martial prowess, physical fitness, a working knowledge of religious fundamentals, and be above reproach however humble their means; and if found guilty of serious infractions, automatically exiled to *Cities of Refuge* as they are worse (hypocrites) than hardened criminals. This will serve as a grave deterrent.

Q. Shari'ah Law must be the law of the land including its Supreme Court. There can be no civil court in an Islamic Nation. Knowledgeable men and women of recognized and *proven* wisdom (generally over the age of 60) should be at its helm and at Cabinet Level, with a cadre of peers in each governmental department conducting the affairs of State. A Board of Censors, wise in the ways of God's Peoples, should be assigned for life to the Chief Minster's office. Their criticism and persons should be held inviolable, as it once was among the courts of Chinese and Roman Emperors.

R. Democracy of the general indescrimate franchise should be outlawed and any franchise given solely to proven Matriarchs and Patriarchs above the age of 40, as in the day of Sirah. This will end representation by uneducated mobs of immature opinions, upstarts and mountebanks and the unwisened unmarried flock (marriage being the sunnah). Anyone actively *seeking* (campaigning) for public office should be automatically excluded from any seat of authority.

S. The Premier, Chief Minister or Caliph should be continually humbled by accountability to a council of elder statesmen schooled in Islamic Principles and *world affairs*, and as guided by the Court of Shari'ah and subject to the

ENDNOTES

Censor's (Grand Mufti) criticism. There can be no Jacobin separation of Church and State or tyranny such as offered by Sarawak's CM Taib.

T. Sedition and graft need to be dealt with severely and with speed. No one is above the Law. Therefore, immunity from prosecution should be suspended at all levels without a statute of limitations. Lawyers who attempt to twist the law should be permanently disbarred, exiled, or sent to dwell with their colleagues in crime.

U. Men should be held accountable for work. There should be no free handout to able-bodied/minded men except if they are indebted or in need due to a lack of employment caused by oppression, monopoly, or inept governmental direction.

V. All forms of gambling must be proscribed.

W. In commerce with non-Muslim states, the latter's influence should stop at the border of entry with no honor paid to envoys save that of civil (courteous) decency.

[xxiii] See; *Trinity, The Metamorphosis of Myth; The Hand of Iblis; Cain's Creed, The Cult of Rome*, Omar Zaid

[xxiv] A common standard banqueting tradition with reclining at table while drinking 'mixed wine' ran across many seemingly disparate cultural practices. 'Mixed wine' was the central, reliable means of accessing the intense mystic altered state throughout antiquity. Ancient 'mixed wine' specifically meant visionary-plant mixtures, such as Psilocybe mushroom wine. *The Entheogen Theory of Religion,* 2007, Michael Hoffman.

[xxv] *Tasawwuf* basically consists of dedication to worship, total dedication to Allah Most High, disregard for the finery and ornament of the world, abstinence from the pleasure, wealth, and prestige sought by most men, and retiring from others to worship alone. This was the general rule among the Companions of the Prophet (Allah bless him and give him peace) and the early Muslims, but when involvement in this-worldly things became widespread from the second Islamic century onwards and people became absorbed in worldliness, those devoted to worship came to be called *Sufiyya* or *People of Tasawwuf* (Ibn Khaldun, *al-Muqaddima* [N.d. Reprint. Mecca: Dar al-Baz, 1397/1978], 467)…

For all of the reasons we have mentioned, *Tasawwuf* was accepted as an essential part of the Islamic religion by the '*ulama* of this *Umma*. The proof of this is all the famous scholars of *Shari'a* sciences who had the higher education of *Tasawwuf*, among them Ibn 'Abidin, al-Razi, Ahmad Sirhindi, Zakariyya al-

ENDNOTES

Ansari, al-'Izz ibn 'Abd al-Salam, Ibn Daqiq al-'Eid, Ibn Hajar al-Haytami, Shah Wali Allah, Ahmad Dardir, Ibrahim al-Bajuri, 'Abd al-Ghani al-Nabulsi, Imam al-Nawawi, Taqi al-Din al-Subki, and al-Suyuti. Among the Sufis who aided Islam with the *sword* as well as the pen, to quote *Reliance of the Traveller*, were such men as the Naqshbandi sheikh Shamil al-Daghestani, who fought a prolonged war against the Russians in the Caucasus in the nineteenth century; Sayyid Muhammad 'Abdullah al-Somali, a sheikh of the Salihiyya order who led Muslims against the British and Italians in Somalia from 1899 to 1920; the Qadiri sheikh 'Uthman ibn Fodi, who led jihad in Northern Nigeria from 1804 to 1808 to establish Islamic rule; the Qadiri sheikh 'Abd al-Qadir al-Jaza'iri, who led the Algerians against the French from 1832 to 1847; the Darqawi faqir al-Hajj Muhammad al-Ahrash, who fought the French in Egypt in 1799; the Tijani sheikh al-Hajj 'Umar Tal, who led Islamic Jihad in Guinea, Senegal, and Mali from 1852 to 1864; and the Qadiri sheikh Ma' al-'Aynayn al-Qalqami, who helped marshal Muslim resistance to the French in northern Mauritania and southern Morocco from 1905 to 1909. Among the Sufis whose missionary work Islamized entire regions are such men as the founder of the Sanusiyya order, Muhammad 'Ali Sanusi, [and Omar Mukhtar] whose efforts and jihad from 1807 to 1859 consolidated Islam as the religion of peoples from the Libyan Desert to sub-Saharan Africa; [and] the Shadhili sheikh Muhammad Ma'ruf and Qadiri sheikh Uways al-Barawi, whose efforts spread Islam westward and inland from the East African Coast ... (*Reliance of the Traveller*, 863).

It is plain from the examples of such men what kind of Muslims have been Sufis; namely, all kinds, right across the board—and that *Tasawwuf* did not prevent them from serving Islam in any way they could. To return to the starting point of my talk this evening, with the disappearance of traditional Islamic scholars from the *Umma*, two very different pictures of *Tasawwuf* emerge today. If we read books written *after* the dismantling of the traditional fabric of Islam by colonial powers in the last century, we find the big hoax: Islam without spirituality and Shari'a without Tasawwuf. But if we read the classical works of Islamic scholarship, we learn that Tasawwuf has been a Shari'a science like *tafsir*, *hadith*, or any other, throughout the history of Islam. The Prophet (Allah bless him and give him peace) said,

> "Truly, Allah does not look at your outward forms and wealth, but rather at your hearts and your works" (Sahih Muslim, 4.1389: hadith 2564).

And this is the brightest hope that Islam can offer a modern world darkened by materialism and nihilism: Islam as it truly is; the hope of eternal salvation through a religion of brotherhood and social and economic justice outwardly, and the direct experience of divine love and illumination inwardly.

The Place of Tasawwuf in Traditional Islamic Sciences
Sheikh Nuh Ha Mim Keller, 1995

xxvi "Abu'Sa'id took up his metal vase and threw it into the air, whereupon instead of falling down it stayed up in the air. "What is the reason for this?" he asked…"What is the violent force?" "Your soul!" replied Ibn Sina, "Which acts upon this." - *Tawhid and Science*, Osman Bakar, 2009, p. 97 from S.H. Nasr's, *Islamic Cosmological Doctrines*, p. 194.

xxvii Muslims believe that there is a basic indivisible subunit (the smallest subunit) upon which bodies are formed. Bodies can be broken down into smaller units until the indivisible subunit is reached. It is the smallest indivisible part, which has to exist as a matter existential necessity. They called it "al-jawhar alfard" (singular entity). The idea of a so-called never-ever land in relation to subatomic regions is not a fact it's rather fictional rubbish. Muslim theologians have said that this Greek originated idea of bodies dividing without a basic indivisible unit negates creation and conflicts with the Qur'an. In fact, it leads to blasphemy. – Mustapha Karalli, op.cit.

xxviii **_Authentic Tasawwuf and Sufiya'_**

Towards the conclusion of my humble endeavor, I feel obliged to clarify what we, the Ahl-us-Sunnah wal Jama'ah, classify as pure *Tasawwuf*. When we pronounce the word, we only represent the version in perfect harmony with the *Qura'an* and the *Sunnah* of the beloved Prophet ﷺ, which was also followed by all our eminent pious predecessors and scholars. We do, though quite sadly, acknowledge the existence of certain groups and individuals, who have used this subject as a scapegoat for the fulfillment and nourishment of their carnal whims and desires, therefore, segregating themselves from the mainstream '*Tasawwuf*'. They have introduced many filthy, false and erroneous ideas into this field that contradict the bases of Shari'ah, thereby depriving it of its original beauty and glamour. These false beliefs include bowing to the 'Sheikhs' or the 'Peers', prostrating to the graves, dancing and singing etc. from which this blessed command of Allah is not only exempt, but is also strictly censorious and deprecatory of. We, the Ahl-us-Sunnah wal Jama'ah, vehemently denounce their evil practices as well as their false innovations in the field of *Tasawwuf*.

Similarly, when making mention of the *Mashaikh* (masters of Tasawwuf) and Sufiya', we only correspond to those are known to possess the true fear of

ENDNOTES

Allah and pure love for Him and His Prophet ﷺ; who wish to live their lives according to the Prophet's ﷺ lifestyle in all aspects and walks of life; who strive for and wish to pass their last breath in the state that their Lord is pleased with them. On the other hand, we severely disapprove of those who have decided for themselves the grandeurs of this world in trade of those pertaining to the hereafter. We rigidly loathe even comprising them under the category of the honored title of 'Sufism'.

Hadhrat Maulana Yusuf Motala Saheb,
Inter-Islam Publications, 2009; inter-islam.org

[xxix] **Sufism** has numerous branches or *tareeqahs*, such as the Naqshbandiya, Qaadriya, Chhishtiya, Saharvardiya, Shaadhiliyyah, Rifaa'iyyah, Rehmaaniya, Rizviya, Subhaniya, Gausiya, Teejaaniyah, Sanusiyyah, Sahiliyyah etc. the followers of which all claim that their particular *tareeqah* is on the path of truth whilst the others are following falsehood. Islam forbids such sectarianism. Allaah says (interpretation of the meaning):"… and be not of al-mushrikoon (the disbelievers in the Oneness of Allaah, polytheists, idolaters, etc), of those who split up their religion (i.e., who left the true Islamic monotheism), and became sects, [i.e., they invented new things in the religion (bid'ah) and followed their vain desires], each sect rejoicing in that which is with it." [*al-Room* 30:31-32] Moreover, you see some of them making dhikr by only pronouncing the Name of Allaah, saying, "Allaah, Allaah, Allaah." This is *bid'ah* and has no meaning in Islam. They even go to the extreme of saying, "Ah, ah" or "Hu, Hu." The Sunnah is for the Muslim to remember his Lord in words that have a true meaning for which he will be rewarded, such as saying Subhaan Allaah wa Alhamdulillah wa Laa ilaaha illa Allaah wa Allaahu akbar, and so on… With regard to the question of the whether the Sufi shaykhs have some kind of [spiritual] contact, this is true, but their contact is with the *shayaateen*, not with Allaah, so they inspire one another with adorned speech as a delusion (or by way of deception), as Allaah says (interpretation of the meaning):

> And so We have appointed for every Prophet enemies – shayaateen (devils) among mankind and jinns, inspiring one another with adorned speech as a delusion (or by way of deception). If your Lord had so willed, they would not have done it…" [al-An'aam 6:112]… And Allaah says (interpretation of the meaning):

> … And, certainly, the shayaateen (devils) do inspire their friends (from mankind)… [al-An'aam 6:121]

ENDNOTES

> Shall I inform you (O people!) upon whom the shayaateen (devils) descend? They descend on every lying, sinful person.
>
> [al-Shu'ara 221-222]

This is the contact that is real, not the contact that they falsely claim to have with Allaah. Exalted be Allaah far above that.

(Mu'jam al-Bida', 346 –359).
Tassawuf or Sufism: The Innovation Within; Web. 1 Mar. 2010

ˣˣˣ See: *Some Aspects of Sufism,* S.N. Al-Attas, op.cit., p. 25.

ˣˣˣⁱ **On The Boy Scouts, Baden Powell & the Occult Connection with Jesuits, Freemasonry, Egypt & Zionists**

The *fleur-de-lis* is a stylised symbolic representation of the Lilium Candidum lily – the "Madonna lily", which has been described as "a royal flower of the ancient world without equal". This flower once grew close to Sumer on the nearby slopes of the southern Zagros Mountains. In summarising his analysis on the Sumerian connection of the lily symbol with Egyptian royalty, archaeologist & author, David Rohl, writes in his book "Legend: The Genesis of Civilization": "The heraldic plant motif of Upper Egypt is a lily which grows only in temperate mountain zones. This royal symbol is clear evidence of the foreign origins of the first pharoahs" (p. 383). He follows up this research in his subsequent tome "From Eden to Exile: The Epic History of the People of the Bible".

The deity of the Sumerian city of Eridu was Enki, symbolised by the goat & associated with the zodiac sign of Capricorn, while the deity of the ancient Egyptian city of Mendes was actually the ram-headed Banebdjedet. 19th century French occult author and magician, Eliphas Lévi, created what became an iconic image that he called the Baphomet of Mendes that is unmistakably ancient in its symbolism, as we can see from the photos of reliefs from Egypt&Sumer below.

ENDNOTES

← Fleur de Lis, Esneh Temple, Egypt, second century B.C.E. Brooklyn Museum

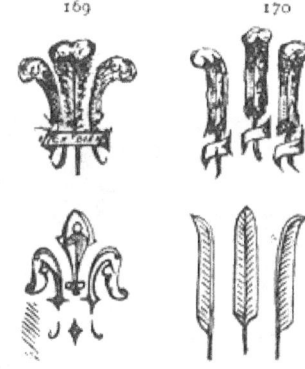

fig. 170 Prince of Wales's Feathers, from the Tomb of Edward the Black Prince, in Canterbury Cathedral. This badge presents the idea of the 'Fleur-de-Lis', 'Ich Dien!'--'I serve!' Fig. 171 represents the Egyptian Triple Plumes, which are the same badge as the 'Fleur-de-Lis' and the Prince of Wales's Feathers, meaning the 'Trinity'.

Figs.: 169, 170, 171

Buckingham Palace Gate; Scouting World Crest; Boy Scouts of America Logo; Flag of Quebec;

A diagram showing the resemblance of the flower of the Madonna Lily to the Star of David (the blue outline). This flower once grew close to Sumer on the nearby slopes of the southern Zagros Mountains. In summarizing his analysis on the Sumerian connection of the lily symbol with Egyptian royalty, archaeologist & author David Rohl [xxxi] writes in his book *Legend: The Genesis of Civilization*, Arrow Books Ltd. 1999, ISBN 0.09.979991.X:

The heraldic plant motif of <u>Upper Egypt</u> is a lily which grows only in temperate mountain zones unknown to African flora. This royal symbol is clear evidence of the foreign origins of the first pharaohs" (p. 383)

He follows up this research in his subsequent tome *From Eden to Exile: The Epic History of the People of the Bible.*

ENDNOTES

The Jesuits' Saint Louis University logo is especially illustrative of this horns & flame evocation in what is ostensibly a fleur-de-lis.

The New Israeli Shekel coin has the Madonna lily on its obverse.

The organizational pattern of achievement in Scouting and the Scottish Rite are similar: Tenderfoot, First Degree; Second Class, Second Degree; First Class, Third Degree; followed by stages of merit, like Chapters or Degrees, the one culminating in the Eagle, while the other culminating in the Double Eagle.

That the pattern in Scouting achievement resembles advancement in Freemasonry is no surprise. A scholar has pointed out that "the founder of the Boy Scouts, Lord Baden-Powell, was very closely inspired by the Masonic model, a fact that allowed the French Boy Scout organization to preserve its unity while grouping together Catholic, Protestant, Jewish, and lay associations." Scouts "trail," Masons "travel." To one who has experienced the progressive movement of both, the similarities of "trailing" and "traveling" are self-evident.

ENDNOTES

A close friend of "B.-P.:' the poet Rudyard Kipling, was made a Mason in India. Their friendship led "B.-P." to use Kipling's series of stories in The Jungle Book as the background theme for Cub Scouting. In England a number of Masonic Lodges have membership predominately composed of Brethren associated with Scouting. They hold an annual reunion in London, sponsored by one of the Lodges, where they wear their Scout uniforms and display their Masonic regalia.

Truly, Lord Baden-Powell's name may be counted among the great benefactors and philanthropists of humanity celebrated by Freemasons everywhere.

> "Lord Baden-Powell must clearly have approved of Freemasonry, for he presented to the first lodge to bear his name (No. 488, Victoria) the Volume of Sacred Law which is still in use. Its fly leaf was thus inscribed by him: 'With best wishes for the success of the lodge in its good work, Baden-Powell of Gilwell. 12th May 1931'. His grandson, Hon. David Michael Baden-Powell was initiated in this lodge and remains an active member."[2]. Lodge records show him to be a Past Master of the lodge.

> There are six masonic lodges named after Baden-Powell, all in Australia—but they were formed by scouts, not by Baden-Powell. Baden-Powell Lodge No. 505 has published a booklet entitled *Freemasonry and the Scout Movement*(1982). They can be reached through: United Grand Lodge of Queensland, Box 2204 G.P.O..Brisbane, Queensland 4001, Australia.

1. *Frederick Smyth, Ars Quatuor Coronatorum: Transactions of Quatuor Coronati Lodge No. 2076, vol. cii.* London: 1990. p. 264.
2. .*Ars Quatuor Coronatorum:* Transactions of Quatuor Coronati Lodge No. 2076, vol. civ. London: 1991. p. 257.
3. 3. "Freemasonry and the Scout Movement" by George W. Kerr, *Ontario Mason,* 1994, *Philalethes,* December 1995. *Cf.*. Web.
4. 4. Detail from an oil painting by David Jagger, 1929. It was presented to B-P on August 6, 1929 at the III World Jamboree at Arrowe Park, Birkenhead, England. The original is displayed in the conference room at World Headquarters (WOSM) in

[xxxii] Theomania also embraces the Christian "Born Again' movement, which has revived itself for the last 100 years beginning on the famous Azuzza St. Revival in California early last century. This is, however, an ancient phenomenon which was also observed in Europe during the 17th Century:

— The theomaniacs [1689] could then be counted by hundreds; men, women, children, all of them believed they were inspired and imbued with the breath of the Holy Spirit. Punishment of fire, the rack, the torture, even massacres directed to their extermination, all torments possible to invent to repress the violence of their fanaticism only augmented the force of evil which they employed. In the year 1704, the Marechal de Villars saw entire cities infested with theomaniacs. They exhibited sudden droppings down as though death-struck, sighs, groans, shrieks and vociferations, on recovering then broken sentences uttered in unearthly tones and tongue, violent contortions, desperate struggling with the spirit, followed by submission and repentance… all brought into play. The number of believers in their power soon became considerable… after a time the sect died away after reports circulated by their own votaries that they were nothing more than the instruments of designing men, who wished to disseminate Socinianism [a form of Humanism] and destroy orthodoxy … Towards the end of 1732, those who were in convulsions began to foretell what was to happen, to discover secrets, to make speeches, pathetic exhortations, sublime prayers; even those who at other times were wholly unable to perform any such things … The insanity lasted without interruption until the year 1790. The Convulsionaires and the Camisards were only manifestations of the Gnostics such as have existed in esoteric branches of various sects ever since the days of paganism; including the Albigenses, The Moravians, Anabaptists, Quakers, Shakers, Methodists etc.,

Their name is Legion'.| H. Madden, Phantasmaia, vol. II, p. 530, quoting L.F. Calmeil (1845) vol. II, p. 304.
Also see Lady Q. Occult Theocracy, Chapter 23 on the Waldenses.

xxxiii Dr. Muhammad Rahman Al-Ansari Al-Qadiri, *A Philosopher Having a Scientific* Mind; Proceedings, Islamic Science and the Contemporary World, Conference at ISTAC, KL, Jan. 2008. Pub. ISTAC, IIUM, 2008, p. 142.

xxxiv Reductionism the practice of analyzing and describing a complex phenomenon, especially a mental, social, or biological phenomenon, in terms of phenomena which are held to represent a simpler or more fundamental level, especially when this is said to provide a sufficient explanation. - New Oxford Dictionary

xxxv This refers to the various well documented Secret Societies that have systematized their metaphysics and applied these principles pedantically to both science and politics. See: *The Hand of Iblis*, by Omar Zaid, AS Nordeen, 2009.

xxxvi *Hadiqatyl-Azhar*, Shaykn Ahmad Al-Fatani, taken from *Some Epistemological Considerations of Malay Traditional Discourse Promoting Scientific Culture and Knowledge*, Muhammad 'Uthman El-Muhammady,

ENDNOTES

Proceedings, Islamic Science and the Contemporary World, Conference at ISTAC, KL, Jan. 2008.Pub. ISTAC, IIUM, 2008, pp 207, 209.

xxxvii But the Jesuits alone shroud themselves intentionally in a darkness, which the laity are completely forbidden to penetrate, and the veil is not even uplifted to many of the members. There are among them a large number who have taken merely three vows, *but not the fourth*, and who are in consequence, not at all, or at any rate, not properly instructed regarding the true principles, institutions and liberties of the order; this secret, on the other hand, is entrusted, as is known to His Holiness, to only a small number, and whatever is especially important is known only to the Superiors and the General.'

M. F. Cusack, *The Black Pope*, 1896

xxxviii Another order that is almost completelyTurkish but whose founder was again Persian is the Baktashiyyah, founded by Hajji Baktash Wall (d. 1338) from Khurasan. The order was organized in Anatolia in the fourteenth century and given its definitive form in the sixteenth century by Balim Sultan, a figure so important that he was called the second master of the order following Hajji Baktash himself. The order incorporated certain elements of Christianity and was strongly Shi'ite with devotion to the twelve Shi'ite Imams, especially 'Ali and Ja'far al-Sadiq. Some within the order even divinized 'Ali. They also incorporated the science of symbolism of letters, which the extremist movement of the Hurufiyyah had spread in Anatolia. The eclecticism of the Baktashiyyah is also revealed in their incorporation into their practices of certain shamanic elements and in the belief in the migration of souls. The Baktashis established their mother zawiyah or tekke near Kayseri in Anatolia, but their order spread all the way to Albania as well as L~aq and Egypt. Within Turkey they influenced popular piety· greatly while gaining special social prominence because of their exclusive religious influence among the Janissaries, who constituted such an important element of the Ottoman army. In 1826 Sultan Mehmet II destroyed the Janissaries, and this in turn led to the destruction of many Baktash1 sites, but the order was revived in the middle of the nineteenth century, especially in the Balkans, with a major center near Tirana in Albania. This order along with others was banned in Turkey by Ataturk, and the Communist takeover of Albania dealt a heavy blow to it there. Nevertheless, the order continues and the shaykhs of the order, called babas, are still found in certain regions of the Balkans and even inTurkey.

The garden of truth : the vision and practice of Sufism, Islam's mystical Tradition.
Chapter: THE SUFI TRADITION AND THE SUFI ORDERS (pp 205–06);
S.H. Nasr, Hapers & Colins, 2007

ENDNOTES

[xxxix] *Lighthouse* is an occult Freemasonic term indicating *hidden light* or Illumination. Rida openly agitated against the Ottomans for the British cause and praised the Young Turks!

[xl] Radio Farda – October 10, 2004: Based on the research on violence against women in Iran conducted nationally, 66% of families are subject to such studies. The report indicated that in 30% of the cases, 10% end in lethal or permanent injuries. The research indicated that most violence occurs in the first year of marriage or during the pregnancy of women. This research was conducted in 28 states and 12,500 women along with 2000 men were interviewed during the study. The research also indicated 63% of the marriages are forced marriages.

[xli] *My Dear Beloved Son or Daughter*, "Ayyuhal Walad" from His Three-Volumes Collection of Short Books "Majmu'a Rasail Imam Ghazali" Translated into English By Irfan Hasan, From the Urdu Translation of the Book, p. 13.

[xlii] "No End In Sight: The American Occupation of Iraq" — Documentary Film by Charles Fergusen, Magnolia Pictures, 2007. Includes testimony from Secretary of State Richard Armitage, Ambassador Barbara Bodine, Lawrence Wilkerson, Chief of Staff to Collin Powell, and Gen. Jay Garner, as well as prominent analysts, journalists and Iraqis.

[xliii] **Metaphysics** (from Greek, 'the things after the physics', from the ordering of Aristotle's works): That branch of philosophy that studies the most general categories and concepts presupposed in descriptions of ourselves and the world. Examples are causality, substance, ontology, time, and reality. Metaphysical questions have a very broad scope. Whereas the physical scientist might ask 'How does x cause y?', the metaphysician asks 'What does it mean for anything to cause anything else?' Whereas the chemist might investigate particular substances, the metaphysician asks what it means to be a substance, and whether there is one basic substance, or many. Metaphysical questions can become the subject of more specialized philosophical inquiry. We can ask whether our actions are subject to causality, which gives rise to the problem of free will. And the question of whether our mental experiences involve a separate substance from body is a major issue in the philosophy of mind. Although metaphysics dates back to the ancient Greeks, there have been occasions on which its status as a legitimate inquiry have been questioned. The rise of science in the 17th century led to attempts by some philosophers, such as Hume and Locke, to limit the claims of metaphysics, and earlier this century scientifically minded philosophers, such as the logical positivists, claimed that metaphysical assertions were meaningless. (Oxf. ENC) — the branch of

philosophy that deals with the first principles of things, including abstract concepts such as being, knowing, substance, cause, identity, time, and space. Metaphysics has two main strands: that which holds that what exists lies beyond experience (as argued by Plato), and that which holds that objects of experience constitute the only reality (as argued by Kant, the logical positivists, and Hume). As per Aristotle: later interpreted as meaning the science of things transcending what is physical or natural. (Oxf. Dict., 10th Ed.)

[xliv] **Theodor W. Adorno** was one of the most important philosophers and social critics in Germany after World War II. Although less well known among anglophone philosophers than his contemporary Hans-Georg Gadamer, Adorno had even greater influence on scholars and intellectuals in postwar Germany. In the 1960s he was the most prominent challenger to both Sir Karl Popper's philosophy of science and Martin Heidegger's philosophy of existence. Jürgen Habermas, Germany's foremost social philosopher after 1970, was Adorno's student and assistant. The scope of Adorno's influence stems from the interdisciplinary character of his research and of the Frankfurt School to which he belonged. It also stems from the thoroughness with which he examined Western philosophical traditions, especially from Kant onward, and the radicalness to his critique of contemporary Western society. He was a seminal social philosopher and a leading member of the first generation of Critical Theory. Unreliable translations have hampered the reception of Adorno's published work in English speaking countries. Since the 1990s, however, better translations have appeared, along with newly translated lectures and other posthumous works that are still being published. These materials not only facilitate an emerging assessment of his work in epistemology and ethics but also strengthen an already advanced reception of his work in aesthetics and cultural theory. — Stanford Encyclopedia of Philosophy

N.B. Prof. Adorno also declared Philosophy to be obsolete due to the disastrous effects of the Marxist exercise.

[xlv] **Rasputin:** (Russian for "debauched")
"The Khlysty sect drew their greatest strength from mystery, and in order to preserve this mystery, to protect their truth from any profanation, the founders of the new doctrine prescribed that their adherents should strictly observe in externals the forms of the "false faith," Orthodoxy, and even distinguish themselves by special zeal in observance."
(Fülöp-Miller, Rasputin the Holy Devil, p. 19).

At the age of 18, Rasputin under went a religious trans-formation of sorts. He decided that it was God's will that he should study religion. He was supposed to have been introduced to the Khlysty sect – they preached that one could

ENDNOTES

attain forgiveness only if one immersed them self in sin. They also preached that a person could only be close to God after numerous and heavy sexual encounters. Rasputin grabbed onto this doctrine as if it were his personal holy grail, and he started practicing this faith with full vigor...

The murder of Rasputin was a big blow to the Jesuit's scheme for the "conversion" of Russia. They lost a vital insider who could produce a Jesuit heir to the throne plus stack the government with Roman Catholic sympathizers.... Whenever a nation closes the door to the Jesuits, the result is always an atheistic regime to take its place. In England, after the Glorious Revolution, they introduced atheism with the teachings of Charles Darwin. The same pattern was followed in Russia with the Bolshevik Revolution of 1917.

De Jonge, Alex. *The Life and Times of Grigori Rasputin*. Coward, McCann & Geoghegan, New York, 1982.

From the time he was "seduced" at 14 by some girls near his village, he never ceased to find female partners, although his wife seemed willing to ignore them. His daughter, Maria, however, gave an accounting of hundreds of them, ranging from nobility, actresses and military wives to chambermaids and prostitutes.... Allegedly Rasputin had gained the attention of Aleister Crowley. Crowley who would be later called "The Beast" was a mad man, the type of person who would make the Marquee De Sade look like a Red Cross volunteer... It is not known who was the master and who was the student in the Rasputin/Crowley combination, but there are heavy suggestions that these two men had several love affairs with each other – after all, they were from the same mold...

According to the Russian secret service the Khlysty believed that sin was a necessary first step towards redemp-tion, and thus sexual excess in the group was rampant. Whether Rasputin joined the Khlysty sect or not, he did come to believe that sin was a necessary part of redemption...

They gathered in crypts, indulging in flagellation, mad dancing and orgiastic sex. Only after sinning could they repent and come closer to God. This mix of religious piety and sexual hedonism, 'driving out sin with sin', was a notion that never left Rasputin. During his participation in "sacred orgies" instead of being exhausted, he seemed to save more energy, and this is the reason that explains his sexual strength. Many people believe, that through his sins (sex) he obtained his holiness, and that he proceeded in initiations that transformed his miraculous "ego".

Fülöp-Miller, René. *Rasputin the Holy Devil*. The Viking Press, New York, 1928; Also see: *The Power and Secrets of the Jesuits*. George Braziller, Inc., New York, 1956.

ENDNOTES

[xlvi] Those who've mastered the religious sciences mentioned in the manner of Ghazali, et.al, as has Shaykh 'Abdallah b. Bayyah, most of who are not faculty members of any Muslim University, but rather dwell in the remote regions.

[xlvii] *Confessions of an Economic Hit Man* by John Perkins and published in 2004. It provides Perkins' account of his career with consulting firm Chas. T. Main in Boston. Before employment with the firm, he interviewed for a job with the National Security Agency (NSA). Perkins claims that this interview effectively constituted an independent screening which led to his subsequent hiring by Einar Greve, a member of the firm (and alleged NSA liaison) to become a self-described "economic hit man". The book was allegedly referred to in an audio tape released by Osama Bin Laden in September 2009.[1]

[xlviii] Sala'u'din pursued every Knight Templar he could find to death without mercy. These were the precursors for the Freemasons and Knights of Malta who Suileman the Magnificent also pursued without mercy, as did the Mamluks. This group and its several off shoots still plague the Levant as follows:

Sun., November 23, 2008 Cheshvan 25, 5769 Haretz.com. Shimon Peres: State president, Nobel laureate and now - knight, by Anshel Pfeffer

LONDON - President Shimon Peres yesterday added 'Knight' to the long list of titles he has acquired over the years. Peres received the honorary knighthood of the Order of St. Michael and St. George from Queen Elizabeth II in Buckingham Palace in London yesterday. Further coverage on Page A4. Peres also met yesterday with Prince Charles, British Prime Minister Gordon Brown and Foreign Secretary David Miliband.

May. 24, 2006 (CWNews.com) -
Four of the newest members of the College of Cardinals, after receiving their red hats from Pope Benedict XVI (bio - news) on March 24, have received high honors from the Knights of Malta. Cardinals Agostino Vallini, Andrea Cordero Lanza di Montezemolo, William Joseph Levada, and Franc Rodé received the Grand Cross of Honor and Devotion from Fra Andrew Bertie, the Grand Master of the Order of Malta. The honor—one of the highest available in the Order—was conferred on the four new cardinals who are currently stationed in Rome, and are now members of the Knights of Malta. Pope Benedict XVI is also a Knight of Malta, having receiving the same honor in 1999. He is the second Pontiff to be a member of the Order, following Pope Pius XII.

[xlix] Oxford Dictionary, 10th Edition

ENDNOTES

[l] The implication here is that if an observed phenomenon appears to counter accepted scientific definition, the phenomenon remains subject to divine laws not yet comprehended by the observer.

[li] Prof. Nasr is Islamic Chair at George Washington University, an Institution steeped in Freemasony. Freemasons are governed by Hermetic Fellowships of Jesuits and Kabalists. "The George Washington University, like much of Washington, D.C., traces many of its origins back to the Freemasons. The Bible that the presidents of the university use to swear an oath on upon inauguration is the Bible of Freemason George Washington. Freemasonry symbols are prominently displayed throughout the campus including the foundation stones of many of the university buildings. The Freemasons feel a special bond in helping the school throughout its history financially." (See: "Building the University: Freemasonry, SJT, and GW"" by GW Hatchet. Its founders and Presidents have all been Freemasons of the highest degrees. Graduates included Secretary of State Colin Powell, former Chairman of the Joint Chiefs of Staff General Peter Pace, former FBI Director J. Edgar Hoover and former Secretary of State John Foster Dulles, and cult leader L. Ron Hubbard (Scientology), all Freemasons and major players in the Globalist Conspiracy.

[lii] "The Secularization of Science as the Problem of Humanity." *Proceedings*, Islamic Science and the Contemporary World, Conference, ISTAC, KL, Jan. 2008. Pub. ISTAC, IIUM, 2008, p. 67.

[liii] Collapse of the American Empire: Swift, Silent, Certain
Commentary: Historians warning of a sudden 'thief at night,' an 'accelerating car crash' by Paul B. Farrell,

March 09, 2010, Market Watch: "One of the disturbing facts of history is that so many civilizations collapse," warns anthropologist Jared Diamond in "Collapse: How Societies Choose to Fail or Succeed." Many "civilizations share a sharp curve of decline. Indeed, a society's demise may begin only a decade or two after it reaches its peak population, wealth and power."

Now, Harvard's Niall Ferguson, one of the world's leading financial historians, echoes Diamond's warning: "Imperial collapse may come much more suddenly than many historians imagine. A combination of fiscal deficits and military overstretch suggests that the United States may be the next empire on the precipice." Yes, America is on the edge. Dismiss his warning at your peril. Everything you learned, everything you believe and everything driving our political leaders is based on a misleading, outdated theory of history. The American Empire is at the edge of a dangerous precipice, at risk of a sudden,

ENDNOTES

rapid collapse. Ferguson is brilliant, prolific and contrarian. His works include the recent "Ascent of Money: A Financial History of the World;" "The Cash Nexus: Money and Power in the Modern World;" "Colossus: The Rise and Fall of The American Empire;" and "The War of the World," a survey of the "savagery of the 20th century" where he highlights a profound "paradox that, though the 20th century was 'so bloody,' it was also 'a time of unparalleled progress.'"

Why? Throughout history imperial leaders inevitably emerge and drive their nations into wars for greater glory and "economic progress," while inevitably leading their nation into collapse. And that happens suddenly and swiftly, within "a decade or two."

You'll find Ferguson's latest work, "Collapse and Complexity: Empires on the Edge of Chaos," in *Foreign Affairs*, the journal of the Council of Foreign Relations, a nonpartisan think tank. His message negates all the happy talk you're hearing in today's news—about economic recovery and new bull markets, about "hope," about a return to "American greatness"—from Washington politicians and Wall Street bankers.

'Collapse of All Empires:' 5 stages repeating through the ages:
Ferguson opens with a fascinating metaphor: "There is no better illustration of the life cycle of a great power than 'The Course of Empire,' a series of five paintings by Thomas Cole that hangs in the New York Historical Society. Cole was a founder of the Hudson River School and one of the pioneers of nineteenth-century American landscape painting; in 'The Course of Empire,' he beautifully captured a theory of imperial rise and fall to which most people remain in thrall to this day. Each of the five imagined scenes depicts the mouth of a great river beneath a rocky outcrop." If you're unable to see them at the historical society, they're all reproduced in Foreign Affairs, underscoring Ferguson's warnings that the "American Empire on the precipice," near collapse.

First. 'The Savage State,' before the Empire rises
In the first, 'The Savage State,' a lush wilderness is populated by a handful of hunter-gatherers eking out a primitive existence at the break of a stormy dawn." Imagine our history from Columbus' discovery of America in 1492 on through four more centuries as we savagely expanded across the continent.

Second. 'The Arcadian or Pastoral State,' as the American Empire flourishes
The second picture, 'The Arcadian or Pastoral State,' is of an agrarian idyll: the inhabitants have cleared the trees, planted fields, and built an elegant Greek

temple." The temple may seem out of place. However, Cole's paintings were done in 1833-1836, not long after Thomas Jefferson built the University of Virginia using classical Greek and Roman revival architecture.

- As Ferguson continues the tour you sense you're actually inside the New York Historical Society, visually reminded of how history's great cycles do indeed repeat over and over. You are also reminded of one of history's great tragic ironies -- that all nations fail to learn the lessons of history, that all nations and their leaders fall prey to their own narcissistic hubris and that all eventually collapse from within.

Third. Consummation of the American Empire

The third and largest of the paintings is 'The Consummation of Empire.' Now, the landscape is covered by a magnificent marble entrepôt, and the contented farmer-philosophers of the previous tableau have been replaced by a throng of opulently clad merchants, proconsuls and citizen-consumers. It is midday in the life cycle.

The Consummation of Empire' focuses us on Ferguson's core message: At the very peak of their power, affluence and glory, leaders arise, run amok with imperial visions and sabotage themselves, their people and their nation. They have it all.

But more-is-not enough as greed, arrogance and a thirst for power consume them. Back in the early days of the Iraq war, Kevin Phillips, political historian and former Nixon strategist, also captured this inevitable tendency in Wealth and Democracy:

> Most great nations, at the peak of their economic power, become arrogant and wage great world wars at great cost, wasting vast resources, taking on huge debt, and ultimately burning themselves out." We sense the "consummation" of the American Empire occurred with the leadership handoff from Bill Clinton to George W. Bush.

Unfortunately that peak is behind us: Clinton, Bush, Henry Paulson, Ben Bernanke, Sarah Palin, Barack Obama, Mitt Romney and all future American leaders are merely playing their parts in the greatest of all historical dramas, repeating but never fully grasping the lessons of history in their insatiable drive for "economic progress," to recapture former glory ... while unwittingly pushing our empire to the edge, into collapse.

Four. Destruction of the Empire

Then comes 'The Destruction of Empire,' the fourth stage in Ferguson's grand drama about the life-cycle of all empires. In "Destruction" "the city is ablaze, its citizens fleeing an invading horde that rapes and pillages beneath a brooding evening sky." Elsewhere in "The War of the World," Ferguson described the 20th century as "the bloodiest in history, one hundred years of butchery." Today's high-tech relentless news cycle, suggests that our 21st century world is a far bloodier return to savagery. At this point, investors are asking themselves: How can I prepare for the destruction and collapse of the American Empire? There is no solution in the Cole-Ferguson scenario, only an acceptance of fate, of destiny, of history's inevitable cycles. But there is one in "Wealth, War and Wisdom" by hedge fund manager Barton Biggs, Morgan Stanley's former chief global strategist who warns us of the "possibility of a breakdown of the civilized infrastructure," advising us to buy a farm in the mountains. "Your safe haven must be self-sufficient and capable of growing some kind of food ... well-stocked with seed, fertilizer, canned food, wine, medicine, clothes, etc. Think Swiss Family Robinson." And when they come looting, fire "a few rounds over the approaching brigands' heads."

Five. Desolation ... after the Empire disappears
Finally, the moon rises over the fifth painting, 'Desolation,'" says Ferguson. There is not a living soul to be seen, only a few decaying columns and colonnades overgrown by briars and ivy." No attacking "brigands?" No loveable waste-collecting robots from Wall-E? The good news is the Earth will naturally regenerate itself without savage humans, as we saw in Alan Weisman's brilliant "The World Without Us:" Steel buildings decay. Microbes eat indestructible plastics. Eons pass. And Earth reemerges in all its glory, a Garden of Eden.

Epilogue: 'All Empires ... are condemned to decline and fall'
In a Los Angeles Times column, Ferguson asks: "America, a Fragile Empire: Here today, gone tomorrow, could the United States fall that fast?" And his answer is clear and emphatic: "For centuries, historians, political theorists, anthropologists and the public have tended to think about the political process in seasonal, cyclical terms ... we discern a rhythm to history. Great powers, like great men, are born, rise, reign and then gradually wane. No matter whether civilizations decline culturally, economically or ecologically, their downfalls are protracted."

We are deceiving ourselves, convinced "the challenges that face the United States are often represented as slow-burning ... threats seem very remote." "But what if history is not cyclical and slow-moving but arrhythmic?" asks Ferguson. What if history is "at times almost stationary but also capable of accelerating suddenly, like a sports car? What if collapse does not arrive over a number of centuries but comes suddenly, like a thief in the night?" What if the collapse of the American Empire is dead ahead, in the next decade? What if, as with the 2000 dot-com crash, we're in denial, refusing to prepare?

ENDNOTES

- Ferguson's final message about America's destiny comes from *Foreign Affairs*: "Conceived in the mid-1830s, Cole's great five-part painting has a clear message: all empires, no matter how magnificent, are condemned to decline and fall." Throughout history, empires function "in apparent equilibrium for some unknowable period. And then, quite abruptly ... collapse," a blunt reminder of the sudden, swift, silent, certain timetable in Diamond's "Collapse" where a "society's demise may begin only a decade or two after it reaches its peak population, wealth and power." You are forewarned: If the peak of America's glory was the leadership handoff from Clinton to Bush, then we have already triggered the countdown to collapse, the decade from 2010 until 2020 ... tick ... tick ... tick ...

[liv] "The believers in their love, mutual kindness and close ties are like one body; when any complains, the whole body responds to it with wakefulness and fever." — Muslim, *Mukhtasar Sahih*, p. 472, #1774

[lv] "Muslim nations on the whole remain—in Tun Mahathir's pithy and forthright words—"poor, backward, weak, disunited and dependent on non-Muslims for all kinds of things including their own security."

The Role of Governments, Muddathir Abdel Rahim, ISTAC Conference Proceedings op.cit., p. 180

[lvi] *Ibid,* p. 181

www.ingramcontent.com/pod-product-compliance
Lightning Source LLC
Chambersburg PA
CBHW081126170426
43197CB00017B/2762